Shadow and Substance in British Foreign Policy
1895–1939

Cedric James Lowe
1930–1975

Shadow and Substance in British Foreign Policy 1895–1939

Memorial Essays Honouring C. J. Lowe

edited by
B. J. C. McKercher and D. J. Moss

The University of Alberta Press

First published by
The University of Alberta Press
Athabasca Hall
Edmonton, Alberta
Canada T6G 2E8

Copyright © The University of Alberta Press 1984

ISBN 0-88864-046-3 (hardcover)
    0-88864-090-0 (paperback)

Canadian Cataloguing in Publication Data

Main entry under title:

Shadow and substance in British foreign policy, 1895-1939

ISBN 0-88864-046-3 (hardcover)
    0-88864-090-0 (paperback)

1. Great Britain - Foreign relations - 20th century - Case studies. 2. Lowe, C.J. (Cedric James), 1930-1975. I. McKercher, Brian. II. Moss, D.J. (David J.), 1938- III. Lowe, C.J. (Cedric James), 1930-1975.
DA566.7.S52 1984   327.42   C84-091040-1

All rights reserved.
No part of this publication may be produced, stored in a retrieval system, or transmitted in any form or by any means, electronic, mechanical, photocopying, recording, or otherwise, without prior permission of the copyright owner.

Typography and cover design by John Luckhurst/GDL
Typesetting by The Typeworks, Vancouver, British Columbia
Printed by John Deyell Company, Lindsay, Ontario, Canada

CONTENTS

Contributors	vii
Acknowledgements	ix
Introduction B. J. C. McKercher and D. J. Moss	1
Elitism and Foreign Policy: The Foreign Office Before the Great War Zara Steiner	19
British Foreign Secretaries and Japan, 1892–1905 Ian Nish	57
British Official Opinion and the Domestic Situation in the Hapsburg Monarchy, 1900–1914 F. R. Bridge	77
Great Britain, France, and the Origins of the Mediterranean Agreements of 16 May 1907 K. A. Hamilton	115
Wishful Thinking: The Foreign Office and Russia, 1907–1917 Keith Neilson	151
The British Foreign Office Between the Wars David Dilks	181
Britain, the United States, and France and the German Settlement, 1918–1920 M. L. Dockrill	203
The British Diplomatic Service in the United States and the Chamberlain Foreign Office's Perceptions of Domestic America, 1924–1927: Images, Reality, and Diplomacy B. J. C. McKercher	221
In Further Pursuit of Lloyd George: International History and the Social Sciences Michael G. Fry	249

CONTRIBUTORS

F. Roy Bridge
School of History
University of Leeds
Leeds, England

David Dilks
School of History
University of Leeds
Leeds, England

Michael L. Dockrill
Department of War Studies
King's College
London, England

Michael G. Fry
School of International Relations
University of Southern California
Los Angeles, California, U.S.A.

Keith A. Hamilton
Department of International Politics
University College of Wales
Aberystwyth, Wales

Brian J. C. McKercher
Department of History
University of Alberta
Edmonton, Alberta, Canada

David J. Moss
Department of History
University of Alberta
Edmonton, Alberta, Canada

Keith Neilson
Department of History
Royal Military College of Canada
Kingston, Ontario, Canada

Ian Nish
Department of International History
London School of Economics
London, England

Zara Steiner
New Hall
University of Cambridge
Cambridge, England

ACKNOWLEDGEMENTS

We would like to thank the following for permission to quote from manuscript collections under their control: the University Library, the University of Birmingham, Birmingham (the papers of Sir Neville Chamberlain); the British Library, London (the papers of Arthur, the first Earl Balfour, Sir Henry Campbell-Bannerman, Robert, Viscount Cecil of Chelwood, and Sir Charles Scott); the University Library, Cambridge (the papers of Charles Hardinge, Baron Hardinge of Penshurst and Samuel Hoare, Viscount Templewood); Christ Church, Oxford (the papers of the third Marquess of Salisbury); the Master, Fellows, and Scholars of Churchill College, Cambridge (the papers of Maurice, first Baron Hankey); the Library, the University of Coleraine, Coleraine (the papers of Sir James Headlam-Morely); the Controller of Her Majesty's Stationery Office (the archives of the Cabinet, Foreign Office, and War Office, as well as the papers of Sir Arthur Balfour, Lord Bertie of Thame, Sir Austen Chamberlain, George, first Marquess Curzon of Kedleston, Sir Edward Grey, Henry, fifth Marquess of Lansdowne, and Sir Arthur Nicolson); the Haus-, Hof-, and Staatsarchive, Vienna (the Politisches Archive and the papers of Baron Alois Lexa von Aehrenthal and Count Albert von Mensdorff); the clerk of the Records, the House of Lords Record Office, Mr. A. J. P. Taylor, the Beaverbrook Foundation, and the present Lord Lothian (the Lloyd George papers and the Philip Kerr correspondence therein); the present Lord Howard (the papers of Esme, first Baron Howard of Penrith); the India Office Library, London (the papers of George, first Marquess of Kedleston); the Library, the University of Leeds, Leeds (the papers of Sir Fairfax Cartwright); the Ministére des Affairs Etrangères (archives and the papers of Jules Cambon, Paul Cambon, Théophile Delcassé, and Pierre de Margerie); the present Lord Salisbury (the papers of the third Marquess of Salisbury and the Cecil MSS at Hatfield House, Hertfordshire); and the papers of the first Earl of Kimberley (the Scottish National Library, Edinburgh).

We would also like to thank the following individuals who were kind enough to offer their help at various stages in the preparation of this book: Dr. Michael Dockrill, the War Studies Department, Kings College, London; Professor W. Roger Louis, the University of Texas, Austin, Texas; Mr. E. Lowe, Professor Lowe's brother; Professor R.C. Macleod, former chairman of the Department of History, the University of Alberta; Dr. K.E. Neilson, Department of History, Royal Military College of Canada, Kingston; and Norma Gutteridge and Mary Mahoney-Robson of the University of Alberta Press. Finally we would like to make note of the special contribution of Mrs. B. Lowe.

B.J.C.M.
D.J.M.

Introduction

Cedric James Lowe died in an automobile accident at Edmonton, Alberta on 26 April 1975. At the height of his intellectual creativity and productivity, his loss was a blow not only to his many friends but to the academic community at large.

He was born in 1930 at Bath, England, the son of a school teacher. Educated first at a local school and then at Swindon, from a very young age his goal was a university education. Nevertheless, instead of proceeding directly to the fulfillment of that ambition, Lowe chose along with many of his contemporaries to satisfy his National Service obligation. For two years, 1948-49, he laboured in the Army's Intelligence Corps, conducting screening interviews with displaced eastern Europeans in Austria. Entrance to University College, London to read medieval and modern history liberated his talents. In 1952 he emerged with a first class honours degree. Having rediscovered his vocation Lowe began immediately to do research in the field of diplomatic history at the London School of Economics, first, under the supervision of Sir Charles Webster and, later, Dame Lillian Penson. The subject of his thesis, 'Anglo-Italian Relations, 1887-1896', necessitated archival work at Rome and was sponsored by a Rotary Fellowship. Upon his return to England in 1954, he accepted the post of lecturer in history at the University of Durham; the completion of his doctorate was consequently delayed until 1958 by the demands of teaching. He moved from Durham in 1964 and returned to the London School of Economics as lecturer in International History and Warden of one of the LSE residences, Passfield Hall. He left England in 1968 to become Professor of History at the University of Alberta in Canada.

The facts of Cedric Lowe's life give little hint of the important contributions he made to the study of the foreign policies of the great Powers from the Franco-Prussian War to the outbreak of the Second World War. His main interest and the bulk of his work centred on British foreign policy in this period, more specifically on the efforts of successive diplomatists from Disraeli and Salisbury to Lloyd George and Curzon to meet the challenge to British global pre-eminence mounted by the European Great Powers and the United States. Considered in their entirety, Lowe's various studies examined the successes and failures of British policy in the period when Britain's position in world politics was marked by a decline in its economic and naval power. Lowe argued effectively and eloquently that this decline was not apparent to successive British prime ministers or foreign secretaries, nor to those in the governments of other Great Powers, who made foreign policy at that time. Moreover, he remained convinced that this decline, especially to the degree that occurred after the Paris Peace Conference of 1919–1920, was not inevitable. One of his favourite admonitions to both his students and colleagues alike whenever the 'inevitability' of British decline was brought out in discussion was: 'In politics, especially foreign policy, nothing is inevitable.' This notion underscored all of his analyses of British foreign policy.

Lowe never suggested, however, that there were no limitations on the exercise of British diplomacy. Quite simply, there were. Britain was a maritime, not a terrene Power. Diplomatic tactics and strategies devised in the Foreign Office and, less often, debated in the Cabinet had to take into account that British power was based not only on the strength of the Royal Navy to ensure that maritime lines of communication for trade and Imperial defence remained open, but on the ability of British sea power to influence the course of events. As Lowe once perceptively observed about Rosebery:'... the collapse of Rosebery's Armenian projects in 1895 [occurred] when it was discovered that not only was the Mediterranean fleet unable to sail up Mt. Ararat but that it could not even pass the Straits.' But Britain did have a great many attributes and, when it became necessary to find allies and keep them, it was Lowe's opinion that British diplomatists were the disciples of Salisbury:

> Salisbury was fully conscious that the idea of treating each question on its intrinsic merits was an impossible ideal. Diplomacy to him was a market place in which you bought and sold

and he was quite willing to offer to perform what he knew he could reasonably expect to carry out, in return for solid benefits.

Although British foreign policy was his primary interest, Lowe had a number of others. The efforts he made in getting 'The Foreign Policies of the Great Powers' series of books published, and in attracting a wide range of specialists to produce each study, attests to this. In his own case, the course of Italian foreign policy after the *risorgimento* captured his attention. In many ways he was mesmerised by the place of Italy amongst the European Great Powers. His doctoral dissertation on Anglo-Italian relations in the Salisbury era was transformed into his first book, *Salisbury and the Mediterranean*. His last book, *Italian Foreign Policy 1870–1940*, which he had to complete himself after the untimely death of Frank Marzari, was the first comprehensive analysis of the subject in English, giving those scholars and students who do not read Italian an opportunity to consider the diplomatic history of the least important of the European Great Powers.

But like every historian, despite varied interests, Lowe's work seemed to focus on one theme. The question was not to discover what was really happening in the world; that was the domain of those who would unblushingly use hindsight to point out with certainty what was not obvious to those making and implementing policy thirty, fifty, or one hundred years before. The question to be answered was what did those who made or influenced foreign policy think was happening? In other words, for Lowe, the perception of reality was reality. He qualified this in what is probably his best piece of historical analysis—the first chapter of *The Reluctant Imperialists*—where he demonstrated that individual 'taste' is an element that cannot be ignored when trying to judge why particular decisions were made and courses of action followed. By pointing out forcefully to specialists through his articles and books that the perception of reality is fundamental to writing diplomatic history—and impressing this on students and colleagues in his gentle but persuasive way in seminar—Cedric Lowe's contribution to the understanding of the foreign policies of the Great Powers in the seventy years after 1870 cannot be overlooked. It was his concern whilst he lived, and it is his legacy now that he has gone.

Leadership in the academic world was also expressed through his teaching. His vivid, wide-ranging lectures to undergraduates and sympathetic guidance to post-graduates were an inspiration. He was forever throwing out ideas and interpretations that compelled responses from even the quietest of students, whilst those who were capable of offering an original contribution were given unstinting encouragement. Many, in consequence, went on to pursue an academic career for themselves. Concern for the well-being of his students extended to their social lives. As Warden of Passfield Hall he fostered a number of far-reaching innovations, not least of which was the pioneering, some would have said revolutionary, step of admitting women students to the Hall from October 1967. Only a man with his energy could have succeeded in overcoming the numerable obstacles that lay in the successful completion of that task.

As a man and personality Lowe was direct, alert and perceptive, witty and, when so inclined, utterly charming. He was genuinely interested in people. Those who came into contact with him rarely failed to respond to his kindness and affability. His was that rare sort of vitality that encourages commitment and was the source of his own consuming professionalism. In the study of history Cedric Lowe found the ideal medium to express his philosophy. His books reflect his abiding interest in humanity for individual hopes and endeavours, and for human frailty. All who knew him mourn the loss of a scholar, teacher, friend, and man of enduring stature.

As a tribute to Cedric Lowe, each paper in this collection focuses on the perceptions and consequent actions of some of those who made British foreign policy from the mid-1890s to 1939. It is clear that in a volume such as this there can be no pretense about compiling a comprehensive analysis of British attitudes and diplomacy in the almost half century from Rosebery to Halifax. The subject is far too complex. Instead the purpose is to consider a number of case studies in a way that Cedric Lowe would have approved: looking at the attitudes of those who actually made foreign policy, how those attitudes were shaped by and, occasionally, shaped events, and how British foreign policy in a few instances was moulded as a result. This collection seeks to illuminate a few aspects of British diplomacy at a time when Britain's global power faced sustained challenges from the European Great Powers and the United States.

Those who made British foreign policy in the almost fifty years prior to the Second World War were always a relatively small group. At the centre was the prime minister and the foreign secretary. A few prime ministers doubled as their own foreign secretaries—Salisbury between 1895 and 1900 and Ramsay MacDonald from January to November 1924—and once, in the case of the Lloyd George premiership, the prime minister conducted British foreign relations without almost any reference to the foreign secretary or Foreign Office. In other instances the foreign secretary stood by himself because his prime minister was more concerned with domestic affairs; Edward Grey before the First World War and Austen Chamberlain in the latter half of the 1920s are two examples. But as time progressed, especially after the crisis of the First World War, others in Cabinet, as well as civil servants, either sought or were allowed to influence the course of policy. Not surprisingly, the Foreign Office was always closest to the foreign secretary. The power of Foreign Office officials to affect the country's diplomacy increased markedly following reforms in 1905–1906 and 1919–1920, reforms designed to speed up decision-making by an improved registry, a quicker circulation of documents, and that sort of thing. Not only the permanent under-secretary—the civil service head of the Office—gained decided power to affect the course of policy, so, gradually, did the assistant under-secretaries, counsellors, and those who tendered advice at the department level. In addition the diplomatic service, most often the ambassadors at the capitals of the other Powers, was not without some weight given the intimate connection between formulating and executing policy.

Cabinet members, for instance, Joseph Chamberlain during Salisbury's last government and Robert Cecil during Baldwin's second, sought to pursue their own diplomacy or shape that of the foreign secretary into something approaching their own preferences. As the foreign policy of the country became more complex, especially during and after the First World War, it was necessary more often to coordinate the political aspects of diplomacy, the domain of the Foreign Office, and the economic and military ones. In this way, the circle of those who made British foreign policy widened as civil servants in the Treasury and the service ministries took it upon themselves to enter the policy-making process. Warren Fisher, the permanent under-secretary at the Treasury in the inter-war period, typified this trend when the inter-war governments moved to impose stringent policies of retrenchment. By 1939, therefore, a larger number of men participated in the policy-making process than had been the case in 1895. But whether small or slightly larger, this elite was responsible for British foreign policy; to understand that policy, it is important to consider the perceptions of those who made up the elite.

The First World War is the dividing line in this collection — five papers deal with the pre-1918 period and three with the time after 1918. Zara Steiner's piece sets the stage for the first part by considering if there was a collective attitude within the Foreign Office before 1914 to foreign policy in general and the profession of diplomacy in particular. She uses this examination to answer some of her critics who feel that her earlier analyses of the pre-war Foreign Office require qualification. A number of questions are considered about the characteristics of the 'tiny elite' that controlled pre-war British foreign policy, considered in terms of contemporary perceptions of late nineteenth and early twentieth century Britain. Whether there existed a 'shared consensus' about the nature of the world in which they laboured? Whether, indeed, there were common beliefs that affected the course taken by British foreign policy? Also, most importantly, whether it is possible to assume that when discussing the pre-war Foreign Office, there was a collective Foreign Office mind? The answers to these questions suggest strongly that there was a basic sense of unity within the small group that made British foreign policy. Dr Steiner's essential point in this is that despite obvious differences amongst those who staffed this important department of state, everyone from the foreign secretary at the top to the junior-most clerk at the bottom, there was a decided degree of similarity in social background, education, and in the perception that they were all members of good standing in the profession of diplomacy. Together these fostered the notion that the Foreign Office alone understood international politics and could respond best to the challenge to Britain's position — this had really always been there — and they became accentuated as the world seemingly became more complex in the decade after 1904.

In the decade after 1892 a number of significant challenges to British global power arose. The Franco-Russian alliance of 1894 had implications for the European balance of power, the control of the Mediterranean, and the Imperial defence of interests in India and the Far East. There was also the determination of wealthy terrene

Powers with imperial ambitions, notably Germany and the United States, to expand rapidly their navies; this threatened the paramountcy of the Royal Navy. China seemed on the threshold of dissolution, a situation that precipitated a 'scramble' amongst the great Powers for spheres of influence which could be held and maintained once that Empire collapsed. Finally, a number of Powers took the opportunity to exploit British strategic weakness caused by Britain's involvement in the Boer War. Britain had not entered into a formal alliance since Crimea. Now for the first time since the 1850s, British diplomatists and a few influential members of the Cabinet perceived the need to find an ally. The Anglo-Japanese alliance of 1902 was the result of this search.

Ian Nish breaks new ground by considering the 'underlying assessments' that foreign secretaries from Rosebery to Lansdowne had about Japan and how this contributed to the conclusion of the alliance. There was never any suggestion in the minds of the foreign secretaries that Japan was anything other than a regional Power, one possessing decided strength, but still regional. Yet that country came to be seen as a potentially valuable ally to British strategic and diplomatic interests not only in the Far East but, because Royal Navy warships could be deployed closer to home, the world generally. Professor Nish's emphasis is primarily on Lansdowne, who controlled British foreign policy when the alliance was negotiated and signed; but his discussion of Rosebery, Kimberley, and Salisbury is especially useful in the analysis of the Foreign Office's intellectual odyssey to Japan. Just as crucial as the perception of Japan was that of the leading Japanese diplomats who were involved in the negotiation. There was some Foreign Office mistrust. Marquis Itō, for instance, one of Japan's *genrō*, or 'elder statesman', was the principal Japanese negotiator. There was fear prior to the agreement that Itō might present the contents of the secret Anglo-Japanese negotiations to the Russians in an attempt to improve Russo-Japanese relations. These relations had been under decided strain over the question of competing interests in the decaying Chinese Empire. There was also a problem in coming to grips with the way the Japanese — the emperor, the *genrō*, the prime minister, and the Cabinet — made policy. These difficulties made the accomplishment of the alliance a remarkable achievement and offers many insights into the way in which British diplomatists arrived at an image of a distant country, its foreign policy, and the domestic factors that shaped that policy. With this analysis, Professor Nish fills a gap in understanding why the Anglo-Japanese alliance came into being.

The matter of allies and perceptions is also pursued in the third paper. Of all the European great Powers in the period before the first World War, Austria-Hungary posed the least threat to British interests. Indeed during the Boer War when other Powers were exploiting Britain's problems and the Germans were trying to entice Austria-Hungary to pursue an anti-British policy, the Emperor Franz Josef stated publicly that *'dans cette guerre je suis complement Anglais'*. It was the high water mark of Anglo-Austrian relations in the two decades before the war. This is not that surprising for, at that time, Britain and the Dual Monarchy shared a number of common interests centring on the need to prevent Russian exploitation of the weakness of the Ottoman Empire: the British sought to ensure the Russian Black Sea fleet was bottled up behind the Straits whilst the Austrians sought to exclude the Russians from the Balkans, an area Vienna looked on as its legitimate sphere of interest. But by 1914 the situation had changed dramatically, as Britain and Austria-Hungary found themselves on opposite sides at the outbreak of general European war.

This turn-about in Anglo-Austrian relations had a number of causes. F. R. Bridge looks at an important one that has never really been examined before: the view that British official opinion had of Austro-Hungarian domestic affairs from 1900 to 1914 and the changes that occurred in that view. The key to this paper is that Dr Bridge casts his net further than just the foreign secretary and his advisers in assessing what the devising and implementation of British policy towards the Dual Monarchy entailed. The monarchy, key members of the Cabinet, as well as members of the diplomatic service at Vienna and Budapest are all considered. It was obvious at the turn of the century that the internal divisions within Austria-Hungary were creating problems. Slavic peoples within the Empire —the southern Slavs in the Balkans and the northern Slavs in Bohemia and Galicia—had legitimate complaints about not being equal with the Germans and Magyars in political affairs. Until 1905 official British opinion, dominated by the Unionist government of Arthur Balfour, actually had sympathy for Franz Josef's problems given their own difficulties within the Empire; the Boer War was a manifestation of this. But with the advent of a Liberal government and the rise of Grey to the Foreign Office in late 1905, official British opinion began to change. Gradually Anglo-Austrian relations cooled because of a number of well-known factors: the Anglo-Russian entente of 1907; a growing closeness in Austro-German relations in tandem with increasing German influence at Constantinople; and the rise to prominence in the Foreign Office after the 1906 reforms of articulate germanophobes like Eyre Crowe. Dr Bridge demonstrates that official British perceptions of Austro-Hungarian domestic policies, a less known factor, were equally important in the Anglo-Austrian question. This is not to say the advent of a Liberal foreign secretary instantly affected British Austrian policy because of the Slav question in the Dual Monarchy. But suspicions about the ingenuousness of Austrian policies towards the subject nationalities had an impact on Grey and his advisers. In July 1914, when Vienna justified its ultimatum to Serbia on the anti-Austrian efforts of Serbian irredentists, it carried no weight in the Foreign Office. There had been a fundamental shift in British attitudes towards Austria-Hungary since 1900.

In contrast to the Austrian situation, Britain drew closer to France in the period from 1900 to 1914. A nadir in Anglo-French relations had occurred over the Fashoda crisis in 1896, a British diplomatic success that demonstrated French inabilities to support bellicose foreign and imperial policies with effective force. By 1904, in response to German pressure, Anglo-French differences were smoothed over with the conclusion of the Entente Cordiale. This was not an alliance like that with Japan but, instead, an effort to resolve a number of differences in the colonial field including North Africa. However for the British the Entente had the same effect as an alliance—Britain secured another ally to help in fending off challenges to its position as a Power of the first rank—thus, in the decade after 1904, Britain and France were tied closer together. By the time of the July crisis in 1914, the British with only a little hesitation joined the French and Russians in going to war against the Central Powers.

The course of Anglo-French relations in that important decade has been analysed in depth elsewhere; the milestones are well known: the military staff talks which began in January 1906, the Algeciras conference, the Agadir crisis, and so on. K. A. Hamilton examines a little discussed but important one of these milestones in his examination of the Mediterranean agreements of May 1907. Having their origins before Fashoda, these agreements were reached in the first years of the Entente Cordiale when difficulties still existed in establishing an Anglo-French *modus vivendi* in a few important spheres. The difficulty in this case was Spain which, because of its geographic position, was strategically and diplomatically important in maintaining the Mediterranean balance of power. German attempts to influence in their favour decisions made by the Spanish government brought about a concerted Anglo-French effort to tie Spain to their condominium of interests in the region. The Mediterranean agreements, designed to maintain the territorial status quo in the lands bordering and the islands of the eastern Atlantic and western Mediterranean, were the result. Dr Hamilton concentrates on the perceptions of this nettled question that were held by Lansdowne and Grey and the officials at the Foreign Office and in the diplomatic service. The British perceived there to be a decided German threat to their interests in the region, so that their problem was to counter German initiatives and avoid differences with the French which they felt had the potential to damage the Entente. Dr Hamilton's paper examines how British efforts to ensure Anglo-French diplomatic collaboration in the period after 1904, efforts based on the idea of a German threat, helped to solidify Europe into the two alliance coalitions that went to war against each other in August 1914.

Just three months after the conclusion of the Mediterranean agreements, the British and the Russians resolved a number of their outstanding imperial differences in Afghanistan, Persia, and Tibet. This, too, was not a formal alliance; but the Anglo-Russian entente ultimately had the same effect by solidifying even more the European alliance coalitions. However, despite the difficulties that the British and French encountered trying to reconcile their differences and keep united in the face of the German threat, the Anglo-Russian entente was never as firm as its French counterpart. Problems over spheres of influence in Asia were always cropping up. In the last year before the war, for example, differences over the Persian question threatened to inject poison into Anglo-Russian relations and wreck the 1907 agreement. Once war broke out, though, Anglo-Russian squabbles were submerged by the need to ensure sound war effort against the Central Powers. The British and the French needed the Russians in the war to pin down Central Power troops in the east in order to relieve pressure on the western front. To ensure their war effort, the Russians relied on supplies of money and arms from their western allies. As the war progressed, these considerations became accentuated.

Keith Neilson considers a long neglected issue: Foreign Office attitudes towards Russia in the decade after 1907, a period neatly enclosed by the signing of the entente and the Bolshevik revolution. As a whole the Foreign Office, headed for most of this time by Grey, saw Russia as 'a reactionary country'. The Foreign Office did lament tsarist absolutism and cheered whenever 'liberal' leaders and institutions appeared, but reducing Anglo-Russian tensions was crucial to British foreign policy; it was perceived that such reductions would put more pressure on the Germans. Two men served as permanent under-secretary in this decade, Charles Hardinge (1906–1910 and 1916–1920) and Arthur Nicolson (1910–1916). Each had been ambassador at St Petersburg: Hardinge from 1904 to 1906 and Nicolson from 1906 to 1910. Each saw Russia as an effective diplomatic and, if need be, military counter to German ambitions in southwest Asia and Europe; these views influenced British Russian policy. The Foreign Office difficulty was that Russia's domestic situation created as many problems as differences over foreign and imperial policies. The British Liberal Party had a strong radical wing which, led by men like Lloyd George, looked on any ties with the tsar as an absolute negation of all for which 'Liberal' foreign policy stood. Thus Grey and his advisers had not only to respond to Russian policies, they had to be wary of radical criticism.

When the war came and men like Lloyd George assumed key roles in directing Britain's efforts, it was recognised that Russia had to be sustained diplomatically and militarily in spite of its internal situation. This is not to say that British desires for domestic Russian reform subsided—Dr Neilson shows they did not—but it meant that the war came first. The Foreign Office view was to keep Russia militarily viable and aware that its allies would not desert it—the possibly of a separate Russo-German peace was always a worry in the Foreign Office. Dr Neilson demonstrates that even after the fall of the tsarist government and its replacement by Alexander Kerensky's provisional regime, which led to monumental domestic changes, basic British policy remained unaltered. Only with the Bolshevik coup in November 1917, initiating even more fundamental domestic changes, was Britain's unaltered Russian policy scuppered.

Like other aspects of British life, the formal processes that made foreign policy underwent a profound change because of the exigencies of fighting the war. In 1914 the foreign secretary and his advisers, the 'tiny elite' described by Zara Steiner, made foreign policy; by 1918 the onus lay with the prime minister and a small group of his advisers at 10 Downing Street. There were two reasons for this. First, during the war, foreign policy as such ceased to exist, especially in terms of inter-allied relations. More than the Foreign Office and the diplomats, the service ministries, the exchequer, and the supply departments conducted external relations, entering into negotiations and concluding agreements. Traditional processes were supplanted by new ones. Normally this would probably have been temporary, but in 1916 Lloyd George became prime minister in a move to improve British war effort. Brilliant, innovative, and pragmatic, he seized control of foreign policy to conduct external relations through his office—it could save time—using periodic inter-allied conferences to meet other heads of government, face to face, to reach agreements. Lloyd George's dynamism and his penchant to have as much power as possible was the second reason why those formal processes making foreign policy altered, and why the temporary loss of Foreign Office power lasted into the 1920s. The effect of the Lloyd George experiment was that in the interwar period, Foreign Office ability to make foreign policy depended on the political stature of the foreign secretary and his capacity to take for his department as much independence in making and implementing policy as he could. This meant usually that the foreign secretary had to fend off encroachments by other Cabinet members, at times including the prime minister, and powerful civil servants in other departments.

As counterpoint to Zara Steiner's article, David Dilks considers the Foreign Office role in the interwar years and the outlook its members had of the world. Lloyd George's fall saw the balance redressed in favour of the Foreign Office making and implementing foreign policy. Generally, Conservative governments witnessed greater Foreign Office autonomy though, as Anglo-German relations came to dominate British diplomatic thinking after 1936, the foreign secretaries, Eden and Halifax, had to permit greater prime ministerial involvement in policy-making. On the other hand the Labour governments, dominated by Ramsay MacDonald, the prime minister, saw less autonomy. In the National Government of 1931–1935, a coalition of MacDonald Labourites, a smattering of anti-

Lloyd George Liberals, and the Conservatives, John Simon, the Liberal foreign secretary, stood somewhere between the Conservative and Labour extremes and so, too, did the Foreign Office. But the interwar period was a time which saw increasing efforts by civil servants in other departments to influence foreign policy. Maurice Hankey, the Cabinet and Committee of Imperial Defence secretary, and Warren Fisher, the Treasury permanent under-secretary, were two of these. Not only did the Foreign Office have to buy and sell in the diplomatic market abroad, it had to do so more often in the bureaucratic one at home.

The Foreign Office perception of the world in the interwar period was conditioned by two factors: Europe and the Empire. Professor Dilks draws attention to the 'professionalism' of both the Foreign Office and the diplomatic service, the mounting volume of work, and the efforts of some, like Eyre Crowe, to reform the administration of foreign policy. But that policy had to do the same things it had always done—ensure the country's security and protect the Empire. The war seemed to demonstrate that Europe was fundamentally important to British security. But Professor Dilks shows that the postwar Foreign Office did not draw any lessons about this from the experience of 1914–1918. The view still dominated that minimal terrene power could be more than compensated by pre-eminence at sea. In this way attempts to ensure European security by specific British commitments, notably the Locarno treaty negotiated in 1925 by the foreign secretary, Austen Chamberlain, which required a sizable British Expeditionary Force, tended to wither and die. This attitude seemed to set a pattern for British diplomatists till the Polish guarantee in 1939. There was Foreign Office recognition, as there always had been, that the Empire was the *raison d'être* for Britain as a Power of the first rank, indeed, the only truly global Power. This created a state of mind which could never contemplate giving up part of the Empire to consolidate Britain's world interests and, as Professor Dilks shows, it resulted in Foreign Office pursuit of a foreign policy the purpose of which was to preserve the status quo at all costs.

The first test for postwar British diplomacy came at the Paris Peace Conference in 1919. The dominant British personality, especially during the first six months when the German settlement was hammered out, was Lloyd George. This conference in many ways set the stage for great Power politics in the interwar years. It precipitated Franco-German animosity when German territories, some admittedly seized from France in 1870, were taken away and given to the French and the eastern European succession states. It created those succession states, which proved to be as rapacious and bellicose as any of the empires from which they were formed or the victorious Powers to which they were tied. It led to the political — but significantly not the economic — isolation of the United States from international politics. It established the League of Nations as the great hope for open diplomacy; however, the Americans refused to join, the Germans came in 1926 and left in 1933, and the Soviet Russians cynically took up membership in 1934. Of course, Lloyd George and the others who met at Paris attempted to ensure that another 'Great War' on the scale of 1914-1918 would never again occur, but they did so in the diplomatic marketplace and made deals which they believed would best serve their national interests. Their perception of the past and their hopes for the future conditioned their diplomacy.

M. L. Dockrill considers British policy at Paris in terms of what Lloyd George and his advisers, including those in the Foreign Office, hoped they would be able to do to ensure that European security could be maintained. The central consideration was Germany. Britain and its two major allies, the United States and France, had to find a means of reconciling their differing views about the German question. The British perception of the problem, delineated by the Political Intelligence Department of the Foreign Office, was that European stability had to be based on Anglo-American collaboration during and after the conference. Initially there seemed to be little difficulty in arriving at a common Anglo-American position, what Dr Dockrill shows as harmonising 'British self-interest and Wilsonian principles'. This entailed assuring, for the British, that the European balance of power was re-established and, for the Americans, that the principle of national self-determination would be at the fore in redrawing the map of Europe. The problem was that French views differed markedly from the British and American ones: the French conception of European security involved hobbling Germany by annexations of territory, massive reparations payments, and encircling it with hostile states. As the conference progressed, the common Anglo-American front proved to be a chimera; it broke up over the naval question, reparations, and the disposal of German colonial territory. This permitted the French view of European security to gain ascendancy in the drafting of the Treaty of Versailles. Dr Dockrill demonstrates that the British were able to defeat some of the more extreme French proposals but, because they had not thought beyond the policy of Anglo-American collaboration, Lloyd George's and his advisers' vision of postwar European security was not realised. The Americans became isolationist, mistrust between the British and French arose, and the Germans were able ultimately to exploit these divisions to reacquire great Power status.

The American question assumed great importance for the British in the interwar years. The 1920s were an especially difficult time in Anglo-American relations. In the five years after the Peace Conference a number of issues affected the perceptions British diplomatists had of the United States: the American rejection of the Treaty of Versailles, and with it the League of Nations; the naval question at the Washington conference; the Anglo-American debt settlement; and the reparations issue. By 1924 these issues had been resolved and, with the election within a week of each other in the autumn of that year of the second Baldwin government and Coolidge's first full Administration, a period of calm developed in Anglo-American relations. This calm lasted until the summer of 1927 when the failure of the Coolidge conference set in train a crisis in Anglo-American relations over the naval question which was not resolved until the London Navy Treaty of 1930. The Foreign Office, presided over by Austen Chamberlain, had the principal role in resolving this crisis, although the second MacDonald government got the credit for the final settlement. However, the perceptions of domestic America that had emerged in the period of calm did not much alter in the crisis years of 1927–1930. The image of the United States formed in the first half of Chamberlain's tenure as foreign secretary was unchanged in the second; moreover, it was the same during MacDonald's handling of the American question in 1929–1930, since those men who advised the Labour Prime Minister were the same ones who had helped Chamberlain.

The Chamberlain Foreign Office's perception of domestic America that evolved during that period of calm and at the time of the Coolidge conference is analysed by B.J.C. McKercher. The Foreign Office view of the United States was based on information received from the diplomatic service in the United States. Official opinion came chiefly from the Embassy at Washington, presided over by the ambassador, Esme Howard. Assessments of 'public' opinion, which were derived from the American press, came from the British Library of Information at New York, a clearing house for American periodicals and newspapers. The Library of Information was crucial because, given the size of the United States and the Embassy's relative isolation on the east coast, it provided Chamberlain and his advisers with currents of opinion in the South and west of the Mississippi Valley. Dr McKercher shows that the Foreign Office drew a number of lessons about domestic American opinion and its probable effect on the course of United States foreign policy both in general and, more specifically, towards Britain—an under-current of xenophobia that could be easily aroused by the jingo press, the power of the press whether jingo or not, the isolationist attitudes of America towards the political situation in Europe, and the corresponding American interest in economic diplomacy. On the eve of the Coolidge conference the Chamberlain Foreign Office had a decided image of the United States and, over the course of that conference and in its immediate aftermath, the lessons drawn in the period of diplomatic calm seemed to have been correct. In responding to the United States, the Foreign Office divided between those who wanted a strident approach—chiefly in the European departments—and those who thought one of cautious resolve would be best—principally the American specialists in the American Department. Dr McKercher outlines the debate between these two competing views, which began as the conference was in its death throes, and demonstrates how, based on information from the Washington Embassy and the Library of Information, Chamberlain sided with those who sought to avoid stridency in approaching the Americans. This set the tone for Chamberlain's American policies after 1927 and goes far in explaining, in tandem, with the perception of domestic America from 1924 to 1927, why particular policies were pursued during the time of crisis.

The first eight articles of this collection concern case studies of British foreign policy in the almost fifty years before the Second World War, studies which consider the attitudes of British diplomatists, how those attitudes were shaped by and shaped events, and how in a few instances British foreign policy was created as a result. As a concluding article, however, there is offered an insightful, and at times iconoclastic, assessment of the state of the art of diplomatic history. It is Michael Fry's purpose to put the relevance of international history into the context of modern trends in historiography, not to castigate the practitioners of the art but, instead, to say emphatically that this question of attitudes is really fundamental to understanding how and why particular courses of action are taken or, as the case may be, not taken. The crux of Professor Fry's piece is the argument that it is time for international historians to reassert the importance of their subject in the general realm of the social sciences, and to do so at a time when the 'applied aspects' of the subject have especial significance to modern problems. There is no doubt that most social scientists, and not a few historians who labour in fields like cultural, economic, intellectual, and social history, see the art of diplomatic history as 'old fashioned'. But foreign and defence policy and diplomatic strategy derive ultimately from men's minds, minds conditioned by a multiplicity of cultural, economic, intellectual, and social factors and personal experience.

Professor Fry contends, and Cedric Lowe would agree — as would the contributors to this volume as evidenced by their work — that writing diplomatic history is more than simply analysing 'what one damn Foreign Office clerk wrote to another'. It is a process of coming to grips with a number of social science issues in a given period to understand why the men at that moment did as they did. As his jumping off point, Professor Fry considers James Joll's seminal discourse on 'the unspoken assumptions' which always lay behind foreign policy decisions. Joll sees these as 'general ideas in the air'; Lowe would call them 'taste'. Both are really part and parcel of the same thing. The difficulty is that there has never been any attempt to investigate rigorously what exactly 'the unspoken assumptions' at given times are. This has left diplomatic historians and their craft open to attack by social scientists who rightly place emphasis on such rigour. Professor Fry believes that diplomatic historians must address themselves to discover precisely what constitutes 'the unspoken assumptions' prevalent amongst those whom they study and whose policies they analyse. He offers ten research problems which, when tackled collectively, can help answer the question 'why do individuals in office think and behave as they do, and how free are they to behave in preferred ways?' These problems are applied to Lloyd George as a diplomatist, and the conclusions that are indicated as a result offer intriguing insights into the course of British foreign policy whilst he was in a political position either to influence or determine the course of policy. Thus, in this collection of case studies which consider attitudes and diplomacy, this final article on the need for those who write diplomatic history to be rigorous in their approach to understanding the minds of those who make and implement foreign policy is a fitting capstone.

ZARA STEINER

Elitism and Foreign Policy: The Foreign Office before the Great War

Diplomacy in the pre-1914 period was in the hands of a tiny elite. Its forms and practices were very much the product of an aristocratic society that persisted even after that class lost its position of primacy. The problem of identification is not a difficult one, above all in Britain where the cabinet system of government and the well-established claims of successive foreign secretaries to positions of primacy provide a useful starting point. Recent studies of other individuals, departments, and institutions have considerably broadened the diplomatic canvas but none have resulted in a reappraisal of the central role of the foreign secretary and his agents in the making of foreign policy. What were the characteristics of this elite? Was there a shared consensus about the world in which they worked? Was there an operative set of beliefs which affected the choice of diplomatic options? As a form of historical shorthand, one speaks of a Foreign Office view. Does this mean something more than just a collection of individual opinions?

Rupert Wilkinson's definition of an elite as 'a distinctive group holding high status in its community and knit together by a strong group feeling, ethos and style', adequately describes the British Foreign Office and diplomatic service. Its social and educational exclusiveness has been the subject of much comment then and now. Its political leaders, Lord Salisbury, Lord Lansdowne, and Sir Edward Grey (as well as their successors, Balfour and Curzon) belonged to the traditional landed class which had long served the state. The differences between these men, and they were considerable, should not obscure their similarities, nor the common way in which they were regarded. They were thought to be statesmen rather than politicians, removed from the daily political battles fought by their colleagues. The office, itself, bestowed considerable prestige on its holder. Lord Salisbury is said to have preferred it to that of prime minister. Lord Lansdowne welcomed his appointment as a means of restoring a somewhat tarnished reputation. Despite his youth and relative inexperience, Grey had an equally exalted view of his position. It was, in part, Grey's reputation as a 'gentleman in the very best sense of the word' that made him acceptable to large sections of both parties.

Those who served these foreign secretaries came from a similar social caste. The great gap between foreign secretary and the rest of the Foreign Office was one of prestige and function. But the lineage of many in Whitehall and abroad was as respectable as the 'august personages' who sat in the foreign secretary's chair. The Foreign Office and diplomatic service were separately recruited. The diplomat had to have at least a £400 annual private income and earned nothing during his first years of service. As a result, it was generally believed that the diplomats came from a higher social strata than London officials and that the costs of diplomatic life abroad discouraged able candidates. In fact, since the 1850s, the number of aristocrats in both services had markedly declined; it was the bias towards the landed classes that still remained.[1] If fewer scions of the aristocracy applied to the Foreign Office, it still had its share of men of good family. Increasingly, both services were recruiting from the professions; it was the sons of diplomats, officers, barristers, bankers, and clergymen who were successful in the annual entrance competitions. Some of these had themselves come from gentry stock; others climbed from the ranks of the successful upper-middle class. But what was most marked in both career ladders was the relative absence of recruits from the mercantile community and that at a time when the balance in Parliament was noticeably altering. It was in this respect that the political and Foreign Office elites clearly differed. When the radicals of the day spoke of the 'aristocratic bias' of the Foreign Office, they were in fact referring to the absence of men from trading and manufacturing families.

It is undoubtedly true that parental origins and professions rather than schooling provide the real key to Edwardian social distinctions;

the middle classes were already using the public schools as a means of entering the governing classes. Nonetheless, the educational homogeneity of both the Foreign Office and diplomatic service reinforced that sense of group identity which the definition of an elite implies. An overwhelming number of recruits went to a few public schools, Eton above all, Harrow, Wellington, Rugby, Winchester, and Downside (the number of Catholics in the Office and service is a curious feature of the pre-war diplomatic establishment.)[2] Particularly after the Lansdowne reforms of 1904, almost all successful entrants went on to university, most to Oxford, some to Cambridge, the odd man to a Scottish or foreign university. The domination of Eton, admittedly a very large public school, seems to have increased rather than diminished in the early 20th century. Between 1908 and 1914, 9 out of 16 clerks and 16 out of 21 attachés came from this one school. However lazy or industrious such prospective recruits may have been, they, like their political heads, had gone through an educational system geared to moulding a particular kind of man. Horace Rumbold, defending himself against a parental charge of undue national narrowness, wrote to his father:

> Having been brought up at a private and public school in England has made me what it makes everybody else and my attitude of mind is no different to that of thousands of others who have had the same education as myself. We are English, and that's all.... [3]

Whereas in social and economic background, there was little to distinguish most British diplomats from their European colleagues, their education was markedly different. The chanceries of Europe were heavily staffed by men who were legally trained or had attended diplomatic academies. In the English public schools, the study of Latin and Greek continued to hold pride of place. At university, an increasing number of would-be diplomats read history or modern languages.

The whole entrance procedure and the examination system was intended to recruit the kind of man who was fit for a diplomatic career. This meant men who could move in a certain social milieu though it was admitted that in many capitals the social and political elites might not be coterminous.[4] It meant men fluent in foreign languages, especially French. It also meant, in the days when 'lady typewriters' were still relatively few in number, clerks and attachés with good handwriting. One must be careful not to over-stress the 'social accomplishments' demanded for the diplomatic life; they were, more or less, assumed. Competition for both services was real. Entrants into the foreign service between 1907–1914 obtained a higher percentage of marks than successful candidates for the Home and Indian civil services. Both the Foreign Office and the diplomatic service had men of undoubted intellectual distinction — including Firsts in Oxford Schools or Cambridge Tripos. But successful entry depended on an expensive and often lengthy education — public school, university, a year or two abroad, attendance at a crammer, two or even three tries at the examination.

One did not present oneself to the private secretary or the later Board of Selection for permission to sit either examination unless one had the credentials needed. Those who tried for places often knew each other; they had been at the same schools or college, frequented the same pensions (Harold Nicolson's *Some People* conveys the atmosphere of Jeanne de Herault's house in Paris where Nicolson, Vansittart, and many others learned their French) and the same crammers (Scoones' on Garrick Street). There was an intricate network of family relationships augmented by marriage ties. Fathers, sons, and grandsons (the Rumbolds, for instance) appear in the *Foreign Office Lists*. Diplomatic circles provided future wives though these might well extend beyond national borders. A number of attachés even had foreign or American wives, although Henry Bruce's marriage to a Russian ballet dancer was somewhat out of the normal pattern and ended his diplomatic career.

Even more than the actual role of the Board of Selection or the examination, the public image of the Foreign Office type restricted the pool of candidates. Asked why there were so few Scots or sons of rich Nonconformist merchants found in the diplomatic service, William Tyrrell (then Grey's private secretary) replied in 1914, 'They do not present themselves.'[5] It was an answer to be echoed each time the Foreign Office found itself under attack for its social exclusiveness. Belonging to the upper classes did not preclude a wide range of social gradation, from earls and baronets to the sons of barristers and surgeons. Nor did forms of recruitment exclude the singular clerk, Eyre Crowe for one, or the brilliant and erratic Arthur Hardinge, so different in all respects from his cousin Charles. Though in any one year, neither the Foreign Office nor the diplomatic service took in more than three to six young men, both services included men who came to maturity in different decades. T. H. Sanderson, Salisbury's and Lansdowne's permanent under-secretary, entered the Foreign Office at 18 in 1859; Eyre Crowe and William Tyrrell, his post-1919 successors in 1885 and 1889 and their successors, Ronald Lindsay and Robert Vansittart in 1898 and 1902. Generational differences can be a question of decades as well as lifetimes, of common experiences rather than birth dates.[6]

More than social and educational ties created the sense of kinship which marked this part of the foreign policy elite. Diplomacy was a profession; its practitioners believed that the conduct of negotiations between states should be left in the hands of men who were experts in their craft. This view was shared both by foreign secretaries and the men who carried out their instructions. Apart from the prime ministership, the Foreign Office represented the top of the political ladder. It was possibly the most prestigious of all other Cabinet appointments. Traditionally, foreign secretaries remained in office throughout the Ministry's life and often returned again when their parties returned to power. While acknowledging the principles of cabinet control, few foreign secretaries expected that their Cabinet colleagues would concern themselves with the details of foreign policy. Most only consulted the prime minister and a small group of interested colleagues. The more active role of Chamberlain and the Cabinet in Salisbury's last administration was a sign of the prime minister's increasing age. Lansdowne, scrupulous about consulting his colleagues, kept the initiative in his own hands. Grey's task was the most difficult of all for he was faced with a split in both the Cabinet and in his party on foreign policy issues. He avoided confrontation when he could, e.g. over the military conversations with France, and was less than honest in his dealings with parliamentary critics. He disliked the new parliamentary interest in foreign affairs and was never happy about the interventions of his Cabinet colleagues in Anglo-German affairs. Basically, Grey, like so many of his predecessors, thought his office should be free from outside intervention. He did not believe his fellow ministers had the necessary expertise, nor was it the foreign secretary's duty to enlighten or educate his party about the delicate mechanisms which preserved the peace of Europe.

These feelings were shared by members of the Foreign Office and diplomatic service. Men recruited through a competitive system, who spent most of their working lives in one department and who slowly but inevitably moved up a career ladder were bound to develop a strong esprit de corps. A sense of professional elitism became more pronounced in the Liberal period of government. The civil service, in general, was more self-conscious as recruitment became competitive and responsibilities multiplied. Life careers (relatively few men left the Foreign Office though there was some change in the ranks of the diplomatic service) made for professional awareness as did the increasing involvement of the Foreign Office staff in the policy-making process.[7] Men who worked in London rarely went abroad. Exchanges with the diplomatic service were the exception rather than the rule; only at the top of two career ladders was it becoming increasingly common in the early 20th century. Despite the recommendations of successive Select Committees and Royal Commissions, the majority in both services resisted amalgamation on the grounds that their differing functions required different professional qualities. There was a certain amount of friction between the two groups particularly as the senior Foreign Office officials underlined their advisory as well as their administrative roles. Diplomats were 'social butterflies' and prone to 'localitis'. Foreign Office clerks were 'office drudges', 'provincial', and 'uncaring'. There were complaints, still familiar today, about despatches which went unread or advice that was ignored. There were still powerful ambassadors and ministers; the European embassies were still the top of the career ladder. But Whitehall officials close to Grey had opportunities for influence denied the distant diplomat. At the least, in addition to the ambassador's despatch, there was an Office minute or a memorandum. The diplomatic manuals, Calliéres, de Wicquefort, and in 1917, Satow's *Guide to Diplomatic Practice,* still stressed the qualities needed by the envoy sent abroad but in these years, those serving at home were developing their own claims to a special position in the foreign policy elite.

As the Foreign Office expanded (there were still only about 50 members of the diplomatic establishment in Whitehall in 1914), became better organised and more involved in matters of high politics, its mandarin tone became a source of irritation to those outside its doors. Equally powerful in the creation of this sharper sense of professionalism was the negative reaction to the renewed public interest in foreign affairs and a demand for information which neither the foreign secretary nor the bureaucrats thought desirable. The Foreign Office and diplomatic service closed ranks against the Radical-Labour attack on Grey and the entente policy. The creation of the Foreign Policy Committee in 1911 and the 'Grey must Go' campaign of 1911-1912 served to strengthen the self-consciousness of the Office. These forms of professional elitism should be distinguished from the social and educational exclusiveness described earlier. They could be linked but they could also be entirely separate. Eyre Crowe is an excellent example of the professional mandarin. Born and raised in Germany with a German mother and wife, he had been educated abroad and attended neither an English public school nor university. His habits of living were of the simplest and he was totally devoid of any social pretensions. He was a superb civil servant, widely read, with a deep knowledge of past history, a keen interest in the workings of the office, and a sharp eye for detail. He not only had a powerfully logical mind but he was a first-rate draughtsman; his minutes and memoranda are clear and to the point. Crowe was totally identified with the Foreign Office; his highest ambition, realised in 1920, was to become permanent under-secretary. No one was more suspicious of politicians nor a stauncher opponent of all forms of outside interference. Crowe, even in the pre-war period, believed that all 'amateurs' and 'busybodies' — which included almost everyone not in the Foreign Office — should be barred from diplomacy. He argued, and it was a prejudice which he never abandoned, that it was quite unnecessary to bother about the press or public opinion. He despised parliamentary manoeuverings and public campaigns. Few men had a greater influence in fashioning the tone and thinking of the younger inhabitants of the Foreign Office even when in later years they came to reject some of his most deep-rooted beliefs.

The British have, for their purposes, a relatively limited body of men, recruited from the upper stratas of society, educated in a common system of values and beliefs, and highly conscious of their professional qualifications. Can we then explore more deeply their 'unspoken assumptions' as outlined by James Joll in his justly influential inaugural lecture of 1968.

> When political leaders are faced with the necessity of taking decisions the outcome of which they cannot foresee, in crises which they do not wholly understand, they fall back on their

own instinctive reactions, traditions and modes of behaviour. Each of them has certain beliefs, rules or objectives which are taken for granted; and one of the limitations of the documentary evidence is that few people bother to write down, especially in moments of crisis, things which they take for granted.[8]

It has been argued by American social scientists that it is the beliefs men hold rather than the evidence before them that determines their ultimate choice of options.[9] Historical example is used to buttress predetermined conclusions. Experience is assimilated into an existing framework of inherited ideas. As we are dealing with men who can be identified and about whom we have a great deal of information, we should be able to provide a clearer definition of these patterns of belief and thought which shaped British diplomacy in the early 20th century. This approach does not exclude the possibility, indeed the probability, that many actions can be explained as a response to outside events but it does suggest that the latter were seen within an inherited framework which proved surprisingly durable given the pace of external change.

For during the last decades of the nineteenth century, new movements and alterations in the body politic were altering the international scene in which diplomats had to operate. This is not the place to elaborate on themes which have been discussed in a variety of books.[10] There seems to be a general consensus among historians that new and more virulent forms of nationalism spread throughout Europe and appeared in other continents as well. The causes were multiple, some specifically European, others individual and indigenous. The enlargement of the governing elite and the electorate was one factor. Economic changes resulting in a greater awareness of the importance of foreign trade and colonial acquisitions another. Improvements in transportation and communication gave a physical reality to events on the periphery. Increasing literacy at home and the rise of the cheap press (the foundation of the *Daily Mail* in 1896 dedicated 'to the supremacy and the greatness of the British Empire... the articulate voice of British progress and domination') popularised and vulgarised events and emotions which had previously concerned only the few. The spread of Social Darwinian thinking changed the clichés of politics and journalism. If the upsurge of a newly articulated pride in national achievement created its own reaction, the terms of the imperial debate at the turn of the century were somewhat different from those used in 1850.

There was another side to the coin. In the '80s and '90s, there was also a growing awareness that there were new threats to Britain's world power and the pax Britannica. There was the troubling economic depression, the National Fair Trade League, a Royal Commission in 1886, and the appearance of a national best-seller, *Made in Germany* in 1896. There were imperial clashes with other great powers; the rivalries with France and Russia were well-publicised. Fashoda, according to Kennedy Jones, the *Daily Mail* correspondent, was one of the first times the press was actually welcomed at the Foreign Office. There were the scares, real and imaginary, starting with the naval scare of 1884, about Britain's naval strength and the safety of her empire and kingdom. There was the creation of a whole new genre of literature feeding and creating a new interest in invasions and war. Then came the Boer struggle, a colonial war of greater duration and far greater cost than the usual Victorian colonial clashes. Older arguments were revived and dressed in new clothing. The imperial case was more strongly stated, but the sentiments expressed in Tennyson's *Maud* were also refurbished and the moral claims for expansion and dominion re-examined. Was struggle inevitable and beneficial? Was war as heroic and self-fulfilling as suggested by the Odyssey or Kipling's Indian stories?

It was against this mixed background that many of Grey's officials came of age. There was certainly a distinct difference in the way Salisbury and Joseph Chamberlain viewed the same external world. The same contrast can be seen when reading Crowe's memorandum of 1907 and Thomas Sanderson's comments on that memorandum. Harold Nicolson, like Horace Rumbold, attributed the sharper sense of national pride and international competitiveness to his father's schooling.

> He curbed his instinctive tendency towards original or individual thought. He adopted rather, the mental habits of his generation — and among other fallacies, he imagined that virility was among the highest aims of human endeavour. He, thus, in common with the vast majority of his contemporaries came to believe that patriotism was in its turn the sublimation of the

virility ideal—that it was the duty of every Englishman to render his own country more powerful, richer and larger than any other country.[11]

There was a noticeable change in the ethos of the public schools during the late Victorian era, a shift from 'godliness and good learning' to muscular Christianity with its emphasis on sport, manly strength, physical courage, and the corporate spirit. There was the new stress in Speech Day orations and school magazines on patriotism, service to one's country and empire. What had been once assumed now became explicitly stated. Lord Roberts and Lord Wolseley were favoured speakers on the public school circuit. The Naval League sent pamphlets and speakers. The Chief Scout was only repeating a familiar theme when he told his youthful audience:

> It will largely depend upon you, the younger generation of Britain that are now growing up to be the men of the Empire. Don't be disgraced like the young Romans who lost the Empire of their fore-fathers by being wishy-washy slackers without any go or patriotism in them. Play up. Each man in his place and play the game.[12]

This is the period when the public schools founded or expanded their cadet and rifle corps and when the Headmasters Conference unsuccessfully petitioned the Conservative government to make cadet corps service compulsory in their schools. These were the lessons intended for the next generation of politicians, diplomats, civil servants, and soldiers. The old aristocracy were deserting governesses and tutors for the prep and public schools; the upper middle class sent his son to Eton to imbibe the same ethos and goals.

The more aggressive assertion of manly virtue and patriotic fervour reached its height at the turn of the century; soon the philistinism of the schools was to come under considerable attack. Character building was both the implicit and explicit function of the schools; it would be surprising if the new lessons were not learnt. We know far less about the effects of a classical education; the changing preoccupation with Greek rather than Latin texts provides an interesting footnote.[13] Men as diverse as Milner, Cromer, Curzon, and Grey continued to read classical authors long after they left school and university. References to the lessons of fifth century B.C. dot the diaries of statesmen and diplomats. For the few who went beyond construing their sentence, the Homeric ideals might well have provided a lifetime tuning fork. The virtues extolled by Homer were the same found in Alfred Austin and Henry Newbold, in Southey's *Nelson* (a favourite prize day award) and in *Scouting for Boys*.

It is more difficult to gauge the effects of Oxbridge at a time when questions of national preparedness and imperial conflicts were in the forefront of political debate. After all, though the Oxford Union was the nursery of future prime ministers, young men played at, rather than engaged in, politics. It is easy to overestimate the influence of T. H. Green or Jowett; the Master of Balliol's effort to tempt Sir Edward Grey from a life of academic idleness ended in fiasco. There was as much attention paid to sport and gambling as to books; to literature and the theatre as to politics. There are too many individual variations to draw any clear conclusions. Undoubtedly Oxford and Cambridge were part of the Edwardian 'inner circle'; the young men rubbed shoulders with London politicians and journalists and expected to join the favoured few. The life-style of the typical upper-class undergraduate did not, on the whole, lead to any massive rebellions against the code of the public schools, at least not among those who thought of diplomacy as a promising career.

The Grand Tour abroad might in this period include the white Dominions, India, and the United States. But these experiences seem to have strengthened rather than modified upper-class pride in the accomplishments of their country and intensified their sense of national identity. Curiously enough, neither travel nor residence abroad proved an antidote to inherited stereotypes and prejudices. Admittedly, experiences during the Boer War were uncomfortable; autobiographies of the period rarely omit a reference to the extreme Anglophobia found not only in Germany but in France. But even those men born in foreign countries and raised in diplomatic households could be passionately chauvinistic and totally intolerant of foreigners. Men like Edward Goschen and Horace Rumbold were entirely 'English' in their sensibilities. The former was highly sensitive about his foreign antecedents and his diplomatic diary is full of laments for 'dear old England'. Rumbold's youthful contempt for the French, Persians, and Jews, particularly the latter, was soon to include Americans and Poles as he moved about the diplomatic circuit. Experience abroad often confirmed a sense of national superiority that bordered on the xenophobic.

Officials denied they were anti-foreign; they were only pro-British. Hardinge defended Arthur Nicolson from German charges of Teutonophobia in 1910 on just these grounds. Eric Phipps was to make the same claim for Vansittart in 1936. The realities were somewhat cruder. The very definition of British was exceedingly narrow; Scots, non-conformists, Jews, black men, were not welcome as colleagues. There were men who fell in love with a particular foreign landscape or country, who went native in the manner so abhorred by their Foreign Office colleagues. But the easy cosmopolitanism of an earlier generation seems to have disappeared. The general distrust of foreigners did not preclude a love of things French or Italian, marrying foreign wives, speaking foreign languages, or spending most of one's life abroad. But it did give to British diplomacy and diplomats a tone and legacy which has not entirely disappeared. 'An Englishman always has a better sense of fair play than a foreigner,' Horace Rumbold wrote. 'We are the linchpin of the world's political structure.'[14] 'I am quite tired of explaining to Foreigners that we *never* have an intriguing policy. We seldom have a policy at all — but when we do it is always straight forward', Edward Goschen wrote in his diary in 1907.[15] An almost unconscious assumption of moral rectitude is found in Eyre Crowe's famed memorandum of 1907:

> The danger (of a combination against her) can in practice only be averted... on condition that the national policy of the insular and naval State is so directed as to harmonize with the general desires and ideals common to all mankind, and more particularly that it is closely identified with the primary and vital interests of a majority, or as many as possible, of other nations. Now, the first interest of all countries is the preservation of national independence. It follows that England... has a direct and positive interest in the maintenance of the independence of nations, and therefore, must be the natural enemy of any country threatening the independence of others, and the natural protector of the weaker communities.[16]

What seemed like a logical imperative to Crowe might well have appeared to foreigners in a rather different light. The maintenance of the Pax Britannica meant the perpetuation of Britain's world primacy. What British statesmen called the balance of power had allowed their country to become the most powerful imperial nation in the world.

The charges of realpolitik made then and now (notice the parallel with the American position after the Second World War) needs qualification if one is to understand how British diplomats perceived their own actions. Successive generations of schoolboys had been taught to believe that British rule was pacific and beneficent. Even the most ardent spokesmen for empire, Curzon, Milner, and Lytton Bulwer, proclaimed that in empire 'we have found not merely the key to glory and wealth, but the call to duty and the means of service to mankind.' Britain's civilising mission was a trust; the marriage between power and responsibility effected even before the doubters and pessimists made their influence felt. The sense of superiority over other races was tempered by a belief that a new harmony could be effected; this despite the social Darwinian jargon of the day. Lord Salisbury may have been exceptional in his call for co-operation between the races and in his detestation of all forms of racial arrogance but some of the same sentiments can be found in Rudyard Kipling's *The Enlightenment of Pagett MP* (1890).

'Once we fall from our traditional standard of fair play and straight dealing', Victor Wellesley, an under-secretary in the Foreign Office, wrote in 1926, 'then we are lost'.[17] This was very much the sentiment of the pre-1914 generation. Diplomats believed in their inherent right to instruct others because it was for the latter's own good. Arthur Nicolson's comments about Persia, Lowther's complaints about the Turks, even John Jordan's communications to the Chinese reflect the tone of the school-master or aggrieved priest. Lord Curzon never abandoned his Viceregal ways; at the Lausanne Conference, his most successful post-war foray, he lectured, bullied, and threatened as if there had been no world war, no Turkish revolution, and no change in Middle Eastern politics. 'He treated us like schoolboys but we did not mind', Ismet Pasha, the head of the Turkish Delegations remarked. 'He treated the French and Italians just the same.'[18]

This combination of morality and self-interest, concern and contempt also coloured Foreign Office thinking about economic and commercial questions. The Foreign Office had already responded to the demands for a more active policy as British traders were faced with an increasingly competitive position abroad, first in the eighties and nineties and then after a period of prosperity and complacency, again after 1912. The protection of trade and the maintenance of 'a fair field and no favour' had remained a vital British interest long after the structure of the mercantilist state had been dismantled. The relations between the Foreign Office, the financiers and the traders had been hammered out in the high Victorian period when Britain was the workshop and the banker of the world. British firms were both enterprising and successful. It was natural, therefore, that Liberals and Conservatives should have believed, with Cobden, that free trade was a blessing and that it would draw nations together and promote international peace. Also, they should follow the maxim, sanctioned by success, that apart from securing conditions of free and open competition for all, the state should leave to individual enterprise the task of finding and developing its own markets abroad.

These beliefs came under strain and attack when other competitors appeared in world markets. They were, in special cases, to be compromised and even abandoned by the Foreign Office in the period after 1885. But the ideas persisted even when the practice changed. Again Eyre Crowe is a most useful witness:

> Second only to the idea of independence, nations have always cherished the right of free intercourse and trade in the world's markets, and in proportion as England champions the principle of the largest measure of general freedom of commerce, she undoubtedly strengthens her hold on the interested friendship of other nations, at least to the extent of making them feel less apprehensive of naval supremacy in the hands of a free trade in England than they would in the face of predominant protectionist Power.[19]

The senior clerk saw in the arguments for free trade a basic reason why the world could accept British rule.

Even when aware of the increasing erosion of the non-intervention principle, foreign secretaries, officials, and diplomats continued to believe that British trade had to be self-sufficient if it were to prosper and to remain British. Successive foreign secretaries complained that British firms were not aggressive enough and could learn a great deal from their foreign rivals. The same views were expressed by those most directly engaged in commercial matters, the diplomats in the Far East (Ernest Satow and John Jordan), in the Levant, and in Latin America. Younger embassy officials, even in Europe, complained that a large part of their work consisted of getting British firms out of trouble caused by their own stupidity or carelessness. Though willing to intervene at the highest levels to see that British firms and investors were 'fairly' treated, the Foreign Office did not believe that diplomats should 'stump the world for trade' or do British merchants' work for them. Horace Rumbold was more forthright than most when on refusing an assignment to Peru, he wrote, 'So somebody else can take on the job of screwing money out of shady Dagoes'.[20]

The continuing belief in laissez-faire and self-help principles was buttressed by the social snobberies of a profession which excluded men from trade. Diplomatic fears of 'touting' covered a certain disdain for matters commercial. Edward Goschen listed subjects that he hated: statistics, finance, commerce, and boundaries (Diary 17 July 1911). Bruce Lockhardt cites the ambassador in Russia who wrote, 'My dear—Please remember that I am not here to bother with questions of trade.'[21] The examples are numerous and extend far beyond the period under consideration. Ambassadors were concerned with 'la haute politique', commercial treaties could be left to subordinates, and more mundane matters to commercial attachés, commercial secretaries, and consul-generals (who could be diplomats).[22] The consular service as such was a world apart from that of the embassy or legation. The General Consular Service was not really put on a serious professional footing until 1903 and then still remained the Cinderella of the diplomatic world. All the consular services (General, Levant, and Far Eastern) were separately recruited and isolated from the Foreign Office and diplomatic service. By comparison, the French, and even the German services, were better treated and more effectively organised. British diplomats assumed that one did not mix socially with consuls (though even the consular service was reluctant to recruit 'the leavings of trade'); they were not seen at the Foreign Office clubs, Travellers', and St. James's; they were 'second class' citizens in embassies and often stationed too far from capital cities to be part of less exalted missions. Professor Platt writes 'Of the two main European clubs at Constantinople, the Circle d'Orient was the preserve of diplomats, financiers and uppermost levels of societies; merchants and men of the second rank, including consuls patronised the Club de Constantinople.'[23]

Some consuls became ministers and ambassadors. William White from the Levant, Sir Henry Parkes, Ernest Satow, and John Jordan from the Far Eastern Services, made the transition. But these men were members of highly specialised consular elites and had performed political and legal, rather than commercial work, before taking their diplomatic posts in Turkey, China, and Japan. Even these positions were soon reclaimed by the diplomatic service ever hungry for top postings. As late as 1939, Hugh Knatchbull-Hugesson could point to a lack of savoir faire and unpresentable wives as reasons for rejecting amalgamation proposals.[24] Nor were these objections restricted to consuls; commercial attachés, first appointed in the eighties, though recruited from the diplomatic class remained on the fringe of embassy life as Joseph Crowe (Eyre Crowe's father) complained in 1886[25] and Francis Oppenheimer emphasised in his very bitter autobiography, *Stranger Within*, published in 1960.

The Foreign Office, moreover, tended to take a different view of the City than the mercantile community. Lord Rothschild, despite being Jewish, and Lord Revelstoke were received in the highest Foreign Office circles and though Charles Hardinge could not bear him, Sir Ernest Cassel was part of the royal entourage. Sons of bankers joined the Foreign Office and diplomatic service; the Baring family was represented in both. For the most part, it was the Foreign Office which sought the assistance of the City and not the other way around. For it was far easier to raise private money for investment in Canada, the United States or even Latin America than to take the risks of investing in Persia or Turkey.[26] The interests of the Foreign Office and the bankers did not always coincide. Arthur Nicolson, while permanent under-secretary, was to complain that financiers were only interested in profit and indifferent to the interests of their country. The ties between the Foreign Office and the City were informal; only a few financial houses were on the former's calling list but their heads were very much part of the official establishment. The preference given to financial over manufacturing interests set a pattern which lasted well beyond the First World War. It was the fear that the City would collapse and thus set in motion a series of events which might lead to severe social dislocations which so alarmed Sir Edward Grey in July 1914. It was the adverse consequences of a run on gold which led to one of the few pre-war investigations of what might be the effects of a European war. The internationalism, particularly the Anglo-German complexion, of the leading firms worried Eyre Crowe and it undoubtedly intensified Charles Hardinge's open anti-semitism. The City represented a power which the Foreign Office could not and did not ignore.

Sir Maurice Bunsen told the 1914 Royal Commission that half of the time of his diplomatic mission was taken up with commercial work.[27] The papers of Charles Hardinge during the early stages of his diplomatic career, Horace Rumbold, and Eric Phipps, all men serving in European posts, suggest that this testimony was entirely accurate. The work in the non-European capitals was even more weighted in this direction. There was a mass of commercial information coming into the Foreign Office from its diplomatic staff extending from sections of each mission's annual report to detailed memoranda prepared by attachés. The Cairo correspondence is rich in economic data as Lord Cromer grappled with Egyptian finances. Despatches from commercial attachés, numbering only seven at the turn of the century but from highly capable and experienced men, as well as the consular reports were multiple and of considerable value. The three British consul-generals at Hamburg, Frankfurt, and Antwerp were asked by the Foreign Office, on behalf of the Admiralty, to give their views on the likely effect of a blockade on Germany. Summarising their conclusions, Francis Oppenheimer from Frankfurt, warned that Germany could remain self-sufficient in food and would be able to secure the resources needed for war-time industry from neutral countries. Again, Oppenheimer was asked to testify before the Desart Committee in 1913 on the probable consequence of a German ban on the repayment of bank loans, a major share of which were held in London.[28]

The difficulty was not with the collection of information, it was with the processing and distribution of that intelligence. Until it was abolished and its functions handled over to the Colonial Office, the African department handed both political and commercial questions together. The Far Eastern department and the clerks handling Latin American affairs also got a great deal of commercial information. But the great bulk of the consular reporting went to the Commercial department, a 'pass-on' office for the Board of Trade. These reports were not studied in the Foreign Office and almost nothing reached the other political departments. It was the

Board of Trade rather than the Foreign Office that was responsible for overseas commerce, the latter was but a post office. The failure to correct these conditions was to cost the Foreign Office its postwar position when economic diplomacy came to the forefront of international relations. Ambassadors did not see the consular material until it came back along with the confidential print and other reports in a printed form. The attention paid to the reports of diplomats, as distinct from the consuls, on economic questions depended on the mission head, its size, and location. The actual number of men in the Foreign Office and in the diplomatic service actively interested remained limited.

Even these men spoke in the terminology of the high Victorian period. This was, in part, because most still believed in the fundamental wisdom of inherited precepts and regarded departures from the rule regrettable exceptions. But though the Foreign Office might have understood the distinction between 'political' and 'commercial' concessions, it was far less clear to the governments of 'semi-civilised' countries, or, indeed, to those other great powers competing for political and economic influence abroad. For these, too, even Germany, the symbol of the new aggressive economic state, were under similar pressures and often responded in equally ambiguous ways. Though there was a protectionist group at the Foreign Office, the old rhetoric of free trade and non-intervention still prevailed. Rivals might have been forgiven for believing that Britain was having the best of both worlds, and that, once more, morality and self-interest were neatly joined.

The strength of these inherited assumptions limited the foreign policy makers' perceptions of their own time and the future. Though it may be true that the roots of the Anglo-German antagonism can be found in their economic rivalry, this was not the way that struggle was perceived in Whitehall.[29] It is interesting that both Hardinge and Crowe, so different in their upbringings and in their treatment of economic questions should have denied the importance of economic factors. It is not even clear how far the efforts of the Tariff Reform League alerted the clerks, to say nothing of the far-off diplomats, to the need for a fundamental rethinking of Britain's overseas role.[30] The complexities of international trade and finance only marginally impinged on the minds of those brought up in an age when such questions were left to others to resolve. Francis Hurst, the editor of the *Economist*, overstated his case before the

Royal Commission of 1914 but there was a central core of truth in his argument that the Foreign Office attitude towards commerce was that 'of the Homeric heroes or the Samurai of Japan'.

The Foreign Office view of strategic and military problems reflected this same awkward balance between old ideas and new situations. Again one notices a deep reluctance to abandon beliefs that had paid handsome dividends in the past even when aware of changing circumstances and new solutions. Having been taught to think in terms of naval power during one's formative years, how many could examine with an open mind the arguments outlined by Sir Halford Mackinder, whose lecture 'The Geographical Pivot of History' in 1904 has become something of an intellectual landmark. Having arrived at a satisfactory explanation of Britain's predominant position, it was far easier to restate the arguments rehearsed by Captain Mahan. The new ideas were either disregarded or were restated to fit in with older hypotheses. Only such an assumption can explain the strategic muddle in which the Foreign Office, as well as the service departments, found themselves between 1905 and 1914.

Undoubtedly, the Foreign Office was more involved in strategic matters under Grey than at the time of Lord Salisbury's rule. There were not only Cabinet meetings but the Committee of Imperial Defence and its many subcommittees, some of which were chaired by the Foreign Office permanent under-secretary. The major cabinet debates over the fleet and the military conversations with France drew in not only Grey but his chief advisors. The naval issue was at the heart of the liberal period of Anglo-German negotiations until the collapse of the Haldane mission talks. In the spring and autumn of 1912 and then again in the spring of 1914, the usual question was to resurface within the context of the ententes.

It would have been impossible to ignore the campaigns for fleet increases and compulsory military training. Almost to a man, the Foreign Office threw its weight behind Grey in his demands for a decisive margin of naval superiority over Germany. In the post-Boer War years, the subject of military preparedness was very much in the forefront of political debate. For many, the Boer War was *the* decisive event, exposing Britain's military weakness and underlining her diplomatic isolation. Percy Lorraine, as a young man, had actually fought in South Africa; almost everyone at the Foreign Office lived through anxious days and moments of elation. Opinions differed as to the right solution; Arthur Nicolson favoured the case for military service and conscription; Eyre Crowe remained faithful to the idea of a volunteer army. The next years were to be punctuated by crises which provoked both serious and frivolous discussions of war and a vast outpouring of leaders, articles, and pamphlets addressed to just these questions. But the Boer War did act as an important catalyst, one of those turning points which is sometimes forgotten because of the enormity of the events of 1914–1918.

During the Boer War the defence estimates spiralled and were not to return to their pre-war levels before war broke out in 1914. Both Unionists and Liberals were acutely conscious of the need to economise, particularly after 1908 when social service costs added to the financial burden. The Budget fights of 1908 and 1914 showed how central the whole financial question was to the politics of the time. The lack of unlimited funds acted as a check on all defence preparations before 1914. The Admiralty used the German threat to force the Cabinet to sanction its increasing costs (from £33 million in 1906 to £42.9 million in 1912) when it became impossible to modernise the navy within the old limits. But it won its struggle at the expense of Cabinet divisions and a chorus of criticism from within the Liberal party. Haldane shaped the Expeditionary Force to meet a rigid financial ceiling; it was the need to keep expenditure below £28 million that produced a six division BEF and not the army's continental requirements.[31] Grey was drawn into these quarrels; he knew that defence expenditure was not only unproductive but that it was a divisive political issue. Though he joined the battle against the economists, he was fully conscious of the need to keep expenditure as low as was consistent with a necessary margin of safety. Defence spending was 'a form of insurance'.

Grey's advisors were more critical of the Liberal government's balancing act; Hardinge and Nicolson, at least, would have much preferred more money spent on defence and less on the social services. In diplomatic circles, too, there was considerable opposition to Lloyd George's budget and the social reforms which they believed had made it necessary. 'It is unfortunate that the government will not lay the state of the country firmly and openly before the country', Nicolson complained in the autumn of 1913, 'and endeavour to stimulate the public to follow the example of every country in Europe and be ready to make certain sacrifices for their own defence.'[32] The permanent under-secretary and the British ambassador in St Petersburg were haunted by the fear that Britain's entente partners, particularly Russia, would strike a bargain with the Germans if Britain did not demonstrate that she was 'alliance worthy'. Even less anti-Liberal officials were equally adamant that defence spending was essential if Britain was to preserve her great power status.

Interest and concern did not constitute expertise. There were few men either at Whitehall or in the diplomatic service who were actually knowledgeable about strategic questions, although, Eyre Crowe was one of the exceptions. His *Lesebuch* contains many military items; Spenser Wilkinson, the military expert and first holder of the Chichele Professorship of War at Oxford (a sign of the times) was his brother-in-law. But though coming from the same social circles (families often sent one son into the army and another into diplomacy), there was not much contact between the officer and diplomatic establishments. The bulk of the former served abroad in imperial garrisons, above all in India, where no diplomats were stationed. Egypt, then and later, was one of the few places where both met. There were the military and naval attachés, still few in number, who did move in embassy circles. Occasionally, their reports were minuted by the ambassador (as when Frank Lascelles noted that, contrary to his own impression, Captain Dumas reported that the German Naval Bill was aimed at the British) and were read in the Foreign Office (usually by Crowe but sometimes by his seniors) before being sent off to the War Office and Admiralty. There was also Henry Wilson, the dynamic Director of Military Operations who, most unusually, was a frequent visitor at Whitehall and shared with Arthur Nicolson a strong sympathy for Ulster and a natural contempt for the Liberal government. His comment that Grey was 'an ignorant, vain and weak man, quite unfit to be the Foreign Minister of any country larger than Portugal. A man who knew nothing of policy and strategy going hand in hand', gives one an accurate sense of the man.[33]

Diplomats did not consider themselves competent to judge defence questions. A distinction was drawn between diplomacy and strategy. Nevertheless, senior officials were drawn into the strategic debates. Lord Salisbury had taken a somewhat jaundiced view of service questions and opinions; Lansdowne and Grey tended to be more involved and more respectful. There were times when the Foreign Office did intervene and pushed its case with considerable vigour. It was Grey who authorised the military conversations with

France (approved by Campbell-Bannerman but not known to the whole cabinet until 1911) though he did not inform himself about their details. Officials took a strong stand against Churchill's proposals to reduce the Mediterranean fleet in order to strengthen reserves in home waters and both Grey and Nicolson had an important part in the compromise which was subsequently approved. But though numerous instances of Foreign Office participation in defence questions can be cited, there seems to have been a certain reluctance to probe too far in what was, after all, the preserve of the War Office and Admiralty.

Some of this reserve must be attributed to political expediency. Grey clearly did not want to have the question of the military links with France explored in what he knew to be a divided cabinet. But it was surprising, given the fact that Grey, Nicolson, and Hardinge had all expressed doubts about the usefulness of a small BEF in military terms, that they should have accepted without question Henry Wilson's argument that six divisions landed at the right time and place would be a 'decisive' force in checking a German offensive into France. It is also striking that despite the fact that Foreign Office representatives had heard the arguments presented at CID meetings, they never pressed for an understanding between the Admiralty and War Office. It was the Balkan crisis of November 1912 which finally led to an army ultimatum and an Admiralty scheme for transporting troops to France. Doubts expressed to the French about Britain's military contribution never led to further discussions in the CID after the crucial meetings of 23 August 1911.

Part of the answer can be found in an unwillingness to face the realities of the British situation. The Foreign Office knew the constraints within which the War Office was forced to operate; Grey was never sympathetic to the idea of military service and even Nicolson who favoured the campaigns of the National Service League must have realised that conscription would be anathema to large sections of the Liberal party and even dangerous for the Unionists. There were neither the funds nor the manpower available to mount more than a token force; even Haldane's Territorial Army was not attracting the number of volunteers needed to make it a viable reserve. The real point was that, almost without exception, officials and diplomats still thought in naval terms. All were members of the blue water school of strategy; almost all accepted the findings of successive enquiries that the navy was powerful enough to protect the island kingdom against invasion. As long as Britain preserved her naval predominance, both she and the empire would be safe. 'Sea power is more potent than land power, because it is as pervading as the element in which it moves and has its being', Eyre Crowe argued in the 1907 memorandum.[34]

Support for an expeditionary force was in no way seen as an alternative to Britain's traditional strategy. The experiences of the past convinced even those who might have harboured doubts about the future that Britain's great power status depended on her naval supremacy. Foreign Office representatives had heard the devastating arguments made by the generals that amphibious operations were useless and that sea power could not turn the balance against a continental victory by a land power. They were aware, too, of the doubts about the efficacy of the blockade weapon in bringing Germany to her knees in a war of attrition. But none of these arguments led to any abandonment of the most deep-seated assumptions of the past. When in 1912, the question of blockading Holland or Belgium arose, with an eye to cutting off the transit trade to Germany, Nicolson and Crowe sided with Asquith against Churchill and Lloyd George, more concerned with the question of neutral rights than the efficacy of blockading tactics. Men can hear and accept arguments which cast doubt on their assumptions without changing the latter or abandoning their faith in the validity of their beliefs. I do not think that the Foreign Office was lying when its officials argued that Britain's contribution to the war would be in terms of her naval and commercial power.[35] She needed French and Russian troops to check the German armies on the continent of Europe but it would be her naval power which would protect England, keep the sea lanes open for the food and materials needed for the war, and eventually deprive the Germans of these same resources forcing her to abandon her military efforts.

It is this belief that explains the tenacity with which the Foreign Office fought off any attempt at an arrangement with Germany that did not end the possibility of a naval threat. It explains why the Foreign Office always endorsed the Admiralty demand for higher estimates. It explains, also, why, although always fearful that Russia might threaten the lifelines to India, it became the German challenge, real or imagined, to the equilibrium in Europe which came to preoccupy the British diplomatic establishment during the Liberal period of power. The British deterrent remained a naval one whatever doubts might have been expressed by members of the General Staff or queries raised about blockade or the effects of mines, submarines, and aircraft on battleship power. To have admitted that British forces would make no difference on the continent and to have conceded that her naval strength was of limited efficacy would have involved a confession of weakness which few men of the traditional ruling class who came to maturity in the eighties and nineties could have faced. The men who served Grey were far more conscious of Britain's weakness than those who had come to the Foreign Office in the early days of Salisbury's rule. Few in Whitehall, at least, would have echoed Disraeli's boast that 'there was never a moment in our history when the power of England was so great and her resources so vast and inexhaustible.'[36] But it would take at least two generations and the changes wrought by two world wars before the Foreign Office came to a fully realistic appraisal of British power and the inevitable adjustment of means to ends.

It had even been difficult to accept the need for retrenchment in the Mediterranean in 1912; Lord Esher's laments that 'Rome had to call in the foreigners to help her when the time of her decadence approached' touched an open nerve, however much the Foreign Office favoured a naval arrangement with the French in that sea. The logical conclusion to the defence debates was unacceptable in Whitehall; it would have meant that Britain was dependent on France and Russia to save their empire from disruption. The ability to fight wars successfully has always been one of the marks of a Great Power. No one at the Foreign Office contemplated a British abdication of this position at that time.

There was much talk of war before 1914. It was not an illegal act; 'the international law of the time condoned, even enhanced war.'[37] Reference has already been made to those who considered war to be necessary, inevitable, and even desirable and the attempts made to indoctrinate youth so that they would be prepared to fight for their country and empire. This is not to deny the existence of strong counter-currents (the post-Boer War debate intensified feelings on both sides). The radical anti-war movement was strong and vigorous and its appeal extended beyond radical ranks. Norman Angell's *The Great Illusion* in some ways a faint echo of Cobdenite thinking brought up to date, was immensely popular. Angell did not argue that war was impossible but that it was unprofitable, shifting the pacifist appeal from a moral to a rational base. Sir Edward Grey detested war. He believed it the worst thing that could happen to trade. He feared its economic and social consequences. It was the function of diplomacy and the diplomats to preserve the peace. War was a defeat.

Notwithstanding these arguments, war was not unthinkable. There were those both in the Foreign Office and in the missions abroad who argued that a clash with Germany could not be avoided despite the successful resolution of successive crises. Behind Foreign Office pressure on Grey to turn the ententes into alliances was the fear that the collapse of the ententes would leave an isolated Britain face-to-face with Germany. Neither the post-1912 detente nor the assurances of British diplomats in Berlin that the Kaiser and Chancellor wanted peace really removed anxieties about German intentions. The powerful fleet and the maintenance of the balance of power were intended to deter aggression; if they failed, Britain had to be prepared to go to war. After the Austrian ultimatum of July 23, Eyre Crowe wrote: 'Our interests are tied up with those of France and Russia in this struggle, which is not for the possession of Servia, but one between Germany aiming at a political dictatorship in Europe and the Powers who desire to retain individual freedom.'[38] The senior hierarchy of the Foreign Office had no doubts about the proper action to be taken in July 1914.

But what kind of war did they expect? Like most of their contemporaries, the Foreign Office thought in terms of a short war. Britain's recent experience had been with colonial wars; even the Boer War had been of relatively short duration. Even the more historically minded thought of the rapid Prussian victories rather than the American civil war. The cost of keeping huge armies in the field only convinced military establishments everywhere that a war of attrition was impossible in a modern society. All war planning, not only in Britain, but in European capitals as well, was predicated on the assumption that war would be short. The state which could mount the most rapid and powerful offensive would emerge the victor. If the war lasted, all the belligerents would collapse as a result of the economic chaos. The Foreign Office accepted a strategy that was neither coherent nor well-defended because it fit preconceived notions of how Britain would always fight a European War.

There were no preparations in depth for a European war.[39] Despite their demands for action, neither Nicolson nor Crowe assumed that these were necessary. The War Book (Nicolson was the head of the organising CID subcommittee) did not extend beyond the first few days. Despite the Foreign Office wish to assist France and Belgium, it was assumed that the British contribution to the war would be maritime and mercantile. However glorious the battles of war were to be, the British contribution on land would remain limited. The 'British way of warfare' meant the preservation of British trade, the provision of money and munitions to allies and an open blockade. There was no massing of gold reserves, no stockpiling of weapons (War Office expenditure on munitions dropped by over one-third between 1905/6 and 1912/13), no plans for the mobilisation of troops. The war would be over before it would be necessary to assemble men or to enlist the financial and industrial resources of the state. It would be sufficient to ensure 'business as usual'.

What concerned the cabinet was the immediate effects of war. There were the predicted fears of a City crisis, the collapse of the stock market, the foreign exchanges, and the joint-stock companies, fears which led the City to take a strong anti-war stand in July 1914 (mistakenly attributed by Crowe to the machinations of the German commercial houses). Financial collapse would be followed by the cessation of trade, food shortages, unemployment, and social revolution. It was the fear of a general strike (anti-war speeches by Keir Hardie and Ramsey MacDonald and high bread prices) and civil war in Ireland which led the cabinet to retain two divisions when they finally decided on 6 August to send an Expeditionary Force to France. The government did massively intervene to support the London money market; the banks were given sufficient money to lend to traders and to make profits for themselves. But strategic planning referred only to the operational conduct of the war by military and naval forces. The government did not think it needed to do anything more.

To speak of a 'pre-war generation' and to concentrate on views of war involves more than a semantic distortion. The difficulties for the historian are compounded because the rich memoir material was all produced after the Great War. There is a tendency to exaggerate the 'before' and 'after' aspects of Foreign Office and diplomatic life. It was still a relatively commodious life. The atmosphere at the Office remained relaxed, the tone informal, the work of most of the staff, despite the administrative reforms of 1905–1906 and increasing number of clerical workers, neither taxing nor heavy except in moments of crisis or on bad days. In some ways, the 'mental maps' of the diplomatic establishment at home and abroad lagged behind contemporary changes.[40] Britain was an island; the seas her highway, the empire a source of strength. Imperial power, as in the past, depended on naval strength and the maintenance of the European balance of power. In diplomatic terms, Europe was the centre.

The European departments, Western and Eastern, were the most prestigious and important. The European embassies and legations were the most sought-after assignments though in Western Europe there was a well established pecking order with Paris the glittering prize and Madrid and Lisbon considered 'nasty'. Much depended not only on the place and quality of life (reasons which made Vienna a young attaché's dream) but on the ambassador, head of Chancery, and one's rank. The Eastern Department always attracted some of the most interesting men; the 'lure of the East' was very strong, both for Victorians and Edwardians. The Department covered, among other countries, Russia, Turkey, Persia, Egypt, and Central Asia. Russia obviously was central to 'la haute politique'; St Petersburg an excellent posting despite the climate. This was equally true of Turkey. Though the embassy had lost the glamour and influence of Lord Dufferin's time under a series of rather unsuccessful ambassadors, the Chief Dragoman, Gerald Fitzmaurice, 'carried the Near East in his head' (Vansittart) and inspired a whole group of influential diplomats — George Lloyd, Percy Lorraine, Lancelot Oliphant, as well as Vansittart himself. The Chancery was an excellent training ground for young attachés and many young men learned the technical tools of their trade there. Persia, too, was a stepping stone to higher things, much more interesting than Tangier, physically beautiful and always in the Foreign Office eye. Egypt was in a class by itself; Lord Cromer ran the country as if it were a part of the British Empire; men not only enjoyed serving the 'Lord' but repeatedly asked for second tours and left with marked reluctance. Cairo was a world of its own, a fascinating one and the closest diplomats came to actually 'ruling'. (Zanzibar was one of the few alternatives!)

The rest of the world was very far away; the mental images the diplomats had and the projected distance from London bore little relation to the physical realities. In some sense, the Far East was the clearest part of the non-European world. The Far Eastern department was the most 'expert' in the Foreign Office; the foreign secretary depended heavily on the experience of assistant under-secretaries and senior clerks of many years service. Beilby Alston, Walter Langley's senior clerk, was actually sent to Peking on two occasions, in 1912 and 1913, to act as chargé when the ambassador returned home on leave, a most unusual procedure when few men in Whitehall actually had first-hand knowledge of the areas with which they dealt. The Far East also was unique insofar as the diplomatic service was concerned. As in the Levant, the special Far Eastern consular corps meant that there was an elite group of men, familiar with the languages of the Orient, who spent their whole lives and careers in China, Japan, or Siam. As mentioned earlier, ministers and ambassadors (the ministers in Japan and China became ambassadors in this period) were recruited from this service (though Claude MacDonald came from the army via Cairo and Zanzibar before coming to Peking and Tokyo). These were not 'normal' diplomatic appointments. Men like Sir Ernest Satow and Sir John Jordan were old Far Eastern hands. An Italian diplomat wrote of the latter:

> To him, China was not one post among many. It represented the beginning and the end of his career and apologia pro vita sua.... I do not pretend to know what passed in Sir John's mind, but it seemed to me that his world consisted of the British Empire and China, with Russia and Japan looming in the background (sometimes inconveniently near) and a lot of other powers fussing round and interfering in matters which did not really concern them and which they imperfectly understood.[41]

The Far East had a very special magnetism for those sent there. Even that grumbler, Horace Rumbold, felt the 'very greatest regret' when he thought his tour in Japan was over while, many years later, Owen O'Malley returning from a trip in the Soviet Union recorded his relief in being back in 'high civilisation' when he arrived in China. Though to some degree, in London, the Far East was regarded as an extension of the European game, those who handled its affairs saw the world through Far Eastern spectacles. Even in this period, diplomats in Japan and China were already pressing the interests of their respective hosts, a divergence which was to become far more marked in the inter-war period.

The case was rather different with the other non-European departments. The American department had only been separated from the Far East in 1899 and was marginal and small. Anglo-American relations were taken for granted; America's new demands for recognition underestimated, the ties of race and kinship exaggerated. Most Foreign Office men did not think of the United States at all, despite visits and American wives. As Donald Watt has emphasized, the Washington Embassy was recognised as requiring different talents than those needed for Paris, Berlin, or St Petersburg. It was not uncommon for both senior and junior diplomats to fight shy of appointments to Washington. The Americans did not quite understand the rules of the diplomatic game; there was Congress, the press, and a whole dimension of public diplomacy which British diplomats had been trained to shun. Eustace Percy, one of the more successful British diplomats in the United States, describes that quality of public arrogance, the 'Mr. Darcy syndrome' which so irritated the Americans even in that narrow Anglo-Saxon elite in which British diplomats moved.[42] In the difficult years under John Hay and Lord Pauncefote, the British could make concessions to the Americans because they did not take them quite seriously and regarded Cousin Jonathan with a mixture of irritation and paternal pride very different from that which marked Anglo-German disputes. Those outside Whitehall were far more conscious of American power; journalists, politicans, financiers, and investors were more aware of the already shifting patterns of power than those who sat at Whitehall.

Latin America was very remote indeed, the Central America just a blur on the Foreign Office map. One posting, preferably during one's first years was sufficient. To accept an appointment in Latin America was, according to Vansittart, to choose a tombstone rather than a touchstone. Part of the prejudice stemmed from the commercial nature of much Latin American work. Diplomats who went to Argentina, Chile, Brazil, Peru, and Uruguay joined large British colonies there, identified with the country of their posting and formed 'a largely independent sub-system of diplomacy.' Despite the pressure of foreign competition, the Foreign Office remained wary of intervention in economic matters and was content to leave its local representatives free to act as long as they stopped short of giving preferential treatment to any firm or individual. Only a few individuals in the American Department took any interest in Latin American affairs and the private secretary's office where the diplomatic rewards were distributed, rarely stooped to notice that its minister in Chile or Peru deserved a choicer plum.

There was also, at least until the nineties, the African and African Protectorates department where once men like Percy Anderson, its head, had ruled a vast empire as if it were a private domain. But these days were soon ended. In 1900, two departments were created and by 1906 all the African protectorates but Zanzibar had been transferred to the Colonial Office. The African department remained important only insofar as imperial conflicts continued to surface even after the main divisions had been made. Though new maps had been purchased and the senior clerk of the department was highly expert, for most of the Foreign Office and diplomatic service, Africa was the 'Dark Continent' known only by those place names made famous by imperial clashes and the Boer War. The same was true of the White Dominions, though here as in South Africa, family ties and visits gave reality to words in books. Apart from the rare conflict with another power that involved Canada or Australia, the Foreign Office had little to do with the self-governing colonies. The foreign secretary used the meetings of the Dominion heads to outline his views but consultation was the exception rather than the rule. When early in 1911 the British cabinet considered the renewal of the Anglo-Japanese Alliance in the face of imperial disaffection the Foreign Office took the view 'that the maintenance of the Alliance is of such vital Imperial interest that its prolongation should not be dependent on the view of the Dominions, though it might be desirable to explain the value of the Alliance...'[43]

We have already insisted that this was the age of imperialism writ large and that men coming to the Foreign Office in the eighties and nineties would have been strongly indoctrinated with imperialist sentiment. The divisions created by the Boer War and its aftermath and the preachings of the Milnerites did not pass unnoticed by the policy-making elite. Yet because they were not intimately involved in the running of this empire or in the management of its relations, the Foreign Office stood somewhat apart from any of these issues. Moreover, there seems to have been a subtle shift, at the Foreign Office at least, in the general frame of reference during the Liberal period of power. Imperial clashes and bargains were increasingly seen through European glasses; it was for this reason that Eyre Crowe was so opposed to the freedom granted the Colonial Secretary to negotiate an Anglo-German agreement with regard to the

Portuguese colonies. Whereas the diplomats on the spot might be concerned with the problems of the periphery, at home, it was often the European consequences which were of the greatest concern.

The great exception, of course, was India, the jewel of the imperial crown. Sir Mortimer Durand, Lord Curzon, and Charles Hardinge were all Indian Viceroys; the quarrels in Persia, Afghanistan, and Tibet were all important because of the lifeline to that great subcontinent. The concern with the defence of India had been the overriding preoccupation of both the diplomatic and military establishments under Lords Salisbury and Lansdowne. Grey, Hardinge, Nicolson, and Buchanan, the British ambassador in Russia, continued to see the newly forged links with St Petersburg as means of checking Russian expansion, and the preservation of that entente the only way to prevent 'an intolerable increase' in the military responsibilities of India and the Empire. Whether it was these older yet enduring anxieties rather than a new concern with German intentions which was uppermost in Grey's mind is another question. It may well be that we have here one of the dividing lines between an earlier and later generation of British diplomats, measured not in terms of years but formative experience. Though India loomed large, to some, Europe seemed closer. It was the German menace, real or imagined, which seemed ultimately more threatening than the Russian advance into Central Asia and the Far East. It is perfectly true that the two were inexorably linked. If the entent policy did not neutralise the German threat, the possiblity of either a German-Russian bargain or a Franco-Russian defeat became an overriding consideration for the safety of the empire. But the focus came to centre on Berlin, the priorities of diplomatic concern had altered even during the period of detente (1912–1924) when improved relations with Berlin again shifted attention to St Petersburg.

This mental map of the diplomatic world was but a crude approximation of the reality. Individuals each had their own maps and they could be very different. Most walked about in this world with considerable ease. The foreign secretary knew his voice carried weight in London and abroad. The British diplomat was an important personage. This was equally true of Francis Bertie, shouting down the telephone to his Chancery head, as it was of Arthur Hardinge, whose practical-minded subordinates used to bustle in his wake, bringing order out of administrative chaos or John Jordan dressing for dinner when vacationing alone in the Chinese hills 'because one does dress for dinner if one is the British Minister'. There are numerous comments in the diplomatic correspondence that suggest that many diplomats felt they belonged to an 'embattled elite' and that their country might be entering a period of decline. There is a good deal of adverse criticism of the radical wing of the Liberal party, the increasing power of the trade unions and Labour, about Lloyd George and the assault on the Upper House, and bitter complaints about the presence of 'men dressed in blue serge suits, their women-kind like maids out for a Sunday' who were assembled for Foreign Office receptions. An uneasiness about the future underlay the more assertive nationalism mentioned earlier. This was the diplomatic counterpart to Foreign Office demands for a 'firm foreign policy' and a *quid pro quo* for any British concession. A diminishing number read the diplomatic map with Lord Sanderson's detachment and balance.

> If the mere acquisition of territory were in itself immoral, I conceive that the sins of Germany since 1871 are light in comparison to ours, and it must be remembered that, for an outside point of view, a Country which looks to each change as a possible chance of self-aggrandisement is not much more open to criticism than one which sees in every such change a menace to its interests, existing or potential, and founds on this theory continued claims to interference or compensation. It has sometimes seemed to me that to a foreigner reading our press the British Empire must appear in the light of some huge giant sprawling over the globe, with gouty fingers and toes stretching in every direction, which cannot be approached without eliciting a scream.[44]

One must be careful not to exaggerate the awareness of an adverse shift in the domestic and foreign balance of power. Diplomats, in particular, were often cut off from many of the currents which fed the malaise of the pessimists. When they thought of home, they thought in terms of their youth, of country houses, nannies and governesses (there is some truth to the contention that diplomats were made in the nursery) and public schools. Some had inherited or purchased estates, not on Lord Curson's scale, but of more than respectable extent. Many, it is true, were deeply concerned about money. As a third secretary, Rumbold received a salary of £450; fourteen years later he was only earning £50 more. Here was a constant theme and worry. But relatively few were in the diplomatic service who did not have sufficient reserves to see them through periods of financial embarrassment. Whatever the fears about rising income tax, militant suffragettes, and rebellious working men, this was still a protected elite.

The main problem for most diplomats had little to do with Lloyd George's budget or the appearance of foreigners contesting British claims to power and influence. It was boredom. In all but a few posts, the work could be finished in the morning. There were then the long afternoons and evenings to fill. Even in European capitals, society was restricted and there was a whole range of posts where native circles were 'off limits'. Rennell Rodd's embassy in Rome was unusual in its intellectual and eclectic atmosphere. Being a fourth at bridge at the ambassador's table nightly or four-course luncheons with a different wine served with each course, but always with the same table companions, had its drawbacks. It was hardly surprising that diplomats took to polo, tennis, and golf, travelled huge distances on and in every kind of conveyance, painted, wrote verse, plays, and travel books, hunted and fished, and complained endlessly in a stream of letters to relatives, friends, and colleagues.

More than one contemporary has noted the arrogance of the British representatives abroad. The cause and extent is difficult to gauge; the tone of command was clearly becoming less acceptable as it became more marked and there is an element of caricature even in the most admiring accounts of Horace Rumbold or Percy Lorraine. This might well have been a response to the more competitive atmosphere of the late Victorian and Edwardian times. Or it may be due, as Lord Eustace Percy, son of the seventh Duke of Northumberland, 'born with the biggest of all possible silver spoons in my mouth' claimed, that the nineties saw a breakdown of good manners, 'the tone of a no longer really leisured class was being set by its younger, rather than its eldest sons, and in consequence the manners of the "nobility and gentry"... were becoming the manners of the club and the mass, rather than of the drawing room.'[45] These changes did not pass unnoticed in the columns of the *Nation* and the *Economist*.

Diplomats abroad moved in restricted circles. Their daily lives reinforced the natural conservatism of men who had chosen the diplomatic career. Distance isolated them, however, from the disruptive changes in the body politic at home and they did not always fully grasp their implications. This was not true of the Foreign Office man who witnessed the strikes of that hot summer of 1911 when the Agadir crisis reached its climax and who lived through the industrial troubles of 1912. Even Sir Edward Grey, whose social sympathies were somewhat broader than those of his most senior advisors, warned listeners of the growing power of the industrial workers who 'will not stand being played with, nor allow their problems of existence to be pushed on one side by international questions'.[46] Again in the summer of 1914, Grey, like John Morley, raised the spectre of 1848 by predicting that war would lead to a collapse of industry and trade and to a social revolution which would engulf the industrial nations however victorious they might be in the European struggle. The cabinet was clearly thinking along such lines as it prepared its defences against a general strike or widespread labour unrest in August 1914.[47]

Such concerns were not restricted to the foreign secretary. His officials, too, were acutely aware of the damaging effects of the domestic disruptions of the post-Agadir period. Arthur Nicolson feared the new strength of the trade unions and the power of the Labour and radical forces. He attributed the weaknesses of Liberal foreign policy to its internal divisions and correctly understood that no Liberal cabinet would turn the ententes into alliances which he believed to be the only safe course for Britain to follow. It was not only that officials assumed that the average Englishman was 'muddle-headed, sloppy and gullible' when it came to foreign affairs but that they feared that the Liberal party was too rent and the social fabric too stretched for the nation to prepare adequately for a war which was well within the realm of the possible. It is far more difficult to judge how far such men felt threatened by the rising tide of domestic and industrial unrest. Arthur Nicolson, like Charles Hardinge who echoed his fears, was more strident in his anti-radical sentiments and anxieties than most of his colleagues. The political sympathies of the Foreign Office establishments were mixed; there were Liberals as well as Unionists and even a few future Labour party members in its ranks. The majority may have been, by upbringing and profession, the natural supporters of the status quo. They may have sensed that the compromises of the past would not be sufficient to preserve their Britain. But like Sir Edward Grey most were secure enough to believe that only a great catastrophe would shake the foundations of the state and topple that structure of which they were so consciously proud.

There was a Foreign Office mind. It was shaped when England was at the height of her power and when the landed and middle classes had effected a successful modus vivendi. It was predicated on the assumption that British power had been wisely and humanely used and that the Pax Britannica had brought peace and prosperity to large sections of the known world. There were still echoes of these 'unspoken assumptions' when Harold Nicolson spoke in the House of Commons on 5 October 1938.

> I know that those of us who believe in the traditions of our policy, who believe in the precepts which we inherited from our ancestors, who believe that one great function of this country is to maintain moral standards in Europe, to maintain a settled pattern of international relations, not to make friends with people who are demonstrably evil, not to go out of our way to make friends with them but to set up some sort of standard by which the smaller powers can test what is good in international conduct and what is not—I know that those who hold such beliefs are accused of possessing the Foreign Office mind. I thank God that I possess the Foreign Office mind.[48]

The realities of international politics were already eroding this position many years before the advent of Hitler. But these unwelcome changes could still be fit into a deeply ingrained pattern of thought and feeling.

NOTES

1. Z. S. Steiner, *The Foreign Office and Foreign Policy, 1898–1914* (Cambridge, 1969), Appendix 3, pp. 217–21. See the corrections made in Ray Jones, 'The Social Structure of the British Diplomatic Service 1815–1914', in *Histoire Sociale – Social History*, XIV, no. 27 (May 1981): 59–66. As may be clear from the following discussion, I do not accept all of Professor Jones's conclusions.
2. Seven of 220 diplomats in the period 1815–60 and five out of 284 for the period 1860–1914 went to one of the major Roman Catholic schools. At least two clerks entering the Foreign Office between 1898 and 1914 were Catholics. See Jones, 'Social Structure', 53, 61, and Steiner, *Foreign Office and Foreign Policy*, pp. 217–8. The subject requires further investigation.

3. M. Gilbert, *Sir Horace Rumbold: Portrait of a Diplomat, 1869–1914* (London, 1973), pp. 24–5.
4. Cd. 7749, Fifth Report of the Royal Commission on the Civil Service, London, 1914. Testimony of William Tyrrell, Q. 40, 910.
5. Ibid. Q. 40, 918; also Q. 40, 912.
6. See the interesting discussion in Donald Watt's book, *Succeeding John Bull: America in Britain's Place, 1900–1975* (Cambridge, 1984), Chapter 1.
7. The best description is in Ray Jones, *The Nineteenth Century Foreign Office, An Administrative History* (London, 1971), pp. 111–135.
8. James Joll, *1914: The Unspoken Assumption* (London, 1968), p. 6.
9. Robert Jervis, 'Political Decision Making: Recent Contributions', *Political Psychology* (Summer 1980): 98.
10. C. J. Lowe and M. I. Dockrill, *The Mirage of Power, British Foreign Policy, 1905–1922*, 3 vols. (London, 1972); Paul Kennedy, *The Rise of the Anglo-German Antagonism, 1860–1914* (London, 1980) and the first section of *The Realities Behind Diplomacy* (London, 1981); David Dilks, *Retreat from Power* (London, 1981) Vol. I; Z. Steiner, *Britain and the Origins of the First World War* (London, 1977); and many more.
11. H. Nicolson, *Lord Carnock: A Study in the Old Diplomacy* (London, 1931), 3rd printing, p. x.
12. Quoted in J. Springhall, *Youth, Empire and Society* (London, 1977), p. 58.
13. I have only found one discussion of this theme in R. M. Ogilvie, *Latin and Greek: A History of the Influence of the Classics on English Life from 1600 to 1918* (London, 1967), pp. 134–171.
12. M. Gilbert, *Sir Horace Rumbold*, p. xiii.
15. *The Diary of Edward Goschen, 1900–1914* edited by C. H. D. Howard, 1900–14, (London, 1980), Camden 4th series, Vol. 25, p. 151.
16. G. P. Gooch and H. W. V. Temperley, *British Documents on the Origins of the War, 1898–1914* (London, 1928), Vol. III, Appendix A, pp. 402–3. (Hereafter, cited as 'B.D.').
17. F.O. (Foreign Office Archives, Public Record Office, London), 371/11653, Memorandum by Wellesley, 20 August 1926 quoted in W. R. Louis, *British Strategy in the Far East, 1919–1939* (Oxford, 1971), pp. 140–1.
18. Nevile Henderson, *Water Under the Bridges* (London, 1945), p. 188.
19. B.D., Vol. III, p. 403.
20. M. Gilbert, *Sir Horace Rumbold*, p. 100.
21. R. H. Bruce Lockhart, *Memoirs of a British Agent* (London, 1982), p. 78.
22. For an example of how embassies used the £100 given for the employment of a commercial secretary, see H. J. Bruce, *Silken Dalliance* (London, 1946), pp. 124–5; also *The Diary of Edward Goschen*, p. 164.
23. D. C. M. Platt, *The Cinderella Service, British Consuls since 1825* (London, 1971), p. 2, but see also the same author's *Finance, Trade and Politics 1815–1914* (Oxford, 1968), which has been corrected only with respect to details by his own subsequent work and by those works cited in footnote 26.
24. Platt, *The Cinderella Service*, pp. 240–242.
25. Ibid. p. 20.
26. D. McLean, *Britain and her Buffer State* (London, 1979), Royal Historical

Society, Studies in History Series, no. 14; 'Commerce, Finance and British Diplomatic Support in China, 1885-6', *Economic History Review*, 2nd series, 26 (1973); M. Kent, 'Agent of Empire', The National Bank of Turkey and British Foreign Policy, *Historical Journal*, 18 (1975).
27. *Royal Commission on the Civil Service*, Q. 38, 062.
28. F.O. 371/673, Oppenheimer to Grey, 28 September 1909; see D. French, *British Economic and Strategic Planning, 1905-1915* (London, 1982), pp. 29 and 67.
29. Paul Kennedy, *The Roots of the Anglo-German Antagonism* (London, 1981), p. 466.
30. There was a protectionist group at the Foreign Office. See the comment by Rumbold that in 1904 'many of the higher officials were tariff reformers' in M. Gilbert, *Rumbold*, p. 48.
31. E. M. Spears, *Haldane; An Army Reformer* (Edinburgh, 1980), p. 195.
32. Quoted in H. Nicolson, *Lord Carnock*, pp. 402-3.
33. C. Callwell, *Sir Henry Wilson: His Life and Diaries* (London, 1927), Vol. 1, pp. 98-9.
34. *B.D.*, Vol. III, p. 402.
35. For a very different reading of the material see K. Wilson, 'British Power in the European Balance 1906-14' in D. Dilks, ed. *Retreat from Power* (London, 1981), Vol. 1, pp. 21-42.
36. Quoted in K. Bourne, *The Foreign Policy of Victorian England, 1830-1902* (Oxford, 1970), p. 403.
37. C. Parry, 'Foreign Policy and International Law' in F. H. Hinsley, ed. *British Foreign Policy under Sir Edward Grey* (Cambridge, 1977), p. 92.
38. *B.D.*, Vol. XI, no. 101.
39. D. French, *British Economic and Strategic Planning*, pp. 42-8.
40. For the concept and definition of 'mental maps' see Alan Henrickson 'The Geographical "Mental Maps" of American Foreign Policy Makers', in *International Political Science Review*, 1, no. 4 (1980); 495-530 (but especially 498-500).
41. D. Varé, *Laughing Diplomat* (London, 1953), p. 119.
42. Lord Percy of Newcastle, *Some Memories* (London, 1958), pp. 19-20.
43. Quoted by I. Nish, 'Japan and North-East Asia, 1905-1911' in F. H. Hinsley, *British Foreign Policy under Sir Edward Grey* (Cambridge, 1976), p. 366.
44. *B.D.*, Vol. III, Appendix B, p. 430; see the interesting interpretation presented by J. A. Grenville in D. Read (ed.) *Edwardian England* (London, 1982), pp. 162-180.
45. Lord Percy, *Some Memoirs*, p. 20.
46. K. Robbins, *Sir Edward Grey* (London, 1971), p. 248.
47. *B.D.*, Vol. XI, no. 86; J. Morley, *Memorandum on Resignation* (London, 1928), pp. 5-6; D. French, *British Economic and Strategic Planning*, pp. 85-8.
48. Hansard, *Parliamentary Debates*, 5th Series, Vol. 339, 434.

IAN NISH

British Foreign Secretaries and Japan, 1892-1905

It is natural for historians to be interested in the underlying assessments that a foreign ministry makes of another country with which it has dealings. One of the difficulties that any foreign government has is to ensure that the assessment is accurate since it is often hard to understand the domestic political forces at work in another country. My concern in this paper is with Japan, a country remote from Britain and therefore more difficult to assess than a nearer country. It may be taken as representative of the countries of Asia during the period of late nineteenth century imperialism that sought to enter into international diplomatic relationships and found that they could only do so on European terms and were assumed to be states on the European model. My second concern is with the British perception of Japan, the accuracy of it, and the way of handling her. I shall be dealing with the Japan policy of four foreign secretaries, Lord Rosebery, Lord Kimberley, Lord Salisbury, and Lord Lansdowne, who, in turn, presided over the Foreign Office between 1892 and 1905. Were they tolerant, patient, and understanding or were they indifferent and patronizing? I shall be dealing in greater detail with Lansdowne's handling of Japan in 1901, arguably the time when Japanese domestic politics had the greatest impact on Britain through Marquis Itō's manoeuvres in Europe.

Lord Rosebery and his successor, Lord Kimberley, served as foreign secretaries between 1892 and 1895 in a period of declining fortunes for the Liberal party and were in office for comparatively short times. They did not have a special grasp of things Japanese. Their prime object tended to be to prevent Russian encroachments in north-east Asia, while working towards an Anglo-Russian *rapprochement* elsewhere in the world. During the tenure of the 'Rosebery-Kimberley duo' war between China and Japan broke out in August 1894. This created special tensions for Britain which had been involved in the 'modernization' of both countries. The war went in favour of Japan; and Russia, Germany, and France on 23 April 1895 lodged a protest against the treaty of Shimonoseki and intervened in favour of China. Japan appealed to Britain for support and Rosebery who found that Kimberley tended to defer to his opinions stated his position:

> We have preserved a benevolent neutrality all along, watching carefully on behalf of our own interests... We cannot embroil ourselves in the quarrels of others unless our own interests imperatively demand it. Imperatively I say, because our commerce is so universal and so penetrating that scarcely any question can arise in any part of the world without involving British interests. This consideration instead of widening rather circumscribes the field of our action. For did we not strictly limit the principle of intervention we should always be simultaneously engaged in some forty wars.
>
> However the practical point is this: Japan cannot receive our support and cannot need our advice. She can judge quite as acutely as we can what is the course for her to adopt, and has I doubt not long ago decided it, for this war is directed against Russia more than against China. But she may well wish to be able to boast of our support and that of the United States. She will however obtain neither, and this I doubt not she already knows.
>
> ... Pray then emphasize... that we admire the qualities that Japan has displayed and cordially wish her well (of which we have given her substantial proofs): that we fear her answer will not satisfy the Powers:... that our great interest is peace and that we are convinced that Russia at any rate is in earnest.[1]

In Rosebery's view, Britain had to stay uncommited on the Three-Power intervention issue, because of her world-wide commercial interests. Because of the danger of her being involved in war against European countries over a matter where her interests were so slight, she could not support Japan. There is very little evidence here or in the other memoranda of the time of any special cordiality towards Japan. Nor is there much evidence of Britain worshipping the successful by switching her allegiance to Japan during the war when it was seen how effective the Japanese armed services were. On the whole, the Liberal ministers observed a narrowly nationalistic policy towards Japan, concerned only about maintaining British commerce.

Japan was not regarded as an inferior but seems to have been thought of as one of the powers and treated accordingly. When Japan sent a new and active minister to London by the name of Katō Takaaski on 23 March 1895, he said that it was desirable to have a close understanding between Britain and Japan in order to frustrate Russian plans for the acquisition of an ice-free port in the area.[2] Since Kimberley survived in office only a few months longer, nothing came of this overture, if overture it was.

When the Conservatives came back to power, it was Lord Salisbury (1895-1900) who took over at the Foreign Office. Salisbury was more experienced in the art of foreign policy-making, though his concern had in the past been mainly with Europe. His approach to the office of foreign secretary was essentially paternalistic. He did not leave policy to his subordinates and transacted much of his business at this private home at Hatfield. Since he had no special expertise on Asia, there was not much scope for a coordinated policy towards the problems of Japan and China. When he came to office for the last time as both foreign secretary and prime minister in 1895, it was just after the ending of hostilities between China and Japan when China was grateful to the triumvirate of European powers, Russia, France, and Germany, that had staged the dramatic intervention on her behalf. This left neutral Britain at a disadvantage. In this extract Salisbury gives the new British minister to Japan, Sir Ernest Satow, some guidelines on the approach he should take to the Japanese:

> My impression is that our strategic or military interest in Japan can easily be overestimated. She may no doubt be of use in hindering Russia from getting an ice-free port. But how long would her obstruction be effective? My impression is that the shrewder Japanese Ministers will not be sorry to see enough Russian power in those latitudes to counterbalance the power of England.

I would not therefore thrust upon them any advice — or the hint of any naval or military cooperation either against Russia or China. But this will in no way hinder you from maintaining a most friendly attitude to the Japanese Government. The great advantage for which we should look in their recent development is undoubtedly improved trade; and if, as is sometimes thought, they can be used for obtaining greater facilities from the Chinese, the result would be very valuable. I think you should give great attention to the commerical part of your duties.³

Judging from this, it cannot be said that Salisbury had formed a high opinion of Japan or her value to Britain. He looked on her either in great power terms, as a partner in limiting Russia's expansion, or in trading terms, as a partner in prising open the markets of China. Satow, the oriental scholar-cum-diplomat, may well have winced at the commercial duties which Salisbury urged upon him; but clearly the foreign secretary was inclined to steer him away from high policy, from promoting suggestions about 'a closer understanding'. It was common ground between them to regard Japan as a possible agent in Britain's struggle against Russia in Asia — but that was for the present less pressing. Salisbury made no mention of an alliance: his reference to 'the most friendly attitude' carried with it no hint of a special British relationship with Japan. Satow did not dissent from this assessment, thinking that the Japanese had no present intention of seeking some special relationship with Britain, and was content to act within his brief. The new Japanese minister in London, however, continued to cultivate the Conservative statesmen like Joseph Chamberlain who were not satisfied for Britain to remain 'without a friend in the world'.

It would be misleading to suggest that Salisbury's perception of Japan remained unaltered until October 1900 when his term at the Foreign Office ended. He was never static in his views and was always testing the ground. In any case he seems to have shared his Foreign Office portfolio increasingly with Arthur Balfour. Expressed in another way, Balfour happened to stand in for him at times of major far eastern crisis. This was the case in 1898 when Britain took the lease of the island and territory of Weihaiwei and the New Territories at Hong Kong and again in April 1899 in the run-up to the Anglo-Russian agreement over the Manchurian railways. These were Balfourian conceptions which were adopted by the less placid members of Salisbury's cabinet and thrust on the foreign secretary himself.[4] This applied also when Britain encouraged Japan's participation in the international military expedition for the suppression of the Chinese Boxers. In the summer of 1900 Britain, involved in the South African war, found herself and her commerce threatened in China by the outbreak of the Boxer disturbances. Salisbury, under pressure once again from his cabinet colleagues, responded commerically: offering in August 1900 a loan to the Yangtse viceroys to ensure that the Boxers were effectively controlled in that area, the centre of British commerce in China; and offering Japan up to one million pounds on 14 July if she would despatch 20,000 Japanese troops to China for the relief of the legations at Peking.[5] This last was the action steered through by Balfour and St John Broderick in Salisbury's absence. It put Japan in a mercenary relationship rather than one of partnership, let alone one of alliance.

In October 1900 Salisbury gave up the post of foreign secretary, though he held on to the prime ministership. It was stated that Lord Lansdowne would take over 'the conduct of Foreign Office details', the implication being that Salisbury would not rest content to be merely an observer in international affairs.[6] Indeed there turned out to be more cabinet interference in foreign affairs under Lansdowne than under Salisbury but that did not mainly come from Salisbury himself. Lansdowne was more sympathetic to and more knowledgeable about the East than his predecessors, because of his imperial experience in Canada and especially in India. Because of his War Office experience under the Salisbury ministry, he was inclined to bring in the strategic element. Also, in the management of the Office, certain changes can be seen. Being less experienced as a minister and politician, Lansdowne seems to have been content to work through his subordinates. He relied especially on Francis Bertie, the assistant under-secretary, on east Asian matters. In 1899, there had been an Office reorganization in which the Far Eastern or China department was set up.[7] This led to more expertise and specialization in the treatment of Japan and China at a time when these countries were beginning to play a vital role in world affairs. This meant that policy reflected less the quirky views of the foreign secretary reached in isolation than the debates and arguments within the Office.

It fell to Lansdowne's lot to serve as foreign secretary at a time when relations with Japan required constant attention. This was because of the hard-fought negotiations which extended from November 1901 until the alliance was concluded in January 1902. These negotiations, which were difficult enough in themselves, were complicated by the concurrent negotiations being carried on in France and Russia by Marquis Itō, one of Japan's 'elder statesmen'.

There could be no dispute about Itō's importance in Japan. After being in and out of high office for three decades, Itō had been prime minister for the third time in 1900–1901. But his tenure had been marred, firstly, by his illnesses which led to his frequent absences from Tokyo and, secondly, the chronic divisions within the cabinet over Korea and Manchuria. He was succeeded as prime minister by General Katsura, a minor figure by comparison, while he withdrew to become the senior 'elder statesman', one of a group of experienced statemen who advised the emperor. Within this group of cautious men there were those who sought some political settlement with Russia over north-east Asia. They successfully persuaded Itō, who wanted to go abroad to recover his health, to go to Europe and even to Russia. This proposal was put to Katsura in September in vague terms and interposed no objections, though it is questionable if he would have had the power of veto in any case.[8]

Itō's activities presented a new dimension of difficulty for Britain. Hitherto Rosebery, Kimberley, and Salisbury had on the whole treated Japan as a state where decisions were made in ways not too dissimilar to European states. But Itō's journey confronted Lansdowne with the new problem of decision-making in Japan, especially the role of the emperor and elder statesmen and, on the other hand, the role of the cabinet. Which would prevail? Without this unfamiliar aspect of Japanese statecraft, Britain would have found the negotiation of the Japanese alliance difficult enough: not only was Britain likely to assume commitments which were comparatively unknown for her but the Japanese would by the alliance enter the international diplomatic fold for the first time. But it was doubly difficult when Britain had to cope during the negotiations with a dual diplomacy on the part of Japan.

There can have been no more difficult question for the British government than to understand the relationship between Itō as a genrō and the Japanese cabinet of Katsura. Their difficulty was compounded by the fact that Katsura left the relationship between Itō's journey and cabinet authorization as vague, informal, and undefined as possible. Indeed it might be said that Japanese statesmen of the day themselves did not know how great or how small was the power of the genrō. It depended on the prerogatives of the Japanese emperor; and these were indeterminate. Each time the genrō insisted on some privilege, it had to be tested by a sort of power struggle. How then was a foreign government to determine who was calling the tune: the genrō or the cabinet? It was a vexing problem of international relations, Japanese government, and foreign policy.

The question was a vital one for the British cabinet because Itō's journey could have an influence on the conclusion of the Anglo-Japanese alliance. The alliance negotiations had begun in July 1900. On 6 November Lansdowne had presented the Japanese with the first British draft. He had no alternative but to wait until the Japanese responded. It was only on 12 December that Japan made even a tentative reply. During this interval of over a month, Itō visited St Petersburg, the capital of the country which was the 'enemy' contemplated in the alliance treaty draft. On 4 November Itō had reached Paris from the United States; on 22 November he set off from Paris for St Petersburg, having been told by Katsura to go there with all speed. He there had talks with Witte and Lamsdorf, the two leading Russian statesmen, as well as audiences with the tsar. He handed over the draft of an agreement and repaired to Berlin in order to await the Russian reply. This much was not known at the time and has only been pieced together subsequently.[9]

While Lansdowne was keeping Itō's movements under fairly close scrutiny, he took them philosophically. It cannot be said that he panicked or that the pace of the alliance negotiations was accelerated because of them. Lansdowne, to be sure, made enquiries from Tokyo, Paris, and St Petersburg but recognized that he would have to let the Japanese decision-making process take its course. This it duly did when the cabinet finally approved on 12 December a counter-draft which was relatively close to what Britain had originally proposed.

It would appear that there were certain factors which gave Lansdowne confidence. They were inspired guesses rather than certainties and might be called the 'unspoken assumptions'. One of these assumptions related to the role of the emperor in Japanese politics. The Meiji constitution of 1889 was a public document. It seemed to give the emperor supreme power over the actions of the Japanese state. But very few Japanese or foreigners understood how this operated or how the genrō, his group of intimate advisers, assisted in exercising his prerogatives. Britain had no reason to doubt that in practice the Japanese emperor possessed absolute power. The problem was to know how far he exercised it through the extra-constitutional group of elder statsmen and how far they had to be consulted on all important aspects of state. The true relationship between the elder statesmen and the emperor could only be gleaned from rare experiences, such as the report of Sir Claude MacDonald, the British minister to Tokyo, about a banquet held on the occasion of the visit of the Royal Navy squadron to Tokyo in autumn 1905. He wrote that:

> His Majesty chatted most amicably with everybody all around. The Imperial Princes, Arisugawa and Kanin who sat on either side, treated him with marked deference but Marquis Itō and Count Inouye (the latter sat next to me) seemed to speak on absolute terms of equality and cracked jokes which made this direct descendant of the Sun roar with laughter. It was a great revelation to me and one which pleased me very much for though a Mikado he seems very human.[10]

The second unspoken assumption was that Itō was on his world tour for the purpose of securing a loan for Japan. The evidence for this theory was persuasive. First there was the firm view that Japan had needed a foreign loan during Itō's cabinet and that her financial predicament later in 1901 was such that a foreign loan was still indispensable. Second there were the reports from along Itō's route. It was said that in Chicago Itō had to feign illness in his hotel to avoid the attentions of local bankers. Then in New York he had been much in the company of those from Wall Street and had engaged in parleys with Pierpoint Morgan. As he moved to Paris, the financial capital of continental Europe, rumours of a loan grew thick and fast. French politicians were waiting for the penny — or rather the request for a penny — to drop, but, so far as we know, in vain. J. H. Longford, who was the Foreign Office official assigned to Itō during his eventual sojourn in Britain, reported that Itō had been rapturously received by French financiers, 'the idea having got abroad that he had come to raise a loan'.[11]

But there were implausible elements in this story, which was widely believed at the time. It was difficult to see why, assuming that the financial motive was uppermost in Itō's mind, he should direct his footsteps to St Petersburg, hardly the source of large international loans. There are no reliable historical sources which confirm that he discussed the matter in Russia. Indeed from the Japanese side and from the various writings of Itō there is no evidence that he had any mandate to seek out a foreign loan. Woe betide the diplomatic historian who concludes from this inadequate evidence that the story was a complete myth! It would appear, however, that it was not a prime object of his journey.

Itō reached Paris on the evening of 4 November. Hayashi, Japan's minister in London, was instructed on 13 November to cross the channel to meet Itō in Paris and show him telegrams that had been exchanged between Tokyo and London about the alliance. He held discussions with Itō from 14 to 19 November. Clearly both were embarrassed because the informal understanding on the basis of which Itō was travelling did not match the Foreign Ministry line of proceeding with the London alliance which Komura, who had been appointed foreign minister shortly after Itō left Japan, was now following. Hayashi thought that he had won over Itō to the British treaty; but Itō received instructions nonetheless from Katsura, the prime minister, to press on with his journey to St Petersburg, without delaying in Berlin. On 20 November, Itō set off for Russia with all speed.[12]

Returning to London on that day, Hayashi saw Lansdowne who enquired whether he had yet received any reply to the British draft of 6 November. Lansdowne also made judicious enquiries about Itō's journey. But Hayashi had to meet the more open and stinging criticisms of Francis Bertie who has some claim to being the author of the alliance on the British side. Bertie's argument was that the two countries had been engaged in secret discussions for an alliance, whose details would be damaging to both if they leaked out prematurely.[13] Obviously his fear was that Hayashi had passed on details of Britains proposals to Itō in Paris—as of course he had. There was, therefore, the danger that Itō in St Peterburg would capitalize on the 'British terms' by driving a favourable bargain with Russia. This was surely a reasonable inference, though it has to be said that Itō does not seem to have disclosed what he knew in discussions with the Russian leaders.

It was at this point that Lansdowne sent a private telegram to MacDonald asking whether he thought that the delay on Tokyo's part in coming to a decision was connected with Itō's visit to St Petersburg and Berlin. From Tokyo MacDonald replied that there were certain other factors which would account for the delay, notably Komura's illness. He referred to this in conversation with Yamaza Eijirō, a Foreign Ministry official, and drew a multitude of assurances that Itō's journey had nothing whatever to do with the alliance negotiations. MacDonald was right to divine that Itō was being kept posted with what was going on over the alliance. Lansdowne minuted that he 'questioned the accuracy of Mr Komura's description of Itō's mission.'[14] The use by Lansdowne of the word 'mission' suggests that he suspected that Itō's journey carried official authority.

Almost immediately, the foreign secretary sent a further private telegram to the British embassy in Russia to find as much information as possible about Itō who was by this time in the Russian capital. Charles Hardinge, the chargé d'affaires in St Petersburg, expressed it this way:

> I hear from the same official source [which has hitherto proved trustworthy] that the Marquis Itō failed in his mission to raise a Japanese loan in Paris owing to the uncertainty which exists in the French capital as to the relations existing between Russia and Japan in connection with the Corean and Manchurian questions, and that he received encouragement from the French Government to come to St Petersburg in order to obtain assurances from the Russian Government which may satisfy French financiers and thereby facilitate the raising of a Japanese loan in Paris. I gather that it is hoped at the Ministry for Foreign Affairs that the presence of the Marquis Itō in St Petersburgh may facilitate an arrangement between the Japanese and Russian Governments by which Japanese obstruction to Russian projects in Manchuria may be withdrawn in consideration for Concessions to Japan in Corea.

In a private letter to Sanderson on 28 November, Hardinge added:

> I received this morning Lord Lansdowne's private telegram in-

structing me to obtain as much information as possible about the Marquis Itō's visit here, and of course I will do my best, but this is quite the most difficult place I have ever been in to obtain reliable information.... I am on friendly terms with Japanese Chargé d'Affaires and although he is a sly little Jap, I may perhaps be able to get something out of him.[15]

The evidence had certainly accumulated about Itō being in search of a loan. But there is nothing positive to show that Lansdowne swallowed this theory. His assistant, Francis Bertie, wrote at the time 'the Russians cannot get money at Paris *at present*.'[16] How then could the Japanese expect to do so? This may have been the explanation of Whitehall's comparative calmness.

By the beginning of December the Tokyo cabinet had approved the counterdraft to Britain, subject to the approval of the genrō who must be consulted wherever they were. It was therefore necessary for the counterdraft to be delivered in code to Itō. Suspecting that their codes had been broken in Russia or at least that interception was likely, the Japanese decided to send the text to Hayashi in London and get him to send someone to St Petersburg. Matsui Keishirō, the first secretary at the London legation, was chosen for this onerous task. He reached the Russian capital on 3 December, decoded the telegram and presented it to Itō. The elder statesman had by this time held detailed discussions with the Russian foreign minister and finance minister. After he received the draft of the British alliance, Itō, on his own initiative and without instructions, passed over in writing on the 4th the skeleton of a possible agreement with Russia over Korea. Meanwhile Itō, in view of the favourable reception of his Russian hosts, urged Tokyo to delay delivery of the counterdraft to Britain, pending the reply from Russia. He expected to receive this after he had moved on to Berlin. The Japanese cabinet and genrō left in Tokyo were therefore in a quandary. But they received information that the alliance negotiations with Britain had been initiated during Itō's own cabinet (October 1900 –June 1901). They therefore rejected Itō's current position on the grounds that it was impossible to contemplate further delay. It only remains to be said that, when the Russian reply was received, it was not as helpful as Itō had been led to expect.[17] The British ambassador, Sir Charles Scott, who had returned to take over from Hardinge, sent a not inaccurate account of Itō's proceedings. He wrote:

> Itō left the capital on 4 December for Berlin and I understand announced his intention of afterwards proceeding to London before returning to Japan.... The Russian Government had evidently not succeeded in obtaining an admission from Itō that there was no connection between the Corean and Manchurian questions and the inferences drawn by the Russian Foreign Office from his persistency in connecting the two questions together seemed to be that either in his own personal view or that of his Government the opposition offered by Japan to the conclusion of a Russo-Chinese Agreement was a useful lever to employ in order to get the Russian Government to acquiesce in the cession to Japan of some additional rights or advantages in Corea.[18]

By the time Itō reached London on 24 December, he had suffered several blows: he had been over-ruled by cabinet, genrō, and emperor; and he had been given an unsatisfactory reply by the Russians. On the positive side he had been warmly received in both Germany and Belgium. His schedule as discussed in Tokyo before he set out had included London but some flexibility had been injected into it and he could always have reneged on the programme on some pretext or another. He now decided to complete the honorific tour as originally planned (though the timing had been advanced by about a week).

Itō was in need of a face-saving device. In fact (though this may be an example of the historian being wise after event), it had been suggested to him by Hayashi when he telegraphed on 19 November after they had met in Paris:

> So long as it is our policy to conclude a Russo-Japanese Convention we should adopt one or other of the following courses: first conclude the Anglo-Japanese Treaty, then notify Britain of our intention to negotiate a convention with Russia and proceed to the conclusion of the convention; or secondly, so long as the Anglo-Japanese negotiations are in progress, you should not discuss a convention with the Russian statesmen, unless they first propose it. In that case you must put them off as best you can.[19]

Itō had replied that he would adopt the second course. In fact he did not do so, proceeding along lines of his own, as we have seen. But, in coming to London, he seems to have adopted Hayashi's first course and pursued it vigorously.

How was Britain to receive this mysterious personality? Clearly Itō was so influential that the British had to try to win him over. Clearly, after the hospitality that had been showered on him on the continent, Britain had to try to do even better. Contrary to many accounts, Lansdowne exerted himself to arrange honours and entertainment for his visitor. On 26 December Salisbury held a banquet in Itō's honour. On the following day Itō had an audience of King Edward VII. On 2 January he stayed at the country estate of the foreign secretary at Bowood House in Wiltshire. This was followed by a 'dinner of 200 places' at the Mansion House given by the Lord Mayor of London where Itō made a pronouncedly Anglophile address. Later, during a reciprocal function given by Viscount Hayashi, Salisbury announced that Itō had been awarded by the sovereign the decoration of GCB. On 4 January he visited the prime minister, Lord Salisbury, at Hatfield House. On 6 January Itō went to say his farewells to Lansdowne at the Foreign Office and was invited to join the Royal Family at Sandringham but had to decline due to his departure from London the following day.

For present purposes, it is important to emphasize the private conversations which took place between Itō and Lansdowne. Unlike Itō's practice in Russia, he allowed Minister Hayashi to be present at the talks. While it would be wrong to pretend that Itō made a clean breast of his doings in St Petersburg, he did explain his thinking on the need for Japan to obtain some sort of understanding with Russia and was disarmingly frank in defending his position. His own version of these discussions contains the following observations:

> Not being one of those who distrust the Anglo-Japanese negotiations I am generally in favour of what has been done. I would only wish that there should be a full exchange of views in advance so that misunderstandings might be avoided. I note that Britain would not under any circumstances relish involvement in war with Russia on account of Manchuria. Before my departure from home Japan seemed to be trying to oppose absolutely any Russian move to push her interests into Manchuria.
>
> There is an agreement in being between Russia and Japan

over Korea [the Nishi-Rosen agreement of 1898]. On account of it Japan is much restrained at present but cannot revoke it. This agreement is something which Japan has borne long enough and cannot allow to continue. I have no idea of any double-handed policy by Japan towards Russia and Britain nor do I support the idea of a Russo-Japanese alliance. I only desire by the most peaceful methods to reach a complete agreement with Russia by moving the milepost of the existing Russo-Japanese agreement just a bit forward in order to protect our country's interests in Korea...

Among the powers there are none but Japan and Russia who feel direct interests in Korea: the one has an adjoining frontier, the other is separated by a narrow channel. At present Japan and Russia face each other from positions of political equality; but one cannot deny that there is a likelihood of conflict, if conditions so dictate, if Korea does not fulfil her obligations as an independent civilised nation, both Powers will compete in order to advise or help her. It is felt that Japan should have these rights exclusively.... In various conversations in Russia, I spoke of the problems of the Pacific generally. But this was the first time that I had heard Russia's declaration of Japan's supremacy there and her denial of any idea of opening hostilities with Japan on that account.[20]

These were interesting conversations as reported by Itō to Tokyo. They accord well with the account left by Lansdowne. The Japanese version like the British indicates that Itō was not Russophile in his conversations with the foreign secretary. Thus, he urged Britain to keep up her naval power in the Far East against Russia. This implies either that he never was or that the response from St Petersburg had to some extent disillusioned him. Lansdowne on his part reacted most considerately. When Itō mentioned the need for some Russo-Japanese negotiations in future over Korea and Manchuria, Lansdowne did not condemn it out of hand as being contrary to the spirit of the forthcoming alliance. Instead he encouraged Japan to go ahead, only asking that the negotiations with Russia should not be out of line with the accord with Britain. It suggests that Lansdowne was genuinely interested in 'defusing' the situation in east Asia, rather than in setting up Japan as a frontier force against the Russians in the east. These conversations were the highpoint of Itō's world trip and probably the most important part of the alliance negotiations. Britain undertook to allow Japan to negotiate with Russia over north-east Asia even after the alliance came into existence, as it did on 30 January 1902.

In retrospect both leaders attributed great significance to these encounters. In a letter of reminiscence written two years later, Itō told Lansdowne that:

> Your Excellency will remember my having told you that in my opinion it was necessary for the maintenance of peace in the Orient to create a more solid and durable understanding between the two countries most interested in the affairs of Korea and Northern China, than those which actually exist and that a solid and durable understanding was possible only on the basis of Russia's cordial recognition of our actual paramount interests in Korea, the existing arrangements being by far insufficient to safeguard our actual interests not to speak of their future development. While my opinion has been shared by our countrymen in general, Russia's high-handed march towards hegemony in this quarter of the globe as well as her strenuous military efforts in the East, have been becoming step by step a serious menace to the safety and the very existence of smaller or weaker states.

Lansdowne's reply also contains an element of self-congratulation:

> I recollect distinctly the conversation in which you mentioned to me your belief that it was necessary that a separate understanding should be arrived at between Russia and Japan as to the affairs of Korea and Northern China. I fully recognised the force of the arguments which you then used as to the advantages of such an understanding.[21]

Obviously Itō's attitude had moved strongly against Russia in the intervening years. But the fact remains that, given the power of the elder statesmen and the delicate diplomatic situation created by Itō's visit to Russia, Lansdowne's tactics had been very skilful. He had not panicked or been stampeded. He had treated Itō seriously as one of Japan's decision-makers who had to be persuaded and consulted. He was able to report favourably to the Tokyo embassy on his overall impression of Itō's visit to Britain:

> Itō's visit went off well and Hayashi assures me that he [Itō] was pleased with his reception, but of course it was most unfortunate that he should have selected the Christmas holidays for this purpose. He spent one night with me in the country and made himself very pleasant.[22]

Speculation about Itō continued well into the future. Valentine Chirol of the London *Times* tried to ferret out Itō's doings in Russia. But Scott reported what the new Japanese ambassador to Russia, Kurino, who had had some communication with Itō in France, told him. It was Scott's view that Japan and Russia had widely differing perceptions of the Itō-Lamsdorf discussions:

> Witte very probably hinted at or even suggested some concrete form of understanding to which Lamsdorf with his greater sense of responsibility would give a more abstract appearance.[23]

But other speculations also continued. Longford, whom we have earlier mentioned as a sort of escort to Itō during his visit to Britain, wrote as late as April:

> I remained a couple of hours with Itō on the night of Viscount Hayashi's dinner to him after other guests had left and what he said then left no doubt on my mind that he had been strongly impressed by the French money market.[24]

Contemporaries found much mystery and uncertainty in Itō's activities. His movements were of course unofficial and secret. On the whole, the secrecy of his negotiations in St Petersburg and London was preserved and only leaked out gradually through diplomatic indiscretions. For a full exposé, contemporaries had to wait for the publication of Hayashi's *Secret Memoirs*;[25] but diplomats had earlier access to the salient features of the story. Indeed within a matter of weeks of the alliance being signed, the British minister in Tokyo was able to report in a private letter some of the background to Itō's actions. MacDonald had learnt it mainly from the lips of Katō Takaaki who had been the foreign minister of Itō's last ministry of 1900-1901 but had found himself often at odds with his chief. In some ways therefore it was a deliberate indiscretion by one who had become disaffected towards Itō. MacDonald reported their conversation in his usual chatty, ungrammatical, and ill-punctuated style:

> [Katō told me that] shortly before I went home last year [August 1901], Hayashi received instructions from the Itō cabinet (Katō being the prime mover) to sound H.M.G. on the possibilities of an understanding and Eckhardstein's old idea was made use of. Perhaps you know all this in which case many apologies for inflicting [the matter on] you again. Katō told me confidentially that Itō is exceedingly cautious in all his dealings and it was with the greatest difficulty he (K) could obtain permission to send instructions to Hayashi to open negotiations. PM [Katsura] told me that Itō agreed to conditions of the [Anglo-Japanese] Agreement in the first instance at Berlin. On his arrival at St Petersburg he began to 'wobble' again doubtless owing to the exceedingly friendly reception he got from the Russians, but he stiffened up all right when he got to London.[26]

Thus the picture emerged of Itō as an inconsistent statesman who could not always make up his mind between alternative courses of action. He took up the British alliance while still prime minister, then he dropped it when he passed over his draft to the Russians, then he took up the British alliance again. This is not the picture which emerges from the official biography of Itō, where inconsistency is a charge that the writers would never dare to admit.[27] But it presents a plausible picture of a man struggling to chart a new course for his country. Thanks to information from Itō's friends and leaks from his enemies, therefore, Lansdowne was not in the dark for too long over Itō's secret journey.

This essay has dealt with four successive British foreign secretaries and their perceptions of Japan and Britain's relations with her. Since it was Lansdowne who had to deal with the most difficult aspect of the Japanese problem, we have dealt with his tenure at the Foreign Office in greater detail. There were certain resemblances between the foreign secretaries in question. Rosebery, Kimberley,

Salisbury, and Lansdowne were all land-owning aristocrats. Yet, despite their origins, their memoranda speak of Japan and east Asia in commercial terms and the place of Japan as a source of trade for Britain. This was as true of Salisbury and Lansdowne as of Rosebery and Kimberley and suggests that a mercantile sense was as much a mark of the Conservative as of the Liberal party. This is not to deny that these statesmen were unaware of political overtones: they were all alert to the Russian threat in north-east Asia and inclined to avoid direct British involvement in the area because of her increasing concentration in the real area of her commercial predominance, the Yangtse valley. Even when in 1900 there was a strategic element which had to be added to the commercial and political ones, Salisbury, under pressure from his cabinet colleagues, responded commercially: offering money to the Yangtse viceroys to ensure that the Boxers were effectively suppressed there; and offering money to Japan if she would send a force to help in the relief of the besieged legations at Peking.

With the coming of Lansdowne, the problem had changed and become distinctly more serious. Russia was in occupation of Manchuria and enjoying superior influence in Korea and trying to exercise dominance over the weak government of China. From this point Japan had to be regarded as a political partner. The negotiations for the Anglo-Japanese alliance presented at least two major problems: there was the sheer negotiation of an instrument which was comparatively new to both Japan and Britain and the necessity to deal with a decision-making elite in Japan which was divided in its ideas over priorities. Landsdowne's problem could not have been more difficult to solve; it could not have arisen in a more awkward way.

Cedric Lowe in the final pages of his book, *The Reluctant Imperialists*, places the Anglo-Japanese alliance in its broader setting. He argues that the alliance certainly involved Britain in 'an obligation to go to war in circumstances which were largely outside British control which was a commitment which had not been made since the 1830s in Europe'; yet it was a regional pact to cope with the situation in China and not a general alliance; Lansdowne's role was not to break away from Salisbury's policy of 'splendid isolation' since Salisbury had never in practice been isolationist. Thus, though the Japanese alliance was important, it was not strictly a turning-point.[28] These statements of Cedric Lowe still seem to be valid fifteen years after they were written. What we have tried to add in this essay is the personal dimension: Lansdowne, more than Rosebery, Kimberley, or Salisbury, showed an understanding of Japan. Perhaps he was forced to be understanding and patient by being thrust against his will into the middle of a domestic dispute in Japan over foreign affairs. Be that as it may, he handled the ensuing crisis of Itō's European trip with skill, coolness, and great foresight. Indeed, he turned Itō's visit to Britain artfully to his own advantage.

NOTES

1. Kimberley papers (Scottish National Library, Edinburgh), 10243, Rosebery to Kimberley, 28 April 1895. Readers will observe that in my conclusions that follow, I am in disagreement with Cedric Lowe, *The Reluctant Imperialists* (London, 1967), pp. 192-3, and W. L. Langer, *The Diplomacy of Imperialism* (New York, 1951), p. 185.
2. I. H. Nish, *The Anglo-Japanese Alliance* (London, 1966), p. 37.
3. Salisbury papers (Christ Church, Oxford), Salisbury to Satow, 3 October 1895.
4. Nish, *Alliance*, pp. 54-7.
5. *Nihon Gaikō Nempyō narabi ni Shūyō Bunsho* (Tokyo, 1955), Vol. I, p. 194.
6. Nish, *Alliance*, p. 103.
7. Lowe, *Reluctant Imperialists*, p. 246, points out that Bertie served his apprenticeship in the Far Eastern department.
8. For greater detail, Nish, *Alliance*, pp. 163-70.
9. Nish, *Alliance*, ch. IX.
10. F.O. (Foreign Office Archives, Public Records Office, London), 800/134, MacDonald to Lansdowne, 24 October 1905.
11. F.O. 46/544, Longford to Campbell, 20 November 1901.
12. *Itō Hirobumi hiroku*, 2 vols., (Tokyo, 1928-30), appendix to Vol. I, nos. 15-20; A. M. Pooley (ed.), *Secret Memoirs of Tadasu Hayashi* (London, 1915), pp. 138-44.
13. *Hayashi Memoirs*, pp. 145-7; G. P. Gooch and H. W. V. Temperley, *British Documents on the Origins of the War, 1898-1914* (London, 1926-38), Vol. II, no. 11, p. 100. (Hereafter cited as 'B.D.')
14. B.D., Vol. II, nos. 112-13.
15. B.D., Vol. II, no. 76, Hardinge to Lansdowne, 26 November 1901; Charles Hardinge papers 3 (Cambridge University Library), Hardinge to Sanderson, 28 November 1901.
16. Hardinge papers 3, Bertie to Hardinge, 6 November 1901.
17. More detail in Nish, *Alliance*, pp. 196-203.

18. F.O. 65/1623, Scott to Lansdowne, 11 December 1901.
19. *Hayashi Memoirs*, pp. 144-5.
20. *Itō Hiroku*, nos. 64-5. The Japanese version accords well with Lansdowne's version in *B.D.*, Vol. II, no. 120.
21. F.O. 800/134, Itō to Lansdowne, 9 February 1904; Lansdowne to Itō, 18 March 1904.
22. F.O. 800/134, Lansdowne to MacDonald, 9 January 1902.
23. Charles Scott papers (British Museum MSS Room), Add. MSS. 52304, Scott to Sanderson, 1 May 1902.
24. F.O. 46/660, Longford to Campbell, 26 April 1902.
25. Hayashi's *Secret Memoirs* were published in London in 1915; but earlier versions in Japanese had appeared in the Japanese press, notably in 1913, the year of Hayashi's death.
26. F.O. 800/134, MacDonald to Lansdowne, 16 February 1902. Portions in square brackets are the author's.
27. Kaneko Kentarō, *Itō Hirobumi den*, 3 vols., (Tokyo, 1943).
28. Cedric Lowe, *Reluctant Imperialists*, pp. 248-51.

F.R. BRIDGE

British official opinion and the domestic situation in the Hapsburg Monarchy, 1900–1914

If in 1900 those responsible for the making of British foreign policy were unanimous in their desire to see the Dual Monarchy survive as a Great Power, by the end of the Great War the Foreign Office viewed its dissolution with composure, if not with hearty approval. Indeed, some would argue that the support the British had given to the opponents of the Monarchy in 1918 was a significant factor in bringing about its collapse. Obviously, developments since the outbreak of war, notably the patent enslavement of the Monarchy to Germany by the summer of 1918, were the chief cause of this change of attitude; but these developments were matched by a growth of sympathy in British official circles for the cause of the oppressed nationalities. It is the purpose of this study to examine the extent to which, even before the outbreak of war, these official circles had developed a sceptical view of the internal problems of the Monarchy that prepared them psychologically to accept its disappearance without any particular regret.

At the very highest level of the British foreign policy making process, in formal constitutional terms at least—to wit the monarchy—there was no modification of attitude at all. Both Edward VII and his successor had nothing but admiration for the Emperor Franz Joseph, who during the Boer War had braved the criticism of his subjects to declare publicly, at a ball, that 'dans cette guerre je suis completement Anglais'.¹ Even the tetchy Archduke Franz Ferdinand, at times vociferously Anglophobe, made a good impression when George V welcomed him and his morganatic wife to England in 1912 and 1913: 'You know, I really like the archduke',² the king had told his cousin, Count Mensdorff, the Austro-Hungarian ambassador. In England VII's estimation, Franz Joseph was always 'the doyen of the sovereigns';³ and in 1908 the king sternly reminded Sir Charles Hardinge, permanent under-secretary at the Foreign Office, that 'my personal regard for the Emperor of Austria is so great, that I could not sanction a policy which would cause him either trouble or pain.'⁴ Similarly, in 1912, George V caused the Foreign Office a good deal of trouble with his persistent, if ultimately vain, attempts to insist on honouring the aged Emperor with the first state visit of the new reign.⁵ He liked to talk freely to Mensdorff, reminding him of how Austrians were always better received in England than other foreigners, and Englishmen in Austria: 'so often allies, never foes'.⁶ In August 1914 he was at great pains to assure the ambassador that Great Britain was going to war for the neutrality of Belgium, and not at all for Serbia or Balkan questions.⁷

In fact, in the circles the ambassador moved in — the cosmopolitan society of court and country house — affection for Austria-Hungry even survived the outbreak of war. Mensdorff's royal relatives, his 'affectionate cousins and sincere friends George and Mary', were quite heartbroken at his departure; and Queen Alexandra on taking leave of him wept and kissed him.⁸ Even after four years of warfare, the king could still write consolingly to his old friend:⁹

> I often think of you, my dear Albert, and am sure you know that your many friends in England have not forgotten you....
> I fear your poor country is passing through a very difficult time.

Again, in 1922, when the League of Nations came to the rescue of the bankrupt rump state, the king was naturally 'glad that Balfour was able to do so much for your poor country'.¹⁰ From 1924 the former ambassador's private visits to Sandringham were resumed on an almost annual basis until the king's death. Over the despoliation of the former imperial family, the king could only shake his head, and he and the queen frequently enquired sympathetically after the Empress Zita and her children.[11] Mensdorff was amused to receive from the king, as late as 1929, a letter addressed to him in 'Marienbad, Austria': 'Wenn die Czechen nur wüssten... Quelles têtes ils feraient.'[12] A letter from Queen Mary in 1931 showed that, at this level at least, affection for the old Monarchy was unimpaired:[13]

> You know, as a child I always thought my father was an Austrian, not a Württemberger and in fact he loved Austria far more than his native land, and that is why I have taken such an enormous interest in Austria and Hungary.... It is a pleasure to think that I did once see Vienna in all its glory, and had the pleasure of making the acquaintance of your beloved Kaiser who was always in the eyes of *our* family, Cambridge, Strelitz and Teck 'Der Kaiser' par excellence.

Those more directly responsible for the making of foreign policy were naturally more influenced by political, than by such personal, considerations. Even here, however, it was clear that both Salisbury[14] and Lansdowne, for whom 'the continued existence of the Dual Monarchy was absolutely necessary'[15] in the interests of the balance of power, wished the Monarchy well. There is no trace in their correspondence of any sympathy for the internal forces that were threatening to undermine it. Grey, taking office at a time when Germany was starting to become obstreperous, was perhaps naturally less inclined to sympathise with her allies in Vienna and Budapest. He was, as a Liberal, wont to point to the 'intense race-feeling' ill-advisedly aroused among the South Slavs by Austria-Hungary's Near Eastern policies.[16] Indeed, as this problem became more acute in the years before 1914, the domestic problems of the Monarchy become a further reason for Grey for keeping his distance in addition to consideration for French and Russian susceptibilities. He was struck by a remark in a report from Vienna at the end of 1913, referring to 'some day', admittedly 'in the far distance', 'when things go to pieces here'. 'Austria will be of little use to us as a friend', he wrote, 'if she falls to pieces. One cannot steer with confidence by a star that may dissolve.'[17]

At a lower level, the British ambassadors in Vienna and consuls-general in Budapest, while assiduous in representing the interests of their own government in international politics, were almost without exception, as far as the domestic politics of the Monarchy were concerned, sympathetic to the attitudes of the ruling circles in which they spent their working days. Of the ambassadors, Sir Horace Rumbold (1895-1900) was an old friend of the emperor and Sir Francis Plunkett (1900-1905), a Catholic, was persona gratissima with the Austrians, who tried desperately to secure for him an extension of his term of office beyond retirement age.[18] Sir Fairfax Cartwright (1908-1913) attached immense importance to the social function of the embassy. In 1909 he demanded a replacement for the commercial secretary, whom he thought[19]

> very dull and has no kick and life in him, such as the young 'Comtessen' usually expect to find in a young attache. If we are to keep up the practice of the British embassy here I must have some young man who will go down and be accepted with open arms by the highest Society here. You know how friendly the big people are disposed to be towards members of the British embassy....

Not unnaturally, none of these diplomats had any time for the opponents of the existing social and political order as organized by the 'big people'. Even Sir Edward Goschen (ambassador from 1905 to 1908), a Germanophobe who consorted with the outspoken *Times* correspondent, Wickham Steed, and who had the task of bearding Aehrenthal in the Bosnian crisis, was overcome with sadness when he was transferred from his 'chère Vienne' to Berlin.[20] Finally, Sir Maurice de Bunsen (January-August 1914), while sharply critical of the political morality of the Austro-Hungarian foreign office, and of the severity of Austro-Hungarian rule in Bosnia, participated extensively in the social life of the high aristocracy.[21]

The people to whom their reports were addressed, Foreign Office officials in the corridors of Whitehall, were of course less impressed by the charms of life among the elite that determined the political life of the Dual Monarchy. It was in these circles, rather than among monarchs, ambassadors, or even foreign secretaries–whose comments were largely confined to high politics–that the idea gradually began to take hold that perhaps something might be rotten in the state of Austria-Hungary. Before the Foreign Office reforms of 1906[22], these people had little opportunity to express their views in writing. But even by that date there is evidence that

Eyre Crowe, chief clerk in the Western Department, was well acquainted with the writings of critics of the existing political system; and in the last years of peace a body of opinion was to develop in the Foreign Office that regarded the Dual Monarchy as not only something of a fraud in terms of its constitutional structure, but as a morally bankrupt state in terms of modern European culture and civilisation.

There was little trace of such attitudes in the Foreign Office correspondence of the early years of the century. Then, the Dual Monarchy was in the throes of what was probably the most severe domestic crisis of its existence: the conflict between the ruling elites in Vienna and Budapest over the future development of the 1867 system.[23] Hungarian attempts to modify the Compromise in the direction of a simple personal union between the two halves of the Monarchy, both in military and economic terms, were threatening to render the state incapable of functioning as a Great Power; and its impending demise was being regularly predicted abroad. In comparison with this crisis, the conflict that had broken out between German and Czech nationalists in the later 'nineties was of relatively local significance: it had simply paralysed the parliamentary system in Austria and led to a period of government by emergency decree. Those problems that were to loom so large in 1914 — the South Slav question and the future of Bosnia and the Herzegovina — seemed at this time even less significant.

For example, as consul-general Freeman reported from Serajevo in 1901:[24]

> No impartial person can say that Austria-Hungry has failed in her mission in Bosnia and the Herzegovina. Tranquillity and security reign throughout the country, excellent communications have been established everywhere in the province... Bosnia and Herzegovina when I first knew them were in a worse state than the Asiatic provinces of Turkey, whereas now, not only are they far ahead, in every respect, of all the neighbouring Balkan states, but even of the Austrian province of Dalmatia. In fact, perhaps the greatest reproach to be made to the administration... is that the country has been forced along the path of progress and civilization at express speed, before the people were thoroughly fitted for it.

Of course, good military roads, impressive local government buildings, and smart hotels had a greater appeal for the foreign traveller than for the tax-paying native, but the latter was not completely neglected: the success of the government's tithe reform 'exceeded all expectations'.[25] Although, in 1903 the consul still believed that perhaps 'the government has been inclined to do even too much, has forced on European culture and civilization... and produced thereby much discontent.' Freeman had to concede that 'Bosnia and Herzegovina is by far the best-governed country in the Balkan peninsula, and can be favourably compared with any other European state.'[26]

British official observers were equally well-disposed towards the establishment in their reporting of opposition to the authorities in other areas of the Monarchy in the early years of the century. This no doubt reflects the general desire of the British, in the years before they had settled their disputes with France and Russia, still the most obvious threats to the security of the British empire, to see Austria-Hungary continue as an effective factor in the European balance of power. Moreover, as the Emperor and his ministers in Vienna and Budapest were notoriously well-disposed towards the British cause in the Boer War, whereas the opposition elements throughout the Monarchy were clearly not, it would have been odd if the British had not wished to see their supporters in Austria and Hungary continue to hold the reins of power. In short, British reporting in the early years of the century reflected a desire to see no change in either the great power status or the political leadership of the Monarchy.

Certainly, British diplomats were little inclined to consider whether the national conflicts that were paralysing parliamentary government in Austria might not reflect some deep and perhaps justified dissatisfaction with the 1867 system. According to Sir Francis Plunkett, the 'wild and scandalous' scenes in parliament simply showed 'how completely the house is at the mercy of a band of a few riotous members.' He saw no hope of any 'permanent improvement so long as the Chamber contains members such as those of which it is at present composed, and until it is possible to introduce a more stringent mode of procedure'.[27] To a degree, British observers were simply bewildered by the complexity of the problem. Plunkett confessed that[28] there is no country in which attempts at prophesying the immediate political future prove more often incorrect than in this composite empire, and therefore the only safe course is to wait and see what may be evolved from the general confusion now so painfully rampant.

His successor, Sir Edward Goschen, soon decided that the aims of the various parties 'require an almost life-long study before they can be thoroughly understood'.[29] His predecessor, Sir Horace Rumbold had been equally resigned: 'Nothing short of authority strongly wielded from the centre can save the Monarchy'; but 'unfortunately, vigorous central action has long ceased to exist at Vienna' under the old and disillusioned emperor, and the future was 'dark and uncertain'.[30]

Not that there was any doubt as to where British sympathies lay. Troublemakers were roundly condemned: the German nationalist leaders, Wolf and Schoenerer, were 'little short of traitors to Austria';[31] and Lueger, whom Franz Joseph had twice refused to accept as mayor of Vienna, was 'a very dangerous man, the very type of a clerical demagogue'.[32] 'To the independent observer', the British chargé lamented in 1900:[33]

> It seems well nigh inconceivable that the responsible leaders should be so engrossed in their petty and local ambitions as to continue a policy which is as fatal to the well-being of the masses, whether German or Czech, as it is to the interests of the Empire at large as a great European power.

But it was no consolation to the British when the Czech and German politicans for once combined to forget their quarrels and denounce the government's pro-British stance over the Boer War. In Agram, a pro-Boer resolution was unanimously adopted by a Committee of the Croatian diet. At Prague, according to Rumbold, interest in the war was 'very remarkable', and the government was under fire from an Anglophobe coalition comprising 'the most reactionary and most clerical elements as well as the great body of extreme Radicals and Social Democrats', all united in their 'instinctive hatred of conservative and Protestant England'.[34] Four years later, in the wake of the attack on Russia by Britain's ally Japan, Czech mobs were again on the streets of Prague, demonstrating outside the British and United States consulates.

In these circumstances, it is not surprising that British reporters tended to be as scathing about the 'senseless quarrels' of the nationalities[35] as they were laudatory of 'the almost inexhaustible energy and patience of Dr. Koerber',[36] the Austrian prime minister from 1900 to 1904; and sympathetic to his successors, Gautsch, who faced 'almost superhuman' tasks,[37] and Beck, 'certainly one of the best representatives of the Austrian official class'.[38] Although, in his concluding report in 1905 Plunkett could only endorse Rumbold's verdict of 1900 that 'the jealousies and quarrels of the various contending nationalities continue to threaten the prosperity, and even the existence of this composite empire' and his 'belief in the traditional good luck of Austria' allowed him to hope that she would yet see better times.[39]

In Hungary, Rumbold was dismayed to see that the opposition's programme 'dangerously approaches the personal union pure and simple to which a large proportion of the Hungarian nation aspires';[40] while to Plunkett, it was 'incomprehensible that there should be any sane person either in Austria or in Hungary anxious to advocate a policy of separation', which must not only spell disaster for the Monarchy in economic terms, but 'deprive it of all influence in the counsels of Europe'.[41] As regards particular issues, such as the Boer War, Plunkett[42] gathered that in Hungary

> in upper and government circles the feeling towards England is apparently most friendly and hearty; but I am told that among the bourgeoisie and the professor class, the... pro-Boer feeling is very general.

Certainly, the British were appreciative when in the Budapest parliament the prime minister, Szell, stoutly defended his government's decision to sell horses to the British for use in South Africa, and condemned the attacks on England, 'whose sympathies Hungary had enjoyed in the days of her troubles' in 1848-1849. Lansdowne made a point of thanking Szell, 'the more so as we are not used to such kindly and sympathetic words' from the continent.[43]

It was with unconcealed dismay, therefore, that the British followed the campaign for an independent Hungarian army, which led to the fall of the Szell government in May 1903. Plunkett even went so far as to warn a Hungarian politician that the concessions being contemplated by the new government 'seemed to me a long step towards the creation of two armies and might be a dangerous move towards the separation of the two kingdoms'.[44] He hoped that the new prime minister, Tisza, would employ 'energetic means' against the 'venomous obstruction' of the opposition.[45] But he had to admit that 'no one sees how order is to be made out of this rampant confusion';[46] and he was sincerely distressed 'at the sad state of impotency to which the oldest constitutional country on the continent sees itself reduced'.[47] Tisza's decision to hold elections at a time of such feverish excitement seemed to Plunkett 'a courageous but possibly dangerous policy';[48] and his worst fears were confirmed when in January 1905 the 'fatal elections' resulted in a resounding defeat for Tisza that portended further 'evil effects' for the relations between the two halves of the Monarchy.[49] At any rate, Franz Joseph was unable to find a government that could secure a parliamentary majority until the summer of 1906, when, by threatening to implement a drastic suffrage reform to the benefit of the nationalities, he cowed the opposition parties into taking office with a more moderate programme. The crisis in Hungary moved even Edward VII to write some of his rare minutes on the despatches: 'a very serious state of things'; 'the Emperor's position is indeed deeply to be pitied.'[50]

By this time, however, there were others who thought that there might nevertheless be two sides to the question. In Budapest, consul-general Stronge decided that Tisza's defeat perhaps simply reflected the fact that 'the mass of the Magyar population is and probably always has been hostile to the Compromise of 1867'; and that the emperor-king was lucky that the victorious Independence Party was in the hands of 'one so moderate and conciliatory as M. Kossuth'.[51] In Vienna, Goschen bluntly declared the root cause of the crisis to be 'the tendency in Austria to regard Hungary as an Austrian province and the amply justified contention of Hungary that she is to all intents and purposes an independent kingdom.'[52]

These indications of a rather more critical tone in British reporting coincided not merely with the appointment of the Germanophobe Goschen to the Vienna embassy, but with a perceptible shift in Austria-Hungary's international position in relation to British interests.[53] The year 1905 had seen not only a German challenge, in the First Moroccan crisis, to Britain's new-found friendship with France, but the destruction for the time being of Russia's capacity to threaten the British empire by land or sea. By 1906, the British were well on the way to a settlement of their extra-European differences with Russia, and coming to see themselves as seriously threatened by the naval policy of Germany. The Kaiser's notorious 'brilliant second' telegram, thanking the Austrians for their support in the Moroccan question, had not gone unnoticed in London, where the new Liberal government also looked askance at the bullying attitude adopted by Austria-Hungary towards Serbia in commercial questions, and her reluctance to risk an upheaval in the Near East by supporting British demands for radical reforms in the Sultan's Macedonian provinces. In broad international terms, therefore, the ground was already to some extent prepared for a less uncritical approach towards the Hapsburg Monarchy.

On the domestic front, the failure of suffrage reform in Austria to produce a viable parliamentary system was matched by a new struggle within Hungary. There, the settlement of the extremely dangerous crisis between the emperor-king and the coalition of opposition parties was followed by a growing conflict between the new 'Coalition' government (which adopted even more extreme Magyarization policies than its predecessors) and the emergent nationalities within the kingdom. Compared to the crisis of 1903–1906, however, this posed a far less dramatic threat to the existence of the Monarchy and the European balance of power. As a result, liberal sympathies in England could be given more free play.

Finally, the administrative reforms in the British Foreign Office after 1906 gave even quite junior officials considerable opportunities to express their views on these matters; and these officials were, by virtue of their environment, less inclined than diplomats in Vienna or Budapest simply to reflect the views of the established authorities in the Monarchy. In 1907, for example, the ambassador[54] reported in some dismay the 'bitter disappointment' of

> all those who saw in Universal Suffrage a panacea for all the defects of the old system, and who proclaimed so loudly that the 'People's Parliament' would be a parliament of earnest and businesslike men, a parliament in which scenes of violence, racial struggles, and obstruction would be things of the past.

> Never since I have been in Vienna, have the debates been characterized by so much personal insult, so much contempt for the chair, and so many disorderly scenes as during the present session.

The chargé d'affaires agreed:[55]

> The numerous national and political groups have continued their unedifying and senseless squabbles with a total disregard for public business and the scenes which have occurred on several occasions have been scarcely inferior in disorder and violence to those which distinguished the year 1898.
>
> The sittings devoted to the vote on account showed the same characteristics which for some time past have marked all debates on financial questions, namely that every conceivable subject except finance was discussed. The same may be said in respect to almost any business laid before the house, for the Austrian M.P. appears to have an invincible disinclination to speak on the particular matter which should be under consideration. If a Canal Bill is introduced, the question of the appointment of a schoolmaster in Galicia would not improbably occupy the attention of the Chamber, while a mining bill might conceivably occasion an animated debate on horse-breeding. Whatever the subject may be, speakers are perpetually interrupted by the members of hostile parties with usually impolite and often indecent and blasphemous remarks which are duly reported in the press without comment or reprobation. A visit to the Chamber reveals a scene of such noise, confusion and disorder that one can only wonder that the procedure of this Assembly, which produces the maximum of talk but the minimum of work, has not been drastically reorganized long ago.

In the Foreign Office, however, this tale of woe elicited only the dry, if sensible observation from an assistant clerk: 'I do not see what grounds there can have been for hoping that a Parliament elected under universal suffrage would prove more orderly than those under the old system.'[56]

Indeed, for a few months in 1906 the British even considered taking advantage of the Hungarian crisis for their own purposes, as a possible counter to the German threat. As early as January the parliamentary under-secretary, Lord Fitzmaurice, noted[57] that Kossuth had disavowed any expansionist ambitions in the Balkans: this was 'very interesting and very important'. If the Coalition came to power in Hungary, 'they would prove a very formidable obstacle to the Drang nach Osten policy, if that policy were taken up from Vienna and supported from Berlin.' He was still of the same opinion in May:[58]

> Germany cannot have an active policy in the Balkan peninsula, or Asia Minor, or the Persian Gulf unless she is certain of the support of Hungary. A continuous chain must run from Berlin to Vienna and so to Constantinople and Bagdad. Consequently, the development of things in Hungary is of special interest now.

When, therefore, in August, the Hungarian emigré, Dr. Emil Reich, wrote to the Foreign Office pleading for closer links between Great Britain and Hungary, more British investment to develop Hungarian industry, and the establishment of more consulates there, Fitzmaurice recommended that his ideas were 'well worthy of consideration'. 'It would be difficult indeed for Germany to dominate Asia Minor... unless she had what might be called a friendly line of communication.'[59] Grey himself had his doubts: Reich's proposal was 'very interesting, though some of it sounds rather visionary':[60] and the traditionalist Barrington, formerly Lansdowne's private secretary, warned that 'we had better not get too intimate with this society lecturer who is not very highly thought of.'[61] Nevertheless, on 22 August the foreign secretary ordered the consul-general in Budapest to report on the possibilities:[62]

> It has lately become increasingly apparent to H.M.G. that the relations existing at present between this country and the Kingdom of Hungary are not proportional to the political and economic position in the Dual Empire held by the latter state, a position which moreover bears every sign of increasing in importance in the near future.

The consul's reply was not encouraging. He suggested that perhaps new consulates might be established in Agram and Clausenburg (in Croatia and Transylvania); but as for the rest, the only English population in Hungary, according to the consul, consisted of 'trainers, jockeys and governesses'.[63] The Foreign Office for its part naturally shrank from showing too much interest in such sensitive areas as Croatia and Transylvania—'this would not facilitate an entente with the Hungarian government':[64] and an incident in September sharply reminded them of the dangers of meddling in the hornets' nest of Hungarian politics. An unofficial visit to Budapest by some Liberal MPs—members of the Eighty Club—gave great offence in Austria when the visitors not only refused an invitation to visit Vienna, but made speeches in support of Hungary's struggle for independence.[65] In London, Crowe was immediately on his guard:[66]

> This is the line of policy into which Dr. Reich wants to drive us, and we should disavow the untimely manifestation. If and when Hungary does establish her 'national independence' it will be time enough to define our attitude and position towards Austria and Hungary.

Grey was inclined to shrug the matter off: 'the world must get used to independent visits by unofficial organizations'; but the arch-conservative permanent under-secretary, Sir Charles Hardinge, took a sterner view: 'these missions will do serious harm some day, owing to the wrong impressions they create abroad.'[67] He was further exasperated when an Austrian newspaper explained that the visit was a result of the conversion of Edward VII (who had recently granted an audience to Count Albert Apponyi) to the views of the Hungarian Independence Party. Although a 'nice letter' from the Austro-Hungarian ambassador eventually calmed the infuriated king, Hardinge was left lamenting that 'the free press is a terrible *fleau*, from which we all have to suffer.'[68] Meanwhile, a Munich paper asked what the British would have said if, in the days of Parnell, Austrian politicians had gone to Dublin to talk to Home Rulers, whereupon Barrington admitted that 'the criticisms of the visit of the Eighty Club are not unfair.'[69] By this time Hardinge had had enough of the idea of establishing closer links with Hungary: 'I think for political reasons it would be well to drop the proposal for the present. It can always be revived later.'[70]

As racial conflicts intensified in Hungary, and as the Coalition government began to pursue increasingly severe Magyarization policies, some British observers began to express a decidedly critical attitude towards the Hungarian regime. True, the reports from Vienna and Budapest continued to show sympathy for the authorities; but inside the Foreign Office strong-minded junior officials took advantage of the new filing system, under which each incoming dispatch was provided with a 'jacket' for comments, to express very different opinions. Eyre Crowe, in particular, was a man of decided views:[71]

> The constitution of the Austro-Hungarian Monarchy is based on the principle of the ascendancy of the Germans in Austria and of... the Magyars in Hungary. The difficulties of the numerous other races who are becoming more and more restive... have hitherto found expression chiefly in Austria...

According to Crowe, they were also making themselves felt in Hungary too. He noted that 'In the proper adjustment of these race questions lies the vital problem of the Monarchy.'

Not that the British Foreign Office as yet felt any direct interest in the success of any of the parties in dispute. In Crowe's view, the Hungarian education law of March 1907 was 'a remarkable engine of coercion. No wonder that the other "Nationalities" are up in arms. But their opposition can hardly be expected to prevail.' Grey, more familiar with British than with Hungarian parliamentary procedure, merely noted that 'the other Nationalities cannot be worth much if they stand it.'[72] Crowe was more realistic:[73]

> The paramount position of the two races which respectively dominate the two halves of the Monarchy is so strong that there is no great possibility of the federalists gaining much ground.

When, in May, the decision of the Coalition government to insist on the use of Magyar on the Croatian railways drove its erstwhile Serbo-Croatian allies to turn to Austria for support, Crowe thought for a time that:[74]

> There are signs of the Coalition Party's regime coming to an end. The Hungarians have had their own way for so long, and have so misused their ascendancy, that if the Austrian half of

the Monarchy will only firmly assert itself and obtains the Emperor's support, the Hungarian bubble may perhaps be pricked sooner than has hitherto been expected.

He was sharply critical of the Magyars' handling of the negotiations:[75]

> The Hungarian government have an infinite genius for making any legal requirements, which are not to their taste, mean the exact opposite of what they say.

The ensuing deadlock might[76]

> prove the beginning of a serious conflict within the Hungarian state. Hitherto the Magyar minority has invariably succeeded in keeping down all opposition to their oppressive authority.

However, not all British observers were prepared to endorse such views or the views of Wickham Steed, the *Times* correspondent in Vienna, or of R. W. Seton-Watson, who gained international prominence in the autumn of 1907 with his exposure of Magyar brutalities in handling a riot at Czernova in Slovakia. On the contrary, the consul-general at Budapest spoke up boldly for the authorities and condemned the British press:[77]

> The Vienna correspondent of the *Times* is more especially looked upon as the avowed enemy of this country.... The difficult position of a Magyar government should be impartially considered. It represents racially only a minority of the nations, yet a minority which has always been the dominant one. This racial domination is being continually threatened. Once undermined, the fate of the country will be sealed, and instead of a vigorous and thriving Magyar Kingdom a loose conglomeration of conflicting racial elements would come to the fore — an easy prey to the designs of ambitious neighbours.

Panslavism was 'spreading apace'; and 'this government can surely not be blamed for acting zealously and for punishing with due severity all those who agitate or conspire against the unity, nay the existence, of the Hungarian state.'

In the Foreign Office, the affair elicited only neutral comments:[78] the Czernova incident 'will further increase the hatred of Magyar rule in Hungary'; 'Mr Clarke sympathizes with the Hungarian government, maintaining that the domination of the Magyar element is the only salvation of the Kingdom.' Even Crowe, some eighteen months later, could take a dispassionate line:[79]

> [It was] only natural that the agitation of the several nationalities which feel oppressed, and *are* in many respects oppressed, by the Magyars in Hungary and by the German party in Austria, should appear treasonable in the eyes of the ruling parties...

These parties feared that any move in the direction of federalism, according to Crowe, would threaten 'their predominant position. From their own point of view, that is quite intelligible.' Hardinge agreed:

> The Hungarians feel uncomfortable as they are in a minority and they realise how they are hated by the Slav and Roumanian nationalities living side by side with them. The situation is an unnatural one from the ethnological point of view, but it will probably right itself in time.

The years 1908–1909 marked a further stage in the alienation of British official opinion from the authorities in the Dual Monarchy in all respects. In the international field, the British found themselves supporting Russia and Serbia against what they regarded as Austro-German expansionism in the Bosnian crisis; and in 1908, in contrast to 1900 and 1904, the demonstrations on the streets of Prague were pro-British. (In November, a Czech mob attacked the house of Aehrenthal's brother and threw the Austrian flag into the Moldau: 'the mob then raised the cry of "Long live Serbia", and cheers were given for England, while the union jack was paraded round the town.')[80] As the dispute raged between Austria and Serbia, Grey and Hardinge were coldly dismissive of the Austrian argument that Siberia had after all no *locus standi* in the annexation question: this might be valid 'in strict logic', but it 'entirely overlooks the question of national sentiment'.[81] For some months after the end of the crisis the British remained suspicious of Aehrenthal's supposed expansionist ambitions, and actually welcomed the prospect of a renewal of domestic strife in the Monarchy as a restraining factor. Even when the bitterness had subsided, in the last few years of peace, the Foreign Office's continuing suspicion of Germany precluded any return to the close relations that had existed with Germany's ally at the turn of the century. The renewal of national conflicts in the Monarchy now drew few expressions of sympathy from London. Although the embassy in Vienna and the consulate general in Budapest continued to take their traditional line, they came in for increasing criticism in the Foreign Office. Finally, a series of judicial and political scandals served to undermine, in the eyes of British observers, the moral standing of the Dual Monarchy as an institution worthy of respect and veneration as an element of European civilization.

Certainly it was partly for reasons of domestic policy, in the hope of moderating South Slav discontent, that after the annexation crisis Aehrenthal attempted to improve relations with Serbia and Montenegro. As far as the Foreign Office was concerned, however, Britain had no interest, in terms of the international situation, in seeing him succeed. Indeed Cartwright was expressly forbidden to give him any assistance: 'We are not inclined to encourage a policy by which Serbia and Montenegro should become dependent on Austria, since it is desirable that they should form a barrier to Austrian aggrandizement eastwards.'[82] After all, 'for a long time to come Austria will be dependent on Germany.... Sir F. Cartwright should not be too sympathetic to Austrian plans for winning over Serbia.'[83] Foreign Office officials did not challenge Cartwright's argument that Aehrenthal wanted to increase the prestige of the Monarchy in order to distract the public from 'what are after all only local squabbles.'[84] Indeed, Crowe even admitted that 'Great Britain has everything to gain from a strong Austria-Hungary, on condition that the latter is not dominated by Germany and does not oppress Italy.'[85] Hardinge agreed, but pointed out that Germany would 'leave no stone unturned' to maintain her domination, 'and as long as she is successful, Austrian policy will in the main be dependent on Berlin.'[86] The Foreign Office was by no means disconcerted to note in the summer of 1909 that 'the normal state of bickering between Austria and Hungary has been re-established after the truce' during the annexation crisis, and that Hungary 'looks like being extremely troublesome in the near future.'[87] Hardinge was 'not particularly sorry, as it is a good thing that Austria should be preoccupied for the time being with internal dissentions. No one can wish her to be definitely weakened, but she has shown of late such an exuberance of strength that she can afford to be weakened a little.'[88]

At Budapest, political life in the last five years of peace was turbulent to a degree, with the Magyar ruling elite both internally divided and at loggerheads with the nationalities. It certainly seemed a far cry from the days when British ambassadors could refer to Hungary as 'the oldest constitutional state on the continent'. By June 1911, the consul-general was declaring that 'obstruction in the Hungarian parliament, where closure does not exist, has been brought to a pitch of perfection unknown, I believe, in any other state.'[89] A year later, he was hopeful that the appointment of the strong-minded Tisza as president of the chamber[90]

> will doubtless have a salutary effect and the government will probably now make a determined attempt to alter the standing orders and so put a stop to the continuous obstruction of a small minority.

However, the results were disappointing. When Tisza brought special police into the chamber to silence the opposition, he was fired on by a disgruntled MP, one Kovacs, and Tisza's opposition to electoral reform led to serious riots in the streets of Budapest. True, on this latter occasion, the consul-general[91] could still write in mocking terms of the 'martyrs of liberty' now consigned to prison, and wholeheartedly approved of the government's draconic police measures which had succeeded in instilling 'a wholesome fear' into the 'rowdy elements of the population.' It was significant that in the Vienna embassy Cartwright condemned the 'violence and destruction by the worst elements of the population' of Budapest, but pointed to the 'very general feeling' at Vienna, 'that the lower classes in Hungary have serious reasons for discontent in the indefinite postponement of electoral reform.'[92] As well, if the acquittal of Kovacs in December seemed to some in the Foreign Office 'beyond comprehension', Crowe[93] saw it as

> one of the results of a long period of oppression and unconstitutional government. It arouses the political passions to the extinction of the ordinary feelings of right and wrong.

Similarly, Crowe dismissed the Budapest government's electoral reform bill of January 1913 as 'one of the usual Hungarian shams.'[94] By April, even the consul-general[95] was reporting that:

> the country is sick to death of parliamentary rows and the bickerings of rival politicians....
>
> Any attempt to introduce effectual legislation or to deal with the numbers of crying evils prevalent in this country, has almost disappeared. The government seems to have no time, even if it has the desire, to ameliorate social conditions. Parliament has become an arena where the rival leaders display the fatal facility for oratory common to nearly every Hungarian.

In November 1913, a financial scandal concerning the government's involvement in a casino venture was merely noted in the Foreign Office as indicative of 'the low standard of political morality publicly recognized in Hungary.'[96] True, in June, when Tisza had been appointed prime minister, a junior clerk in London had ventured to remark that 'much constructive work may be expected from a man of Count Tisza's calibre, especially now that he has swept away obstruction.' Crowe, however, proffered a different assessment of the leading statesman of Hungary: 'I do not believe in any constructive work by Count Tisza. He is a reactionary of the deepest dye and never gets on with anybody.'[97]

Certainly, Tisza's handling of the abortive negotiations with the Roumanians of Transylvania in the next few months seemed to bear out Crowe's judgement. According to Max Müller,[98] recently appointed consul-general at Budapest and less susceptible to Magyar arguments than his predecessor,

> the truth is that he [Tisza] is *au fond* as chauvinist and reactionary as any other Magyar politician and though sagacious enough to perceive the danger arising from the present state of feeling among the Roumanians, he cannot bring himself to sacrifice the Magyar fetich of a united Hungarian state in order to conciliate the Roumanians. His promised concessions amounted to nothing.

From this judgement, nobody in the Foreign Office dissented:[99]

Count Tisza offered the Roumanians nothing worth having and will always be prevented from doing so by his instincts and his associates. No real progress has been made.

Progress was made, by contrast, in the handling of Croatia, where Tisza displayed more flexibility than Crowe was prepared to admit. During the period of Coalition rule, relations between Budapest and Agram had deteriorated sharply; and if some people in the Foreign Office found Croatian criticisms of the railway language laws 'very unreasonable' from the point of view of foreign travellers in Croatia, Crowe pointed out that 'the Croatians have the letter of the law on their side.... The general treatment of the non-Magyars by the Hungarian government has been calculated to provoke the most bitter opposition.'[100] By 1912 this opposition had resulted in the suspension of the Croatian constitution. In Budapest, consul-general Grant-Duff[101] sympathized with the authorities and blamed the 'Croatian extremists', who

> acting often under outside influence have been led to many ill-advised acts. During the last few years the terrorism exercised by [them]... has been such that successive Bans have been unable to obtain a majority in the Diet.... Supporters of the union with Hungary, a union which has lasted for several centuries, have been boycotted, insulted, and threatened. The general want of discipline has even penetrated to the schools, where the Authorities have been set at nought by the boys.

The Foreign Office was not entirely convinced. As one clerk pointed out, 'the extremists may by their "terrorism" have prevented successive Bans from getting a majority, but the method of the Bans, when they have the chance, hardly mean free and independent elections; and so far as his vote is voluntary, I suspect the Croatian elector prefers giving it to the Croatian party.'[102] In the summer, negotiations for a settlement were deferred when an attempt was made on the life of the Ban of Croatia—an attempt which, the new consul-general, Max Müller, sternly observed, 'should convince the Hungarian government of the urgency of removing as far as they can the causes of the existing discontent and induce them to hasten the restoration of a consitutional state of affairs in Croatia.'[103] But by November, as negotiations resumed it did seem to some in the Foreign Office that 'the Hungarians are making rather belated attempts towards the conciliation of the Roumanians and the Croats'; and although Crowe stubbornly insisted that 'the efforts are not likely to be genuine',[104] Tisza in fact reached agreement with the Croats on 8 December.

Max Müller[105] was impressed: 'the Hungarian government are to be congratulated on their policy.' The consul-general went on to point out the significance of the Croatian question for the Monarchy generally, both externally, as a result of the recent expansion of the Balkan states at the expense of the Ottoman Empire, and internally:

> As I have before remarked, Count Tisza is evidently alive to the additional danger that the Monarchy incurred during the recent crisis in the Balkans owing to the discontent, if not actual disloyalty, existing among the Roumanian and Slav nationalities within its boundaries, a danger which can only have been intensified by the victories and territorial aggrandisement of Roumania and Serbia.

At least Tisza had settled the immediate Croatian crisis, over the operation of the constitution of 1868; but the 'Croatian question', as posed by those who demanded the abolition of the 1868 arrangements and the reorganization of the Monarchy on a Trialist basis, was as far from a solution as ever: 'no Hungarian government could be a party to any arrangement which would in any way satisfy such aspirations.' In the Foreign Office, too, there was a growing appreciation of the implications of the South Slav question for the future of the Monarchy. The Earl of Onslow, in a long minute on Max Müller's despatch, pointed out that those who had been wont to argue that Catholic Croats and Orthodox Serbs would never be able to co-operate, have been proved wrong:

> They have joined together, and just at the time when the success of independent Servia has rendered her a far more important nation than she was two years ago. In order to realise the importance of this question, one must grasp the fact that some 50% of the whole Serbo-Croatian race are Austrian or Hungarian subjects — there being roughly 4½ million Serbo-Croats in Austria-Hungary to 4 million in the rest of the world. A

break-up of the Empire would mean, (probably) the strengthening of Servia by a large territory and more than doubling her population.

In Austria too, meanwhile, there was evidence enough of serious constitutional difficulties. Cartwright had analysed the problem in 1909:[106] the government was essentially absolutist, 'but Austrian absolutism has had its hands tied by constitutional forms, and so the state machine practically refuses to work.' The constant recourse to government by emergency decree — 'the root principle of this vicious system — had been 'absolutely disastrous to parliamentary procedure' and any sense of responsibility; reform and a settlement of the language question would, however, be 'a herculean task, far beyond any of the governments Austria has yet produced.' Foreign Office comments were even more down to earth: 'parliamentary government in the Austro-Hungarian Empire is a farce.'[107] By 1915 it seemed to London that although[108]

> so far as Austria is concerned, the central government appears to be dealing wisely and firmly with the problems that confront them... there appears for the moment to be no prospect of an improvement in the political situation in Bohemia, and the situation not only in Bohemia and Galicia, but also in Hungary and Croatia, can be summed up in one word, 'deadlock'.

Clearly, Foreign Office views of the political developments in the Dual Monarchy were evolving in a sceptical direction; but it must be said that Foreign Office officials themselves recognized that this evolution was based on information of varying quality and quantity; and that the reports from the embassy left something to be desired in terms of the domestic background to foreign policy. True, even people in the Foreign Office were still feeling their way in these years: Crowe, as late as March 1912, still thought it necessary to inform his colleagues that 'Mr Seton-Watson is the well-known author whose books, written under the pseudonym of 'Scotus Viator', have dealt largely with the Slav grievances against the political tyranny of the Magyars.'[109] When Cartwright asked for a copy of Seton-Watson's recent publication, *The South Slav Question*, the Foreign Office readily agreed that it 'seems desirable that the embassy should have the volume'.[110] However, as the interrelationship between foreign and domestic policy became more patently obvious in the Balkan wars—as the growth of tension with Serbia was accompanied by a clamping down on the Slavs at home, unease about the quality of the reporting from Vienna began to grow. The Foreign Office could indeed deduce that there was 'no improvement in the internal situation; the tendency of the government is to become more reactionary than ever'.[111] But this was not enough for Crowe:

> It is clear that the internal situation is very adversely affected by the way in which the war preparations are made. Austria-Hungary is, above all others, a country where questions of foreign policy are inextricably mixed up with the most important questions of internal policy.... We need more information from Vienna,

and Grey emphatically agreed.[112] As a result, the embassy was told to report more fully, and to send a monthly summary of domestic events; but the results were disappointing. Nicolson's comment on Cartwright's report of 6 April 1913, 'a poor summary. Our information from Vienna on all questions is sadly meagre'[113] re-echoed time and again as the year went on.

One laudable exception, in the eyes of the Foreign Office, was Lucas-Shadwell, vice-consul in Ragusa, who in February 1912 produced the first detailed report[114] on local conditions in Dalmatia, an area which had until then hardly seemed to be a potential source of trouble,—indeed, it had almost escaped the attention of British observers. Lucas-Shadwell, like others in his position, was by no means unsympathetic to the Austrian authorities: when his old school-friend, R.W. Seton-Watson, on holiday in Dalmatia, was wildly feted by the natives of Zara, Split, and Ragusa, Lucas-Shadwell[115] had put himself out to dissuade him from proceeding to Agram at such a critical juncture in the Croatian crisis. His report on Dalmatia is, therefore, all the more striking for its sceptical tone:

> The bulk of the population is anti-dynastic, because it looks upon the dynasty as being anti-Slav and as an essential part of the present regime. The feeling towards the Emperor is one of complete indifference; he is looked upon as a German with German sentiments and as being completely out of touch and sympathy with his Slav subjects. The Dalmatian Slavs feel that

they are treated as an inferior race and they know too well that their country has been entirely neglected by the central government. It can hardly be expected that any affection can be felt for the Emperor who, in the mind of the peasant, is responsible for all this.

Lucas-Shadwell did not suggest that a crisis was actually imminent, noting that the upper-class Slavs were law-abiding, and

> the peasants are too poor and too ignorant to be dangerous. The average Dalmatian has neither the enterprise nor the grit necessary to make him dangerous. On the other hand, they might become most peaceful and even loyal subjects if they were treated with more consideration and if they were accorded the material assistance necessary for the development of their country.

This report impressed even Crowe, who saw to it that Cartwright was 'instructed to inform the vice-consul that it has been read with much interest'.[116]

Finally, in Bosnia, praised by the British as almost a model province some ten years earlier, things were no better. The establishment of consitutional government after the annexation was delayed by bickerings between Vienna and Budapest; then there was the upheaval of the Balkan wars when the triumphs of Serbia, which sought to be the unchallenged leader of the southern Slavs, increased the effervescence in the annexed provinces to fever pitch. The British consul admitted[117] that the precautionary measures of the authorities—the declaration of a partial state of siege and the dissolution of Social Democratic and Serbian 'clubs'— were perhaps justified in terms of military necessity; but he felt they could 'only add strength to the smouldering fire of Servian hatred of Austrian rule'. By October 1913 the Bosnian Diet had still not been convened, as the authorities could not get a working majority. For this the consul[118] was inclined to blame the 'Servian extremists', who had 'distinguished themselves by intransigent impractical opposition to the government'; but the end result was that

> after a troublous existence of little more than three years, for the last ten months of which it has not sat at all, the Diet has drifted, as was perhaps anticipated from the beginning, into

the chronic incapacity for work exhibited by parliamentary assemblies in Austria-Hungary.

The outlook was not promising, especially as

> the victories of Servia have encouraged the growth of national consciousness among the Serbs of Bosnia-Herzegovina. They are in the main submissive to their masters, but there is in them a spirit of resistance which is stirrred whenever Servia strikes a bolder attitude.

This last point was not lost on Cartwright who, as usual, sympathized with the Austrian point of view:[119]

> Servia will some day set Europe by the ears and bring about a universal war on the continent.... I cannot tell you how exasperated people are getting here at the continual worry which that little country causes to Austria under encouragement from Russia. It may be compared to a certain extent to the trouble we had to suffer through the hostile attitude formerly assumed against us by the Transvaal Republic under the guiding hand of Germany.

In the Foreign Office, by contrast, there was scant sympathy for the authorities, and the explosive South Slav question was viewed with some aplomb: there was 'clearly a lot of discontent among the Serbs, but capable leaders are lacking'. It was thought that the situation was 'best summed up'[120] by a Croatian observer quoted in a consular report from Serajevo:

> Here, as elsewhere in the Empire, a constitution is only a make-believe. The Government allows the representatives of the people to fret and fume to their hearts content, while it retains the real power in its own hands. Austro-Hungarian rule in Bosnia-Herzegovina depends entirely on the power of the sword. So long as the Army maintains its present efficiency, the Monarchy will have no cause to apprehend the loss of this province.

If, by 1914, the British had come to the conclusion that the constitutional structure of the Dual Monarchy was a sham, they took an equally sceptical view of the state of the press and 'public opinion'. Fundamental to this scepticism was a long report on the Austro-Hungarian press[121] written in 1906 by Goschen with the assistance of the *Times* correspondent in Vienna, Wickham Steed. Both men were notoriously suspicious of Germany, and Goschen's report laid great emphasis on the activity of the Press Bureau—the Literarisches Bureau of the Ballhausplatz—as pernicious in two respects: not only was the Press Bureau supposed to have a working arrangement with its counterpart in Berlin,

> under which the journalists at Vienna and Berlin have mutually agreed to write in the interests of the other country where those of their own are not involved. This obligation affects practically all the Austrian papers;

the Bureau also 'seems to have the power', even over large and apparently independent papers like the *Neue Freie Presse*, 'to exact the publication of official articles when necessary'. It was significant that in the Foreign Office, Crowe, who had an almost pathological dislike of the Press Bureau, welcomed Goschen's report with enthusiasm as 'a really valuable aid to understanding what appears in the Austrian press'.[122] It was completely in line with this analysis that Goschen declared during the Bosnian crisis that 'Austrian public opinion is formed almost entirely upon what is served up in the newspapers by the press bureau';[123] and that Hardinge told the Austro-Hungarian ambassador straight out that it was 'perfectly well known that the Austrian government have complete control over the press'.[124] They were not alone in this lofty attitude. According to Odo Russell,[125] counsellor of embassy from 1908–1914, public opinion 'in our sense is practically non-existent, owing to the antagonistic elements which go to make up the public in Austria'. The higher classes 'still take but little or no interest in politics and... the press is to a great extent corrupt'. He had himself collected evidence of the brutal methods of the authorities from a journalist:[126]

> [even the writer,] Professor Vambery displayed to Steed signs of abject terror, after a headwashing at the Ballplatz, exclaiming that he did not mind exile for himself, as he was old, but he dreaded the vengeance which might be wrought on his son, a Professor of the University, and as such at the mercy of the

government. This state of affairs is hardly conceivable in the 20th century, but I am reciting facts.

Whether this story was true or not, the opinion was widely held among British observers that, as far as the press and public opinion were concerned, the Dual Monarchy hardly measured up to British standards of civilisation.

It was not an opinion that was universally held, however. Indeed, it led to a lively debate between the Foreign Office and senior British diplomats in Vienna and Budapest. When, in June 1910 some French, German, and Austrian newspapers made unsubstantiated allegations about British policy over Crete, Steed asserted in the *Times* that the Austrian reports were officially inspired. The *Neue Freie Presse*, in a fierce personal attack on Steed, strongly denied this, and Aehrenthal sent for Cartwright to complain about the tone of Steed's reporting in general, and to hint at his possible expulsion.[127] Cartwright had a good deal of sympathy for Aehrenthal's charge that 'if he [Steed] had been a Czech, he could not have shown more violence against the government.'[128] 'He is far too violent against everything Austrian or Hungarian', the ambassador confided to his father, 'and writes as if he were the Apostle of the Southern Slavs. He does much mischief and the sooner he goes to some other post the better.'[129] As for the *Neue Freie Presse*'s denunciations, Steed had, in Cartwright's view,[130]

> brought this attack upon himself by the offensive way in which he tries to discover Machiavelian intentions on the part of the Austro-Hungarian Government. Mr Steed has for some time past displayed an animosity against everything in Austria and in Hungary, which, it seems to me, leads him to lose to a considerable extent his sense of proportion... In my opinion, Mr Steed exaggerates the control the Austro-Hungarian government have over the press. Count Aehrenthal only gives a directive to the press on great occasions.

Two weeks later, he returned to the charge: Steed had been 'absolutely unfair' in reporting as officially inspired some unfounded allegations about British policy that had appeared in the *Wiener Tagblatt* — a low class paper read by servants and common people, full of tittle tattle and sensational items of news, somewhat in the style of the *Daily Mail*.'[131] Nor was Cartwright alone in his views: 'Who is now your *Times* correspondent?', the exasperated ambassador in Constantinople asked Cartwright during the Balkan Wars;[132]

> and why does he write about Constantinople in the way he did in the *Times* of January 1? A collection of the greatest rot I have ever read. It cannot, I imagine, still be Steed, though I often thought he took the record for nonesense.

Cartwright's reply showed that his opinion of Steed had not mellowed with time:[133]

> He is a fanatic against Turkey and an enthusiast for the Serbs, and he dreams of nothing less than a great uprising of all the Southern Slavs in this Empire and a final burst-up of Austria-Hungary. I have had plenty of trouble in calming down many of the alarms which he has caused our Foreign Office by his exaggerated representation of things here.

The 'trouble' Cartwright had taken was not appreciated in the Foreign Office. In the 1910 affair, for example, Crowe was enraged at the 'excessively vulgar and abusive personal attack on Mr Steed in the *Neue Freie Presse*', and considered that 'Sir F. Cartwright takes a rather astonishing line.'[134] It was 'little short of absurd' to say that Aehrenthal interfered with the press no more than the British government did: Aehrenthal 'seems to have made Sir Fairfax Cartwright forget that there is an official press bureau in the Vienna Foreign Office'.[135] Crowe himself wrote to Cartwright on 1 July, castigating the pernicious activities of press bureaus in general, adding that the records of the Vienna bureau were no clearer than any other—'see Agram, Friedjung, etc. etc.'.[136] Grey's private secretary backed him up: 'I can't help thinking that you are rather hard on Steed', he wrote to the ambassador on 26 July.[137] Despite his defects,

> in his exposure of the methods of press bureau journalism he has been *quite* justified and fair.... As regards his strictures on the reptile press methods and machinations, I am sure he is right.

When Consul-General Howard in Budapest chose this moment to

complain about an account in the *Times* by R. W. Seton-Watson on an election riot in Slovakia—'the mere statement of a partisan writer like Mr Seton-Watson... is hardly conclusive'—this drew another fierce minute from Crowe:[138]

> [The consul had] perhaps been unconsciously influenced by the feelings entertained for Mr Steed at the Vienna embassy. Mr Seton-Watson, who writes under the well-known pseudonym of 'Scotus Viator' is an acknowledged authority on modern Hungary and an author of repute.... Mr Howard cannot make us forget that the Austrian and Hungarian records in the matter of corrupt administration and police brutalities are of the very darkest. It would probably not be far wrong to say that there has been no change in this since the days of the notorious Austrian atrocities in Italy and Hungary in 1849. We have the Agram Trial and Dr Friedjung's forged documents still fresh in our minds.

The Agram trial had opened in January 1909, at the height of the Austro-Serbian crisis over the annexation, and had resulted in the conviction of some fifty orthodox Serbian members of the Croatian diet for treasonable relations with Belgrade.[139] Initially, British official comment had been confined to the international implications of the affair. The British minister in Belgrade noted that any improvement in Austro-Serbian relations now appeared 'exceedingly problematical', especially as 'the religious element, which is constantly fed from Russia' could hardly be appeased by economic concessions.[140] In London, Hardinge expressed some concern: 'It will be unfortunate if Servian agitation receives fresh impetus'; but Grey blandly noted that 'it shows what strong forces are at work.'[141] The affair took on a more sinister aspect when it transpired that the documents on which the verdict rested—and on which the historian Friedjung had based a public denunciation of the accused—were forgeries, transmitted to Vienna from the Austro-Hungarian legation in Belgrade. The resultant quashing of the convictions in April 1910 was, Crowe sourly noted, merely 'tardy justice now at last applied for political reasons'; 'a satisfactory ending to a very dark chapter in Hungarian history'.[142] At the end of 1910, moreover, the Serbian authorities proceeded to try and sentence one Vasic, who confessed to having supplied the forgeries to the legation. During the course of this trial the allegation was made which caused a considerable furore in Delegations of the Austrian and Hungarian parliaments in session at the time that the forgeries had been made at the behest of the Austro-Hungarian government. 'No one acquainted with the methods of that government in the past and with the proceedings of the Agram trial would deny that the story is quite probable', Crowe declared.[143] After all, it was 'a very small step from the ordinary machinations of the official press bureau to the forging of documents'.[144] He wrote to the British minister at Cettinje that:[145]

> All press bureaus... naturally lead by an inevitable decline into manoeuvres of this shoddy and dishonourable description, and of all press bureaus, those at Vienna and Berlin are the vilest. Those who deliberately work and use them are responsible for their direct and indirect effects which in my opinion constitute not only the most shameful but also the most dangerous feature of modern foreign politics.

Meanwhile, in the Delegations, Masaryk described the Agram trial as 'a dishonour to a cultivated state'.[146] 'Count Aehrenthal and his officials come very badly out of this business', Crowe observed, which Nicolson thought was 'putting the case mildly'.[147] Although, in the end, Aehrenthal managed to satisfy the Delegations, and even Nicolson suspected the possiblity of a Russian intrigue in the Vasic affair, Crowe was adamant: 'No one can doubt Count Aehrenthal's complicity in the unsavoury intrigues exposed by Professor Masaryk.'[148] It was perhaps no mere coincidence that when he learned, just at this time, of a plan to found a Turco-Hungarian technical school at Budapest, he mockingly endorsed Masaryk's more general conclusions: 'the idea of Young Turks learning Magyar as a passport to civilization, is very comical.'[149] Altogether, in the eyes of the Foreign Office, the whole affair of the Agram trial and its aftermath did lasting damage to the Monarchy's reputation as a civilized state.

What had become an ingrained suspicion of Austro-Hungarian methods surfaced again in June 1913 when the military authorities in Bosnia detained on spying charges, stripped, and searched a British tourist, one Hope-Johnstone, who was collecting examples of Serbian dialects in the company of the clerk to the British consul at Serajevo. (Apparently, Hope-Johnstone's 'unconventional and travel-stained dress, and his taking notes' had aroused the suspicions of an innkeeper and a drunken soldier.[150]) Crowe was not particularly surprised at the incident: 'the Austrian authorities are well known to have peculiar ways of treating foreigners whom it pleases them to suspect.'[151] His suspicions were confirmed when he discovered that in February Berchtold had taken the ambassador to task: the Bosnian authorities had complained to Vienna 'that Mr Freeman, our consul at Serajevo, and especially his clerk, are showing such marked pro-Serbian sympathies that they have reason to complain about their conduct.'[152] Cartwright, true to form, had then obligingly warned the consul 'to be very careful in future not to annoy the authorities in any way'.[153] In view of this, Crowe decided[154]

> that we have here to do with the typically Austrian habit of concocting unfounded charges against any foreign agents whose presence or whose candid and honest reports are believed by them to be unfavourable to their own proceedings.
>
> The record of the Austrian officials in connection with the Agram trials, the Friedjung forgeries, and the more recent inventions concerning the ill-treatment of an Austrian vice-consul in Servia is a particularly black one. I think we should on no account allow our consular officials to be accused without insisting on the most specific particulars, which we could then investigate, and we should decline to listen to any vague and general charges, which are probably trumped up.

Altogether, the general conclusion of the Foreign Office was that 'the treatment by the Bosnian authorities of the... incident is worthy of their past record to which Sir E. Crowe has called attention.'[155]

By the summer of 1914 scepticism prevailed even at the British embassy in Vienna, where Cartwright had been succeeded in January by Sir Maurice de Bunsen. The tone of the new ambassador's reporting of the aftermath of the Serajevo assassinations is significant. De Bunsen was strongly critical of the 'marauding bands' of Catholic Croats with a strong admixture of Mussulman Slavs', who were resorting to violence against the Orthodox Serbs of Serajevo in defiance of 'the feeble attempts of the police to restore order'; while at the same time he felt that in the long run the assassinations were bound to 'cause the police regime of Bosnia-Herzegovina to be rendered infinitely more severe than before'.[156] As for possible international repercussions, he was sceptical in the extreme:[157]

> Those who remember the circumstances of the notorious Agram and Friedjung trials in 1908 and 1909 when the efforts of the Austro-Hungarian Government to justify the expected war with Servia by publishing proofs of a widespread irredentist plot so woefully broke down, will hesitate to accept without adequate proof the wholesale denunciation of the Servian patriotic societies which may now be expected to be made.

The Austro-Hungarian government did, in fact, seek to justify the famous note to Serbia of 24 July by circulating to all foreign governments a formidable dossier listing the misdeeds of Serbian irredentists over the past five years. In the Foreign Office in those hectic days, however, the dossier was simply consigned to the archives unread; and Crowe's reaction was totally consistent with what had now become his settled opinion: 'I doubt if it is worth reading.'[158]

With the outbreak of war, of course, high policy became the sole determinant of British attitudes towards the Monarchy. In the search for allies, Grey, as early as August 1914, was endorsing offers of Austro-Hungarian territory to Italy and Rumania; and when the British in 1917–1918 were toying with the idea of a separate peace with Austria-Hungary, it was with a view to breaking up an intolerable German power bloc in Central Europe that they insisted on the implementation of internal reforms to break the monopoly of power of the German and Magyar elites. When it became clear that the Monarchy had been reduced to a helpless appanage of the German empire, the allied governments, preoccupied above all with the future balance of power, at last acquiesced in the demands of the Monarchy's subject peoples and irredentist neighbours for its destruction.

Of course, since 1918, their successors, both inside and outside the former Monarchy, have had ample occasion to regret its disappearance, both in political and humanitarian terms. Certainly, the injustices and political chicaneries of the pre-1914 Monarchy pale into insignificance beside the mass persecutions and genocide that have marked the history of central Europe in the twentieth century, when images of Czernova and Agram have been eclipsed by Auschwitz, Lidice, and Katyn. Yet none of this could have been foreseen in 1914. The fact remains that in terms of the higher standards of political morality prevailing in the Europe of that day — standards that were reflected not least in the British Foreign Office — the Monarchy was found wanting. In the last decade or so before the war, as far as the perceptions of the British Foreign Office were concerned, there was a marked shift of opinion against the Monarchy as a political and social institution; and this meant that, in those quarters at least, its passing did not occasion the disapproval or regret that might have been expected at the turn of the century.

NOTES

1. G. P. Gooch and H. W. V. Temperley, *British Documents on the Origins of the War, 1898–1914* (London, 1926–38), Vol. I, no. 305. (Hereafter cited as 'B.D.').
2. Politisches Archiv (Haus-, Hof-, und Staatsarchiv, Vienna), VIII, 144 Mensdorff to Aehrenthal, no. 29C, 12 May 1910. (Hereafter cited as 'P.A.')
3. Mensdorff MSS (Haus-, Hof-, und Staatsarchiv, Vienna), K. i, Mensdorff to Lützow, 21 July 1903.
4. Hardinge MSS (Cambridge University Library), XIV, Edward VII to Hardinge, 24 March 1908.
5. F. R. Bridge, *Great Britain and Austria-Hungary, 1906–1914, a diplomatic history* (London, 1972), pp. 195–6.
6. P.A. VIII, 146, Mensdorff to Aehrenthal, private, 2 September 1910.
7. F. R. Bridge, 'The British declaration of war on Austria-Hungary in 1914', in *Slavonic and East European Review*, 47 (1969): 401–22.
8. Ibid.
9. Mensdorff MSS, K. viii, George V to Mensdorff, 17 December 1921.
10. Ibid., George V to Mensdorff, 21 October 1922.
11. Ibid., K. v., Tagebuch, see for example the entries for 21 November 1929, 4 November 1930, 2, 5, 9, 13 December 1934.
12. Ibid., 12 July 1929.
13. Ibid., 26 November 1931 (Transcription).
14. On Salisbury, see C. J. Lowe, *Salisbury and the Mediterranean, 1886–96* (London, 1965); *The Reluctant Imperialists, British foreign policy 1878–1902* (London, 1967).
15. F.O. (Foreign Office Archives, Public Records Office, London), 7/1339, Plunkett to Lansdowne, no. 150, 4 June 1903; and see also C. J. Lowe and M. L. Dockrill, *The Mirage of Power, British Foreign Policy 1902–22* (London, 1972).
16. B.D., Vol. V, nos. 485, 488 are typical.
17. B.D., Vol X/1, no. 316.

18. P.A. I/464, Goluchowski to Mensdorff, 1 June 1904.
19. Cartwright MSS (Leeds University Library, Special Collections), photocopy, Cartwright to Russell, draft, 6 July 1909.
20. C. H. D. Howard, ed. *The Diary of Edward Goschen, 1900–1914*, Royal Historical Society, Camden Fourth Series, no. 25, 1980; Aehrenthal MSS (Haus-, Hof, und Staastarchiv, Vienna), Goschen to Aehrenthal, 5 September 1908.
21. C. H. D. Howard, 'The Vienna Diary of Berta de Bunsen, 28 July–17 August 1914,' in *Bulletin of the Institute of Historical Research*, 51 (1978).
22. Zara Steiner, *The Foreign Office and Foreign Policy* (London, 1969), pp. 79 ff.
23. N. Stone, 'Constitutional crises in Hungary, 1903–1908', in *Slavonic and East European Review*, 45 (1967): pp. 163–82; F. R. Bridge, *From Sadowa to Sarajevo, The Foreign Policy of Austria-Hungary, 1866–1914* (London, 1972), pp. 13–21.
24. F.O. 7/1315, Freeman to Lansdowne, no. 4, 26 June 1901.
25. F.O. 120/825, Freeman to Goschen, 17 August 1905.
26. F.O. 7/1345, Freeman to Plunkett, no. 4, 14 March 1903; no. 12, 18 July 1903.
27. F.O. 7/1323, Plunkett to Lansdowne, no. 96, 10 April 1902.
28. F.O. 7/1352, Plunkett to Lansdowne, no. 234, 17 November 1904.
29. F.O. 7/1363, Goschen to Grey, private, 13 December 1905.
30. F.O. 7/1299, Rumbold to Salisbury, no. 191, 8 September 1900.
31. Ibid.
32. F.O. 371/7, Minute by Lord Fitzmaurice on Goschen to Grey, no. 82, 28 June 1906.
33. F.O. 7/1297, Milbanke to Salisbury, no. 59, 25 March 1900.
34. F.O. 120/763, Rumbold to Salisbury, draft, no. 16 Africa, 27 February 1900.
35. F.O. 7/1325, Plunkett to Lansdowne, no. 282, 20 November 1902.
36. F.O. 7/1322, Plunkett to Lansdowne, no. 84, 26 March 1904.
37. F.O. 7/1363, Goschen to Lansdowne, no. 211, 1 December 1905.
38. F.O. 371/195, Goschen to Grey, no. 22, 8 March 1907.
39. F.O. 7/1362, Plunkett to Lansdowne, no. 106, 5 May 1905.
40. F.O. 7/1298, Rumbold to Salisbury, no. 106, 19 May 1900.
41. F.O. 7/1323, Plunkett to Lansdowne, no. 122, 4 May 1902.
42. F.O. 7/1323, Plunkett to Lansdowne, no. 133, 20 May 1902.
43. Lansdowne MSS (Public Record Office, London), Lansdowne to Deym, copy, 17 December 1902.
44. F.O. 7/1338, Plunkett to Lansdowne, no. 60, 26 February 1903.
45. F.O. 7/1338, Plunkett to Lansdowne, no. 162, 17 June 1903; no. 69, 12 March 1903.
46. F.O. 7/1340, Plunkett to Lansdowne, no. 245, 16 August 1903.
47. F.O. 7/1339, Plunkett to Lansdowne, no. 136, 20 May 1903.
48. F.O. 7/1352, Plunkett to Lansdowne, no. 258, 19 December 1904.
49. F.O. 7/1362, Plunkett to Lansdowne, no. 30, 31 January 1905.
50. Minutes by Edward VII on: F.O. 7/1363, Johnstone to Lansdowne, no. 129, 16 June 1905; F.O. 7/1362, Plunkett to Lansdowne, no. 77, 24 March 1905.
51. F.O. 120/825, Stronge to Plunkett, no. 7, 31 January 1905.
52. F.O. 7/1363, Goschen to Grey, private, 13 December 1905.
53. Lowe and Dockrill, *Mirage of Power*, pp. 27–8.
54. F.O. 7/195, Goschen to Grey, no. 147, 28 October 1907.

55. F.O. 7/196, Carnegie to Grey, no. 174, 24 December 1907.
56. Ibid., minute by G. Spicer.
57. F.O. 368/3, Clarke to Grey, no. 5, 23 January 1906, minute.
58. F.O. 371/7, Clarke to Goschen, no. 60; 15 May 1906, minute.
59. F.O. 371/7, Memorandum from Dr Emil Reich, July 1906, minute by Fitzmaurice.
60. Ibid., minute by Grey.
61. F.O. 371/7, Reich to Foreign Office, 22 August 1906, minute.
62. F.O. 120/829, Grey to Clarke, no. 1, Political, 22 August 1906.
63. F.O. 371/7, Clarke to Grey, no. 1, 7 September 1906.
64. Ibid., minute.
65. Bridge, *Great Britain and Austria-Hungary*, p. 26ff.
66. F.O. 371/8, Henry Norman MP to Foreign Office, minute by Crowe.
67. Ibid., minutes.
68. Hardinge MSS, Hardinge to Mensdorff, [7?] October 1906.
69. F.O. 371/8, Buchanan to Grey, no. 139, 24 October 1906, minute.
70. F.O. 371/7, Boothby to Grey, no. 166, 30 October 1906, minute.
71. F.O. 371/7, Goschen to Grey, no. 65, 9 June 1906, minute by Crowe.
72. F.O. 371/195, Clarke to Goschen, no. 10, 11 March 1907, minutes by Crowe and Grey.
73. F.O. 371/195, Clarke to Goschen, no. 11, 17 March 1907, minute by Crowe.
74. F.O. 371/195, Clarke to Goschen, no. 31, 30 May 1907, minute by Crowe.
75. F.O. 371/195, Clarke to Goschen, no. 29, 18 May 1907, minute by Crowe.
76. F.O. 371/196, Clarke to Goschen, no. 30, 28 May 1907, minute by Crowe.
77. F.O. 371/196, Clarke to Goschen, no. 72, 16 December 1907.
78. F.O. 371/196, minutes on Clarke to Goschen, no. 58, 31 October 1907, no. 72, 16 December 1907.
79. F.O. 371/599, Howard to Grey, no. 19, 14 March 1909, minutes by Crowe and Hardinge.
80. F.O. 371/399, Carnegie to Grey, no. 205, 4 December 1908.
81. F.O. 371/754, Cartwright to Grey, no. 43, 18 March 1909, minutes.
82. F.O. 371/756, Grey to Cartwright, private, 7 April 1909.
83. F.O. 371/756, Cartwright to Grey, no. 54, 1 April 1909, minute by L. Mallet.
84. F.O. 371/599, Cartwright to Grey, no. 62, 14 April 1909.
85. Ibid., minute.
86. Ibid., minute.
87. F.O. 371/600, Cartwright to Grey, no. 77, 1 May 1909, minute by Crowe.
88. Hardinge MSS, Hardinge to Cartwright, private, 4 May 1909.
89. F.O. 371/1047, Grant Duff to Grey, no. 28, 7 June 1911.
90. F.O. 371/1297, Grant Duff to Grey, no. 23, 21 May 1912.
91. F.O. 371/1298, Grant Duff to Grey, no. 24, 24 May 1912.
92. F.O. 371/1298, Cartwright to Grey, no. 70, 24 May 1912.
93. F.O. 371/1298, Grant Duff to Grey, no. 46, 18 December 1912, minutes.
94. F.O. 371/1575, Grant Duff to Grey, no. 1, 1 January 1913, minute.
95. F.O. 371/1575, Grant Duff to Grey, no. 12, 27 March 1913.
96. F.O. 371/1575, Max Müller to Grey, no. 23, 5 November 1913, minute by Nicolson.
97. F.O. 371/1575, Brüll to Grey, no. 18, 14 June 1913, minutes.

98. F.O. 371/1899, Max Müller to Grey, no. 13, 26 March 1914.
99. Ibid., minute by Villiers.
100. F.O. 371/827, Howard to Grey, no. 82, 16 November 1910.
101. F.O. 371/1296, Grant Duff to Grey, no. 13, 4 April 1912.
102. Ibid., minute by Campbell.
103. F.O. 371/1575, Max Müller to Grey, no. 21, 1 September 1913.
104. F.O. 371/1575, Max Müller to Grey, no. 23, 5 November 1913 and minute by Crowe.
105. F.O. 371/1576, Max Müller to Grey, no. 27, 8 December 1913, minute by Crowe.
106. F.O. 371/599, Cartwright to Grey, no. 17, 1 February 1909.
107. F.O. 371/826, Cartwright to Grey, no. 106, 6 July 1911, minute.
108. F.O. 371/1575, Cartwright to Grey, no. 123, 16 August 1913, minutes.
109. F.O. 371/1296, Cartwright to Grey, no. 30, 28 February 1912, minute.
110. F.O. 371/1296, Cartwright to Grey, no. 28, 25 February 1912, and minute.
111. F.O. 371/1297, Grant Duff to Grey, no. 43, 5 December 1912, minute by Crowe.
112. Ibid., minutes.
113. F.O. 371/1575, Cartwright to Grey, no. 59, 6 April 1913; Max Müller to Grey, no. 22, 3 October 1913; de Bunsen to Grey, no. 192, 8 December 1914, minutes.
114. F.O. 371/1297, Lucas-Shadwell to Cartwright, 29 December 1911, enclosed in Cartwright to Grey, no. 35, 19 March 1912.
115. F.O. 371/1296, Lucas-Shadwell to Cartwright, no. 2, 26 February 1912.
116. F.O. 371/1297, Cartwright to Grey, no. 35, 19 March 1912, minute.
117. F.O. 371/1575, Freeman to Grey, no. 5, 17 May 1913.
118. F.O. 371/1575, Freeman to Grey, no. 6, 6 October 1913.
119. B. D., Vol. IX/2, no. 582, Cartwright to Grey, 31 January 1913.
120. F.O. 371/1575, Freeman to Grey, no. 6, 6 October 1913, and minutes.
121. F.O. 371/166, Goschen to Grey, no. 56, 18 May 1906.
122. Ibid., minute.
123. F.O. 120/853, Goschen to Grey, no. 171, 3 November 1908, draft.
124. F.O. 371/599, Memorandum by Hardinge, 14 January 1909.
125. F.O. 371/828, Russell to Grey, no. 189, 26 October 1910.
126. Grey MSS (Public Record Office, London), Russell to Tyrrell, 8 January 1909.
127. Bridge, *Great Britain and Austria-Hungary*, pp. 154 ff.
128. Grey MSS, Cartwright to Grey, private, 24 June 1910.
129. Cartwright MSS, Cartwright to his father, 1 July 1910.
130. F.O. 371/827, Cartwright to Grey, no. 93, 21 June 1910.
131. F.O. 120/874, Cartwright to Grey, no. 107, 7 July 1910, draft.
132. Cartwright MSS, Lowther to Cartwright, 7 January 1913.
133. Cartwright MSS, Cartwright to Lowther, 11 January 1913, draft.
134. F.O. 371/827, Cartwright to Grey, no. 93, 21 June 1910, minute.
135. Ibid.
136. F.O. 371/827, Crowe to Cartwright, 1 July 1910.
137. Cartwright MSS, Tyrrell to Cartwright, 26 July 1910.
138. F.O. 371/827, Howard to Grey, no. 51, 20 June 1910 and minute.

139. C. A. Macartney, *The Habsburg Empire, 1790–1918* (London, 1968), pp. 785–6.
140. F.O. 371/748, Whitehead to Grey, no. 8, 19 January 1909.
141. Ibid., minutes by Hardinge and Grey.
142. F.O. 371/827, Howard to Grey, nos. 27, 30, 4, 11 April 1910, minutes by Crowe.
143. F.O. 371/1046, Barclay to Grey, no. 2, 5 January 1911, minute.
144. F.O. 371/1046, Cartwright to Grey, no. 231, 30 December 1910, minute.
145. F.O. 120/833, Crowe to Akers-Douglas, 6 April, 1911, copy.
146. F.O. 120/875, Russell to Grey, no. 204, 9 November 1910, draft.
147. F.O. 371/829, Barclay to Grey, no. 84, 8 December 1910, minutes.
148. F.O. 371/1046, Cartwright to Grey, no. 34, 24 February 1911.
149. F.O. 371/1046, Howard to Grey, no. 3, 17 January 1911, minute.
150. F.O. 371/1576, Cartwright to Grey, no. 88, 19 June 1913.
151. Ibid., minute.
152. F.O. 371/1576, Cartwright to Nicolson, private, 11 February 1913, copy.
153. Ibid.
154. F.O. 371/1576, Cartwright to Grey, no. 92, 25 June 1913, minute.
155. F.O. 371/1576, Note from the Austro-Hungarian embassy, 14 July 1913, minute.
156. F.O. 371/1899, de Bunsen to Grey, no. 132, 2 July 1914.
157. F.O. 371/1899, de Bunsen to Grey, no. 129, 29 June 1914.
158. Bridge, 'The British declaration of war...', 140.

K. A. HAMILTON

Great Britain, France, and the origins of the Mediterranean agreements of 16 May 1907.

The accords which Great Britain and France concluded with Spain in the spring of 1907 for the maintenance of the territorial status quo in the lands bordering and the islands of the eastern Atlantic and western Mediterranean have attracted little attention from historians of British foreign policy.[1] Yet at the time of their publication in June 1907 they provoked an angry reaction in the Austrian and German press, and caused some consternation in Berlin, Vienna, and St Petersburg.[2] Alexandre Izvolsky, the Russian foreign minister, was at pains to explain to the German ambassador at St Petersburg that the agreement that he was negotiating with Britain aimed only at removing outstanding causes of conflict between Britain and Russia in Asia.

The arrangements Izvolsky described consisted of a parallel exchange of notes between the governments of Britain and Spain, and France and Spain. Sir Edward Grey, the British foreign secretary, exchanged notes with the Spanish ambassador, Señor de Villa-Urrutia, on 16 May 1907 in London that registered the interest of Great Britain and Spain in the preservation of the territorial status quo and their resolve to maintain intact their respective rights over their insular and maritime possessions in 'the Mediterranean and in that part of the Atlantic Ocean which washes the shores of Europe and Africa'. Each government was also committed to communicate with the other if circumstances arose which altered, or tended to alter, the status quo in order to afford the opportunity 'to concert, if desired, by mutual agreement the course of action which the two

Powers shall adopt in common'. That same afternoon notes expressing similar sentiments in almost identical terms were exchanged between the Spanish ambassador at Paris, Fernando de León y Castillo, and the French foreign minister, Stephen Pichon. Grey informed the French ambassador at London, Paul Cambon, that if in such circumstances it should be necessary for the British and Spanish governments to communicate with each other, both would know 'that France takes the same view, and is as firmly resolved to preserve intact her rights over her insular possessions in the regions referred to'. Cambon likewise informed Grey of his government's readiness to concert with the British and Spanish governments.[3]

Three weeks later Paul Cambon asked whether British support would be forthcoming in the event of German pressure being put upon France and Spain in consequence of this exchange of notes; Grey stated that he would 'regard the spirit of the Agreement of 1904 as applying to the provisions of their Notes, and the same support would be forthcoming as we had given in connection with the 1904 Agreement'.[4] The implication was clear. Germany was considered to be the Power which was most likely to challenge their terms, and in that event Grey was prepared to extend to France the same degree of assistance as Britain had afforded to her *entente* partner during the Moroccan crisis of 1905 and the subsequent Algeciras conference. In this sense the exchange of notes represented a broadening of the geographical bounds of the *entente cordiale*. They complemented the secret convention which Spain had already concluded with France on the future partition of Morocco, tightened Spain's relationship with Britain, and created a further barrier to the encroachment of any other power on Spain's possessions.

The German press had few doubts about the purpose of the new accords. Professor Schiemann in the *Preussicher Kreuz Zeitung* complained that a new paragraph had been added to the 'paper blockade' which Anglo-French policy was constructing against Germany. The new agreements, claimed the *Kölnische Zeitung*, were concerned with Germany's further isolation.[5] In Vienna the ultra-German *Deutsches Tageblatt* argued that the chief object of the arrangement was to prevent in time of war a junction of the Austro-Hungarian and German fleets. The notes and the British attitude towards arms limitation and the second Hague conference were, the paper hinted, facets of a policy designed to deprive Germany of the means of defending herself against the diplomatic restriction of her peaceful policy of commercial expansion. Moreover 'there remains the danger that the forcible compression of so much expansive power will create an explosion. That means war.'[6]

Set against such invective, Grey's claim that British policy was 'practically the same as that embodied in the agreement concluded in 1887 between Great Britain and Italy to which Austria-Hungary, with the concurrence and approval of the German Government, immediately afterwards became a party', seems bland and even futile.[7] Only in forms and nomenclature do the Mediterranean agreements of 1907 appear to resemble those of 1887. The latter had established a formal link between Britain and the powers of the Triple Alliance, and had, in the first instance been intended by Lord Salisbury to help him to cope with the problems posed by Russian intrigues in the Balkans and the defence of the status quo at the straits between the Black Sea and the Mediterranean. On the other hand, those of 1907 seem to offer fresh evidence of Britain's desire to work with France in restricting any further increase in German influence in the Iberian peninsula and its adjacent islands. Nevertheless, it is still worth considering the degree to which Grey's diplomacy was in this instance a response to what he perceived to be Germany's ambitions. Was there perhaps some substance in Grey's claim to continuity between his policy and that pursued by Salisbury some twenty years before?

The notion of an Anglo-Spanish agreement on the preservation of the territorial status quo in the regions covered by the notes was in no sense new. Spanish governments had in the past sought British assistance in resisting real and supposed French aspirations in Morocco, and Spain had been associated, albeit tenously, with the Mediterranean accords of 1887. During the following decade, Sir Henry Drummond Wolff, the British ambassador at Madrid, continued to impress upon the Foreign Office the value of Spain to Britain as a friend and potential ally.[8] Spanish proponents of foreign alliances were also inclined to have a somewhat exaggerated impression of the role that their country could hope to play in international affairs. Spain did, however, possess a substantial strategic and therefore diplomatic asset in her geographical position. In an era in which the formation of the Franco-Russian alliance and imperial rivalries in Africa and Asia were leading Britain's naval experts to focus their attention upon the Mediterranean, the Foreign Office could not always afford to neglect the whims of governments in Madrid.[9]

From a strategic point of view friendly relations with Spain were of advantage to Britain because of the menace to her lines of communication if another first class sea Power gained control and influence over Spain's ports and other important locations, not only on the peninsula, but in the Balearic and Canary islands, and on the northern littoral of Morocco.[10] During the 1890s, rumours abounded concerning the designs of other powers upon Spain's continental and insular possessions. France was credited with wanting one of the Canary islands, and Russia was at one time suspected of wishing to acquire the *presidio* of Ceuta.[11] An immediate concern to Britain's service chiefs and the Foreign Office was the vulnerability of the anchorage and harbour of Gibraltar to bombardment from the Spanish mainland. Modern artillery had made it possible for the Spaniards to bring the rock within range of their guns. Indeed, in the spring of 1894 the first sea lord considered organizing an army corps to occupy the hills behind Gibraltar in the event of Britain finding herself at war with France and Spain.[12] Some naval specialists recommended that since Gibraltar was no longer tenable, Britain should exchange it for Ceuta, Port Mahon, or some other place either in the Canaries or on the Spanish mainland.[13] During the Spanish-American war of 1898 when the Spaniards began work upon the construction of concrete gun emplacements and military roads in the vicinity of the bay of Algeciras, Salisbury and his colleagues concentrated their efforts upon trying to persuade them to abandon the task.[14] The Spanish government claimed that the batteries were intended for the defence of its coast against possible American attack. Yet at a time when French influence was in the ascendant at Madrid, and when an Anglo-French confrontation on the Nile seemed ever more likely, the British were in no mood to acquiesce.[15] The Spanish authorities were equally disinclined to yield, and even after the commencement in August of peace negotiations between Spain and the United States, work continued on the batteries.[16] With only doubtful legal grounds upon which to oppose their erection, and reluctant to resort to the use of force, Arthur Balfour, who was temporarily in charge of the Foreign Office, proposed that Britain should offer to defend the Spanish coast in the neighbourhood of Gibraltar against attack in return for the abandonment of the works.[17] To some Spaniards this promised to reduce Spain to the status of a British protectorate.[18] But in mid-September Sigismundo Moret, a former liberal minister of state who had long favoured a closer Anglo-Spanish understanding, suggested to Drummond Wolff the basis of an accord. Spain would promise to assist Britain to the best of her ability in the event of a war and do nothing that would impede her hold upon Gibraltar, in return for a British commitment to defend not only the coast of the bay of Algeciras, but also the Balearic and Canary islands.[19] The idea appealed to Salisbury. 'As we could not allow the islands in question to be taken by another power', he noted, 'the guarantee would hardly add to our responsibilities'.[20] When, however, this proposal was put to the Spanish government at the end of October, it was promptly rejected by the Duke of Almadovar, the minister of state. It was, he claimed, 'practically for an alliance', and it would mean that Spain in her 'shattered state' would incur the hostility of other Powers. The British, he observed, did not propose to guarantee all Spain's territory, and a powerful France, even if she did not attack Spain, might foster 'discontent and even insurrection in the Spanish frontier provinces'.[21]

All that Almadovar could offer was a guarantee that Gibraltar would not be attacked by forces operating from Spanish soil. In return he wanted a British promise not to use Spain's territory in a war with another Power and an undertaking to defend Spain's neutrality.[22] Salisbury dismissed this proposal as 'so illusory as to be almost absurd'.[23] Given the current belief that gun emplacements were essential to long range artillery, and that several months would have to elapse between the laying of the concrete and the mounting of the guns, it made sense for the British to seek a Spainish pledge on the non-construction of such works.[24] But Almadovar's guarantee would have meant nothing in the event of an Anglo-Spanish war, and a self-denying promise such as he required might have limited the options open to Britain's naval strategists in a Mediterranean conflict. 'In the case of a war between England and France', Salisbury thought, 'Minorca would be one of the first subjects demanding our attention.'[25] He also informed Drummond Wolff that he might tell Almadovar that if there had been an Anglo-French war, 'the destruction of the heavy guns which have been in question would have been the first precaution that we should have found it necessary for us to take.'[26]

This warning and the French climb down over Fashoda may well have been effective. Thus, despite his pro-French inclinations, Francesco Silvela, who formed a conservative administration in February 1899, assured the British ambassador that he wished to 'unite with England in maintaining the status quo'.[27] In the following month, Silvela, in return for a British assurance that they desired no further territory from Spain and an undertaking to prevent any hostile landing on the coast of the bay of Algeciras, promised that Spain would discontinue work on the gun emplacements.[28] The Spaniards remained extremely sensitive also to British intentions and acutely conscious of their country's diplomatic isolation. On 14 April, Silvela suggested to the German ambassador at Madrid, Joseph-Maria von Radowitz, that Spain's security might best be guaranteed by an agreement between France, Germany, and Russia. Bernhard von Bülow, the German state secretary, doubted if such an agreement was either feasible or necessary.[29] But a similar approach which Silvela made to the French ambassador, Jules Patenôtre, seemed likely to yield more positive results.[30]

French diplomats needed no reminders about 'les convoitises de la Grande-Bretagne'. They had long suspected the British of coveting the Balearic and Canary islands, and they assumed that in the event of an Anglo-French war the Royal Navy would seize a Spanish port from which to menace France's Mediterranean communications. The presence of a large British community in the Canaries and the frequent visits by British warships to Port Mahon served only to encourage such fears.[31] Thus, when in 1898 Spain's territorial integrity had seemed to be threatened by the combined forces of the Anglo-Saxon world, Paul Cambon's brother, Jules, who was then French ambassador at Washington, had recommended that the Quai d'Orsay should offer Spain a guarantee of her island possessions.[32] Moreover, although a French response to Silvela's proposed tripartite guarantee was delayed by the desire of the French foreign minister, Théophile Delcassé, to consult with the Russians, reports continued to flow from Spain concerning the dangers to which the peninsula might be exposed. Patenôtre warned Delcassé in April of the threat that would be posed to the free passage of French ships through the straits of Gibraltar and to France's communications with Algeria if Britain were to seize Ceuta or Port Mahon. To counter this supposed menace he proposed that the French government should offer Spain assistance in the fortification of these places: a move which he thought would dissipate rumours of French aspirations upon them.

Delcassé personally doubted if it would be possible to assist Spain with the fortification of her ports without offending Spanish susceptibilities.[33] He did, however, favour an exchange of views between Paris and Madrid on matters of common interest, and he readily entered upon negotiations with León y Castillo for an agreement on the future of Morocco.[34] Progress towards the achievement of such an accord was hampered by the reluctance of Spanish politicians to risk alienating Britain. Silvela, who formed a new government in November 1902, proposed on 3 March 1903 to Jules Cambon, successor to Patenôtre, that Spain should conclude an 'entente cordiale et intime' with France and Russia by which the latter Powers would guarantee Spain's possessions in Africa and the Mediterranean.[35] In return, Spain would not conclude any agreement with another Power without first consulting them. Jules Cambon was enthusiastic about this proposal which was similar to that which he had put forward some five years before. Such an undertaking, he observed to Delcassé, would not increase France's liabilities since she could not afford to permit the areas concerned to fall into the hands of another great Power. Moreover, it would, he thought, enable France to combat British efforts to achieve dominance at Madrid.

Delcassé was cautious about entering into such an engagement. Russia was occupied elsewhere and seemed unlikely to want to take on fresh commitments in the western Mediterranean, and Spain was offering very little in exchange for the 'very heavy charge' of guaranteeing her territorial integrity.[36] Yet Jules Cambon persisted. He urged the Quai d'Orsay to ensure that more French warships called at Port Mahon so that the French flag would be shown there as many times as the British, and, in May, the visit of Prince Henry of Prussia to Spain allowed him to raise the bogey of increasing German involvement in the affairs of the peninsula.[37] Finally, in what appears to have been an attempt to force the pace of the discussions with the Spaniards, he settled with Silvela on the terms of a draft convention by which France, Russia, and Spain would undertake to maintain the territorial status quo in the western Mediterranean. He also gained Silvela's consent to an arrangement for French assistance to be given in the fortification of Ceuta and Melilla, and their use by French submarines.[38]

Attractive though this prospect may have been, the draft declaration which Jules Cambon transmitted to Paris on 5 June failed to stimulate Delcassé's enthusiasm.[39] He was already showing more sympathy for the idea of an Anglo-French bargain on Morocco and other extra-European issues, and within five months negotiations were to commence with England on these lines.[40] Spanish politicians were also beginning to adjust their position to take into account the possibility of a *rapprochement* between the two Powers from whose rivalry they had not been slow to seek advantage. Raimundo Villaverde, who succeeded Silvela at the end of July, indicated to the French ambassador that while he was still in favour of an arrangement on the Mediterranean status quo, he would prefer to have Britain rather than Russia as a third party to the agreement.[41] For his part Jules Cambon still hoped that once the Moroccan issue was settled, Delcassé would take up again with Spain the subject of a Mediterranean accord, which, he claimed, would be 'le vrai couronnement' of Delcassé's latin policy.[42]

Shortly after Silvela's resignation the former queen-regent of Spain expressed some sympathy for an Anglo-Spanish understanding. Sir Henry Mortimer Durand, Wolff's successor, pressed the foreign secretary to take the initiative and to prevent Spain from falling into France's arms. In terms which closely resembled those used by his French colleague, he explained 'whatever may be our relations with the French, England and France must, I suppose, remain watchful of each other in the Mediterranean, and in Africa, and it might be very awkward for us to find hereafter a more or less reorganized Spain committed to a French alliance.'[43] Just one week later the Admiralty also made it plain to the Foreign Office that 'no more formidable coalition could be brought against us in the Mediterranean' than that of the 'Latin states — France, Italy, and Spain'.[44] Lord Lansdowne, who had succeeded Salisbury as foreign secretary, was not inclined to follow Durand's advice. Spain was not, however, forgotten in the Anglo-French negotiations on Morocco. Lansdowne was determined that France should not gain a position at the entrance to the Mediterranean, and he insisted on the inclusion of the northern littoral of Morocco in an eventual Spanish zone of influence.[45] Similarly the French strove without success to persuade Lansdowne to uphold the territorial status quo within a five hundred mile radius of the Gibraltar straits. Delcassé professed that this was intended to meet the threat of a German incursion into the area, but Paul Cambon was probably correct in his surmise that the British cabinet 'compris que nous redoutions moins les Allemands que les Anglais eux-même de ce côté'.⁴⁶

Neither the negotiations for the Anglo-French entente nor its conclusion effected any immediate change in the views of Jules Cambon upon the value of closer ties between France and Spain. He appreciated the check which the understanding placed upon the oscillations of Spain between her great continental and maritime neighbours;⁴⁷ he was also aware that the Spaniards might now turn towards Germany: a Power of whose intentions in Morocco and the western Mediterranean he, like Delcassé, was becoming increasingly apprehensive. Moreover, England remained in his eyes a potential threat to France's interest.⁴⁸ Despite the evident readiness of the British ambassador at Madrid to assist his French colleague in promoting a Franco-Spanish agreement on Morocco, Paul Cambon also thought it necessary to warn Delcassé against England assuming the role of 'protectrice de la Peninsule, qui est trop conformé à ses traditions pour qu'elle n'essaie pas de la repondre'.⁴⁹

The officials of the British Foreign Office were similarly aware that the Anglo-French *rapprochement* was no sure guarantee against the re-emergence in the perhaps not too distant future of a hostile France. Indeed, the Franco-Spanish accord of 3 October 1904 by which Spain adhered to the Anglo-French convention on Morocco, was not in their opinion a wholly satisfactory arrangement. Thus, although Spain promised not to alienate any of the territories designated to her in Morocco, there was nothing in the agreement that prevented her from ceding such territories to France or, in the event of a Franco-Spanish war, to any other Power.⁵⁰ This flaw was spotted by Sir Thomas Sanderson, Lansdowne's permanent under-secretary. Prior to the departure of Sir Arthur Nicolson, the newly-appointed British ambassador at Madrid, at the beginning of 1905, Sanderson suggested that there might be an advantage in obtaining from Spain a commitment to Britain not to cede her projected zone of influence to any other Power.⁵¹ 'This engagement', Sanderson subsequently observed, 'should clearly be secret... and we should not be very desirous that the French Government should know of our asking for it.'⁵² But Nicolson thought it 'more prudent to feel the way' before broaching a secret convention, and Lansdowne agreed that he should await a favourable opportunity.⁵³ In any case within three months of Nicolson's arrival at Madrid, the German emperor landed at Tangier, and the Moroccan crisis erupted, highlighting another aspect of the changing situation in the western Mediterranean.

The German seizure of Kiaochow, their acquisition of Samoa, their purchase from Spain of the Caroline and Mariana islands, and the expansion of their navy had already led some in Britain to think that the Germans would soon seek elsewhere for ports and coaling stations. For Francis Bertie, a British diplomat who was to play an important role in helping to keep alive the idea of an Anglo-Spanish understanding, this was but a logical consequence of the emergence of Germany as a first class naval Power. It was equally logical in his view that Britain should seek to contain this threat to her interests.[54] The conclusion of the *entente cordiale* reduced the possibility of Britain having to reckon with a Franco-German naval combination. But Bertie's theorizing was also based upon a doubtful assumption about German naval strategy. Admiral von Tirpitz was far more concerned with concentrating his warshps in northern waters than with dispersing them in the defence of distant ports. Nevertheless, he saw advantage in freeing the German navy and merchantile marine from their dependence upon British coaling stations, and in December 1901 he had recommended to the Wilhelmstrasse that Germany should acquire coaling depots on the north-west coast of Africa. The possibility of Germany securing a position on Morocco's Atlantic coast had already been raised in conversations between the British colonial secretary and the German ambassador in London in 1900.[55] It was perhaps not therefore surprising that reports which began to reach London in 1903 of the growing involvement of German capital in the economic development of Madeira were sufficient to cause Lansdowne to seek assurances from the Portuguese government that it would not grant a coaling station to a foreign Power in any of its islands.[56] Moreover, the Moroccan crisis, and the news that German firms were trying to obtain coaling depots for commercial purposes not only in the Portuguese islands, but also in the Canaries, were readily interpreted in London as fresh evidence of the German government's desire for a coaling station in the eastern Atlantic.[57]

The French, too, came to suspect that the Germans had designs upon the Spanish islands. Pierre de Margerie, who in Jules Cambon's absence was French chargé d'affaires at Madrid, suggested to Delcassé on 29 March 1905 that since Britain was no longer a threat to the Balearics, she might now be associated with France in guaranteeing their neutrality.[58] There was, however, another reason that seemed to make it worthwhile extending France's co-operation with Britain in the Mediterranean. From an early stage in the Moroccan crisis Jules Cambon began to appreciate the value of Britain's friendship as a means of keeping Spain in line with France's policy, and of countering German efforts to separate Spain from France.[59] This seemed all the more important in view of a report that the German emperor had recently suggested to Alfonso XIII, the young king of Spain, that in the event of a Franco-German war he should concentrate his forces on the Pyrenees.[60]

British diplomats also saw in the affair an opportunity for achieving a formal bilateral agreement with Spain such as had been proposed in 1898. Perturbed by the news that Radowitz was trying to discourage the Spaniards from co-operating with the French at Fez, Bertie, who since January 1905 had been British ambassador at Paris, proposed that Britain should use the occasion to secure from Spain a new agreement on Gibraltar. In a letter to Lansdowne of 12 May 1905 he asked if the government could not 'take advantage of the menacing attitude of Germany towards Spain in order to offer to assist Spain in meeting any attack on the Balearic Isles, the Canaries and Fernando Po' in return for Spanish assurances on the future of Gibraltar. He suggested that the government might declare to Spain that it had no territorial desires on any of the Spanish mainland and islands, and if she would undertake not to 'cede, sell, let or otherwise alienate in whole or part any of her islands or allow them to be used by a foreign power as coaling stations or depots', Britain would assist her in defending them. The Spaniards, he thought, should promise that 'no works or gun emplacements' should be erected or laid down that could affect the safety of Gibraltar, its works, Harbours or anchorages'. In other circumstances the French might have been expected to oppose such an exclusive Anglo-Spanish arrangement, but, Bertie contended, they could not at the moment regard it as aimed at them.[61]

In June, de Villa-Urrutia, then Spanish minister of state, accompanied Alfonso XIII on a state visit to London. Lansdowne put to him a proposal for an Anglo-Spanish agreement which was broadly similar to Bertie's recommendation.[62] But Bertie had little sympathy with the manner in which the project was thereafter handled. Even at this stage, the obtaining from Spain of new pledges on Gibraltar seems to have been in Bertie's mind essentially a pretext for an agreement whose main purpose would be to 'keep out from Spanish Islands Germans whether as possessors or concession holders'.[63] Nevertheless, he was also aware that, despite the entente, British and French interests were far from being identical in the Mediterranean. Indeed, he never excluded the possibility of Britain one day having to defend the Spanish islands from the French.[64] When he learned that Nicolson had suggested that he might inform Jules Cambon of the proposed agreement, Bertie immediately protested to the Foreign Office. 'Security for Gibraltar', he claimed, 'is not a *permanent* French interest and its protection from danger on the land side might not always suit the policy of France.' He thought that if the French were informed of the British project they might try to persuade the Spanish government not to accept it in its entirety. On the other hand, he reasoned, if the German government were to learn of the negotiations, they would have another grievance against England and France, for the arrangement would appear to be aimed at excluding them from the islands.[65]

In spite of Bertie's strictures, Lansdowne was unable to restrain Nicolson from communicating the British proposals to Jules Cambon.[66] As a result the latter was encouraged to think in terms of a possible tripartite agreement. Certainly, in his view, France must be a party to any agreement that Britain might seek with Spain.[67] A change of government at Madrid and a succession of relatively weak Liberal administrations inhibited any further progress towards negotiations.[68] The matter of an Anglo-Spanish accord was not seriously considered again in London until the following March, when Grey, the new liberal foreign secretary, was presented with a Foreign Office memorandum which traced the history of previous discussions with Spain.[69] Grey thought that once the Algeciras conference was over, the matter might be reconsidered, and Sir Charles Hardinge, Sanderson's successor as permanent under-secretary, suggested that within a few months talks might be resumed. Nicolson, who had been appointed to represent Britain at Algeciras, even told the senior French delegate that the forthcoming marriage of King Alfonso to an English princess could provide the occasion for such talks: a reaffirmation of Britain's *esprit de suite* that prompted Jules Cambon to remind the Quai d'Orsay of the importance of France's participation in such an arrangement.[70]

Of more immediate concern to the British Foreign Office in the spring of 1906 was the efforts of a German firm to secure landing rights for a telegraphic cable in the Canary Islands.

The early pre-eminence achieved by the British telegraph companies in their operation of a global network of submarine cables had for some years been viewed with jealousy by the continental powers. The Germans, who until the turn of the century had been dependent upon Anglo-American companies for their transatlantic cable communications, had been particularly anxious to obtain their own links with the Americas. In 1900 Feltern und Guilleaume, the largest of the German cable companies, laid a cable from Emden to New York. Then in the aftermath of the Algeciras conference the same company applied to the Spanish ministry of the interior for permission to extend the Emden to Vigo telegraph cable to the Canaries with a view to eventually obtaining for Germany its own cable links with South America and west Africa. The scheme, which was backed by the German embassy at Madrid, was attractive from the Spanish point of view. It offered to Spain a new cable which would supplement the existing overworked and unrealiable one between Cadiz and Teneriffe, for the replacement of which the Spanish government had already budgeted, and the prospect of a cheap and rapid means of communication with South America. The Spanish authorities had to consider whether it might not be better to preserve for themselves the benefits to be had from the use of their territory for the further extension of transoceanic telegraphy, and the effects that the German project would have upon established British and French cable interests.[71]

The British government regarded the German cable project primarily in strategic terms. Its acceptance, the Admiralty claimed, would greatly strengthen Germany's cable communications for war purposes.[72] Yet it is difficult to see what could be done about it, especially as reports from Spain seemed to indicate that the government in Madrid might be prepared to grant landing rights for a German cable. Such a course was favoured by the director general of Spain's post and telegraphs, and on 18 July his recommendations were endorsed by the council of state. Nevertheless, neither the General Post Office nor the Eastern Telegraph Company felt that the British government could apply pressure on the Spanish government to reject the German project simply on the grounds that it menaced a British commercial undertaking.[73] In this situation the Eastern Telegraph Company was encouraged by the Foreign Office to make fresh proposals for a cable connection with the Canaries, and the Spaniards were urged to defer any decision on the proposal of Feltern und Guilleaume.[74]

The British were not alone in wishing to thwart the overseas expansion of the German telegraph system. In December 1904 Alexandre Berard, the under-secretary of state for posts and telegraphs at Paris, had begun to suspect that the Germans were after a concession to lay a cable from Tangier to Mogador. This, he thought, might be linked to the German cable at Vigo and eventually lead to a German cable network throughout Morocco.[75] Moreover, these suspicions seemed to be confirmed when at the Algeciras conference the German delegate insisted upon Germany retaining the right to land a cable on the Moroccan coast.[76] When, however, the news of Feltern und Guilleaume's application for landing rights in the Canaries reached Paris, Berard was less concerned with the future of Morocco than with the pecuniary interests of his department. He had no doubt that the German object was to secure their own cable links with South America and their west African colonies, and that, if achieved, these would threaten the viability of existing French cables, including the cable between Dakar and Penambuço in Brazil. Jules Cambon was instructed to propose to the Spanish government an alternative French cable scheme by which to link the peninsula to the Canaries and Morocco. He also recognized the value of presenting the German project as a menace to French and Spanish interests in the Shereefian empire. He warned the Spanish minister of state against what he interpreted as the first step towards a German cable link with Morocco, reminded him of the agreement that their two governments had concluded in September 1905 to favour Franco-Spanish commercial enterprises in Morocco, and with this in mind he advised the Quai d'Orsay to try to associate a Spanish telegraph company with their plans.[77]

Neither Jules Cambon nor his new British colleague, Sir Maurice de Bunsen, were optimistic about persuading the Spanish authorities to accept an alternative scheme to that supported by the German embassy. Both ambassadors thought that the Spanish government had been trying to improve its relations with Germany in the wake of the Moroccan crisis, and that in the hope also of securing Berlin's acquiescence in Spain's new protective tariffs, had already gone some way towards leading the Germans to expect the fulfillment of their wishes. If they were to stand any chance of defeating the German plan, Jules Cambon and de Bunsen were agreed that they had better collaborate and propose a single project for the laying of a new cable to the Canaries, and the granting to the responsible company of monopoly landing rights.[78] The Quai d'Orsay favoured the idea, and, in late July, Grey accepted a French proposal that the Eastern Telegraph Company should be encouraged to combine with the South American Cable Company, and, if possible, a Spanish firm in preparing an application for the concession to lay a cable between Cadiz and Teneriffe.[79] Unfortunately, neither the French government, nor any of its agencies, showed any urgency in initiating negotiations on the subject. The dilatory approach of the French towards the proposed combination may, as Jules Cambon surmised, have been due to the absence from Paris of ministers and officials during the holiday season.[80] Yet it was also evident that Léon Bourgeois, the French foreign minister, and Louis Barthou, the minister responsible for posts and telegraphs, were reluctant to assume a too overtly anti-German stance at Madrid.[81] It was preferable that France should not appear to take first place in opposing Germany.[82]

During the autumn of 1906 it became increasingly apparent to the Foreign Office and the Quai d'Orsay that the Spanish government was likely to grant Feltern und Guilleaume's application for landing rights. The Spaniards had doubts about whether there was any substance in French claims that the Germans were after a telegraph connection with Morocco. After all, the Germans could always obtain a direct link with Morocco without acquiring landing rights in the Canaries, and as Perez Caballero, the Spanish minister of state, pointed out to de Bunsen, it would be a 'very strong measure' for Spain to stand out against Germany obtaining cable links with South America and west Africa.[83] All this placed the British Foreign Office in something of a quandary about how best to proceed. As Grey cabled to Bertie on 22 December:

> We could not on ground of Eastern Telegraph monopoly alone urge Spain to refuse German concession and make conse-

quent sacrifice. Nor do we regard German wish to have direct telegraphic communication to South Africa and South America as an object we could permanently oppose on its merits.[84]

Opposition to a German controlled transatlantic cable would, Grey feared, 'give unnecessary provocation'.[85] Nevertheless, the foreign secretary was also keenly aware of Britain's obligation to support French aspirations in Morocco, and he was reluctant to do anything that might harm the *entente*. Thus in his instructions to Bertie he explained that if the French were sure that the main object of the German concession was to secure a communication to Morocco which could not otherwise be obtained, Britain would continue to support French objections.[86] 'I should', he wrote to the prime minister, 'like to give a graceful concession to the Germans, but I do not like to do it in a matter which the French think will affect Morocco.'[87]

Some of Grey's officials were taken aback by the course which he was ready to pursue. Algernon Law, the senior clerk with charge of the commercial department, drew his chief's attention to the fact that it had been for some time a policy of the Foreign Office 'to preserve for British telegraph companies the fruit of their early enterprise not merely out of consideration for British commercial interests, but also for strategical reasons'.[88] Moreover, Eyre Crowe in his memorandum of 1 January 1907, pressed the government to abandon any hope of conciliating Germany 'with graceful British concessions... made without any conviction either of their justice or of their being set off by equivalent counter-services'. Instead, he recommended that they should show courtesy and consideration towards Germany in matters of common concern, but with the 'most unbending determination to uphold British rights and interests in every part of the globe'.[89] Bertie was guided by similar sentiments. It was in his opinion 'as much a British as a French interest to keep the Germans out of the Spanish Islands'. He warned Grey that it would not be advisable to let the French think, or to give them grounds for saying, that in order to protect British interests, 'we are using French interests in Morocco and our obligations to support them as a lever wherewith to oppose the laying of a German Cable to the Canaries.'[90]

Bertie was correct in his assessment of the likely reaction of the French to Grey's views. Pichon, who had recently been appointed foreign minister in the government of Georges Clemenceau, quickly concluded that the British intended France to take the responsibility for opposing the German project. It was a role which he, like Bourgeois, had no desire to assume, and on 29 December Jules Cambon was instructed that in the existing circumstances it was above all necessary that France should not appear 'comme soulevant une opposition contre une entreprise allemande dans une intérêt purement et principalement français'.[91] Much as Jules Cambon may have agreed with the object of this communication, he was disturbed by its tone. Had the British learnt of its contents, then, he protested to his brother, it would have seemed to them like treachery, and it would have been 'un coup droit porte à l'entente cordiale'.[92] Nevertheless, he made it clear to de Bunsen and to Perez Caballero that France intended to act 'mais derrière l'Angleterre'.[93]

The impression left in London by this warning was somewhat modified by Arsène Henry, the commercial director of the Quai d'Orsay, who told Bertie on 5 January that notwithstanding a German undertaking not to connect their cable with Morocco, France was still 'strongly opposed' to it.[94] All effective opposition to the German scheme collapsed after Grey learned that its backers were prepared to agree that the cable would not be extended to Morocco, and that in order to avoid the appearance of connecting two points on Spanish soil, it would be laid direct from Emden to the Canaries.[95] Grey was still prepared to support the Spanish government if it wished to reject the German project, and de Bunsen encouraged the efforts of Perez Caballero to reserve for Spain the right to cut the cable in time of war.[96] But by the end of January the Foreign Office had reconciled itself to the idea of the German company securing landing rights in the Canaries.[97] All this was far from pleasing to those in France who had deliberately understated their country's commercial interest in the affair in the belief that they could rely upon Britain to oppose a German transatlantic cable. Barthou still suspected that the British were trying to manoeuvre France into taking a more positive stance at Madrid. If they were not, and all opposition to the German cable ceased, then, he complained to Pichon, France would risk losing the fruits of the 'sacrifices considérables' that she had made 'pour maintenir la lutte qu'elle a engagé contre l'Allemagne dans l'Atlantique'.[98] All was not, however, lost. The brothers Cambon had more than one card up their diplomatic sleeves and were about to play them.

The apparent readiness of the Spanish authorities to yield to German solicitations reawakened the interest of Jules Cambon in an Anglo-French guarantee of Spain and her possessions. Not that the notion had long been absent from his mind. Both during and since the Algeciras conference he had found cause to advocate a tripartite accord as a means of holding Spain to her previous commitments and countering German influence at Madrid.[99] In 1906 Franco-Spanish relations were troubled by Spain's decision to introduce a new and higher scale of tariffs on foreign imports, and the need to negotiate a new commercial treaty with France. Moreover, where Morocco was concerned, the Spaniards were in no mood to follow abjectly in the tow of the French. Thus, despite evidence of mounting disorder in the area around Tangier, they seemed reluctant to envisage collaborating with France in mounting a military operation to defend the European community there. Apprehensive lest delay should bring into question the mandate which France and Spain had been granted for the organization of the policing of the Moroccan ports, the French looked to Britain for diplomatic assistance at Madrid.[100] Jules Cambon was equally convinced that England's friendship was a guarantee of that of Spain, especially in a year in which the royal wedding had made England à la mode. He had no doubts, however, about the drawbacks of a separate Anglo-Spanish understanding. 'Réalisée sans nous', he had warned Bourgeois in May, 'elle constituerait un grand danger: realisée avec nous, je ne doute pas qu'elle n'obtient l'adhésion immediate de l'Italie, et peut-être ce serait un gage de securité et de paix que l'union permanente des Puissances maritimes et liberales du monde.'[101]

During the week before Christmas 1906 Jules and Paul Cambon introduced Pichon to the idea.[102] The moment was propitious. German pressure upon Spain to obtain an early decision on the cable concession seemed likely to make Britain more amenable to a tripartite agreement, and Perez Caballero was inclined towards closer co-operation with France in Morocco.[103] A conversation with Bertie on 22 December provided Paul Cambon with the opportunity to suggest 'that it would perhaps be as well to make some arrangement between France, England and Spain for the preservation of the status quo in the Mediterranean'. But Bertie remained unenthusiastic. Grey, he told Paul Cambon, would favour the proposal, but he would have to contend with the opposition of his colleagues who were 'paralysés par les craintes de responsibilitiés'.

If Bertie had his reservations about a tripartite agreement, he was nonetheless aware that the alarm expressed by Paul Cambon and Pichon over Germany's intentions might furnish Britain with a favourable opportunity to achieve a bilateral accord with Spain. In a private letter to Grey of 25 December he repeated the proposal that he had made to Lansdowne in 1905 for an Anglo-Spanish understanding on Gibraltar and the Spanish islands. Again he emphasized that the defence of Gibraltar was a 'solid British interest', and that a sacrifice to secure it would be justified in 'public opinion in England, and Foreign Powers would have no just cause for complaint'. Once more he explained that if Britain were to get on bad terms with the French they would instigate the Spaniards to put up works threatening Gibraltar, and that an Anglo-Spanish agreement on the rock might in 'ordinary circumstances' meet with French opposition.[104]

What Bertie may not have been aware of was that the whole subject of an understanding with Spain was already under consideration in Whitehall. Prompted, perhaps, by the prospect of French and Spanish military intervention in Morocco, Hardinge had on 8 December drawn Grey's attention to the fact that Spain need not refrain from alienating any of the zone of influence that it had been promised in northern Morocco. To remedy this 'serious flaw' in the Franco-Spanish convention of October 1904, he suggested to Grey that he should remind de Villa-Urrutia, who was now Spanish ambassador at London, of the proposal that Lansdowne had put to him in June 1905.[105]

Grey recognized the value of such an arrangement, but he, like Bertie, also raised the subject of Gibraltar. Reluctant to multiply the country's treaty obligations, he minuted on 12 December that what would exercise a 'determining influence' on his decision was the 'question of the necessity for making future provision for the Security of Gibraltar, and of the possibility of attaining this object by the means proposed'.[106] Yet by 1906 Britain's service chiefs had serious doubts about whether any assurance from Spain concerning the absence or presence of gun emplacements in the vicinity of Gibraltar would be of advantage to Britain.[107] The only effective solution to the problem of Gibraltar's security was in the view of Sir George Clarke, the secretary of the defence committee, to maintain good relations with Spain.[108] Bertie had reached much the same conclusion. He wrote to Grey on 3 January 1907: 'As Gibraltar appears to be at the mercy of mortars placed in Spanish ground invisible from Gibraltar is it not of vital importance to make sacrifices to retain the permanent friendship of Spain and therefore to guarantee her island property?'[109] This was a somewhat different view to that which he had expressed in 1898. Then Bertie had advised Balfour that if Gibraltar was 'useless to us without Spain as a reliable friend... we had better remove our guns &c to some more eligible situation, and blow up as much as we can at Gibraltar.'[110] But whatever may have been his original concern with the fate of Gibraltar, this was now secondary. 'The safety of Gibraltar might', he argued, 'be used as the ostensible reason for an arrangement with Spain though the maintenance of the integrity of Spain in the interests of the balance of power is really quite sufficient justification for a guarantee by us.' He also made it quite clear that the primary purpose of such a guarantee would be to prevent Germany acquiring coaling stations. In the existing circumstances, he claimed, the German government could always establish interests in Spain's possessions, provoke a quarrel between its nationals and the local authorities, and then take an opportunity to seize an island. If, however, Britain were bound to defend the Spanish islands, then, Bertie argued, the Germans would 'take good care not to push matters unless they desired war with us'.[111]

Meanwhile, the chances for Britain achieving a bilateral accord with Spain were diminished by the action of Jules Cambon. Spurred on perhaps by the knowledge that he was soon to be transferred to Berlin, after his return to Spain, Cambon began to explore with Perez Caballero the bases of a tripartite agreement such as he had recently discussed with his brother and Pichon. He thought de Bunsen favourable to the idea, and he proceeded to draft his own *projet de note*. This stipulated that the British, French, and Spanish governments were agreed that it was essential to maintain the territorial status quo in their respective maritime possessions in the Mediterranean and that part of the Atlantic that washed the shores of Europe and Africa; that they would not cede any of these possessions, any fishing rights, coaling stations, or other establishment that could lead to a permanent occupation by a third Power or one of its nationals; and that in the event of one of them receiving a proposal to that end it would communicate it to the other two who would lend their diplomatic support to maintain the status quo.[112]

Although this draft note was intended to serve as the basis for a tripartite agreement, and made no specific reference to Gibraltar, nor provision for military or naval assistance, it did not conflict in principle with the requirements which Clarke had already set for an Anglo-Spanish agreement. Nevertheless, the news when received in London on 8 January that Jules Cambon had made a verbal communication of its terms to Alfonso XIII and Perez Caballero, was resented by Grey and his officials.[113] With the exception of what Paul Cambon and Pichon had said to Bertie before Christmas, there had been no recent communication between the British and French governments on this issue, and though it soon emerged that Jules Cambon had acted on his own initiative, his action nevertheless seemed to circumscribe British diplomacy at Madrid. De Bunsen had deliberately withheld any proposal to Perez Caballero because of the uncertain state of Spanish politics at the time.[114] Under the impression that they would prefer a bilateral accord with Britain, or that at any rate the initiative for an agreement should be British, he doubted if the French ambassador's proposal would have much chance of success.[115] Grey readily accepted this advice.[116] His précis writer, William Tyrrell, considered that it might be better if Britain were to conclude an engagement with Spain including within it provision for Gibraltar, and to let the French join later.[117] This was also Bertie's opinion. On 19 January he observed to Hardinge that he still thought that it had been a mistake on Lansdowne's part to take the French into his confidence in a matter which was purely Anglo-Spanish.[118]

The efforts of Bertie and Hardinge to persuade Grey of the advantages of an understanding with Spain had not been made in vain. On 11 January, in a letter which seemed to echo Bertie's earlier appeal, Grey warned the Prime Minister, Sir Henry Campbell-Bannerman, that Germany would 'continue to endeavour to get an ascendancy over Spain'. The Spaniards were weak and afraid that France might some day, if left to herself, 'squeeze Spain', and therefore looked to Britain 'with the greatest confidence in the honesty of our intentions'. 'I think', he concluded, 'we should give Spain confidence in her position for the future, by offering her an undertaking to protect her islands and Moroccan coast against aggression in return for guarantees to us on her part, which would increase the security of Gibraltar.'[119]

Campbell-Bannerman, though reluctant to sanction any further opposition to the German transatlantic cable scheme, assented to an approach to Spain upon these lines.[120] But Grey was mistaken in thinking that such an offer would be acceptable to Spain. Both Antonio Maura, who formed a conservative administration at the end of January, and his minister of state, Manuel Allendesalazar, preferred an arrangement which would place Spain on an equal footing with two great Powers to one that might look like a treaty of protection.[121]

There was still some scepticism in the Foreign Office about the wisdom of Britain participating in a tripartite agreement. An accord *à trois* would, Hardinge told Paul Cambon on 13 February, have 'une couleur d'alliance politique qui souleverait peut-être certains susceptibilités'. It would be better, he asserted, to seek an agreement which had the appearance of having as its objective the security of Gibraltar.[122] On the other hand, Grey seems to have thought that it might be possible to devise some kind of arrangement that would provide both for an Anglo-Spanish agreement on Gibraltar and Morocco, and a broader pact with France.[123] All this the French ambassador interpreted as meaning that while Grey found a tripartite accord acceptable, he feared the objections of his cabinet colleagues to 'un projet destiné à nous garantir contre les entreprises éventuelles d'Allemagne'.[124] In one sense he was correct. Grey still hoped to fend off criticism of an arrangement with Spain by giving prominence to the value of a further guarantee of Gibraltar's security. Nevertheless, the susceptibilities to which Hardinge referred were not just domestic ones. As he later explained, the chief British objection to a tripartite agreement was the 'necessity which it would entail of absolute secrecy'. Otherwise, he thought, 'it would be seriously resented by Germany who would regard it as aimed at her'.[125] Hardinge wished to uphold the status quo and protect Britain's interests without appearing to encircle Germany with alliances and treaties.

A somewhat different attitude towards an accord with Spain was adopted by the government's naval advisers who persisted in thinking of France as a potential enemy. An Admiralty paper of 25 February maintained that it was desirable to prevent Germany from acquiring naval bases in any of Spain's possessions. But it also concluded that the advantages to be derived from an Anglo-Spanish engagement on Gibraltar and the defence of the Spanish islands 'would be much greater in the case of war with France then they would be in the case of war with Germany, as the two main points in the Mediterranean, viz., Gibraltar and the Balearic Islands are unlikely to be of any great strategic value in the case of a war with the latter Power'. In order to enable Britain to continue to make use of Gibraltar, the Admiralty insisted that it was necessary 'that Spain should be on our side, or at least ready and willing to uphold her neutrality'.[126] Nevertheless, the defence committee agreed on Grey's prompting that it was 'desirable that France should be party to this arrangement'.

By the end of February Grey was still hoping to obtain from Spain some assurance on Gibraltar such as would enable him to justify an Anglo-Franco-Spanish understanding.[127] At Madrid, however, Jules Cambon had already succeeded in impressing upon Maura the advantages of linking Spain to Britain and France by a single diplomatic instrument.[128] When on 25 March de Villa-Urrutia finally took up the subject of an agreement with Grey, he proposed that not only should negotiations proceed on the basis of Jules Cambon's draft note, but that this should be amended so that in the event of aggression by a third Power the signatories should be required to consult with each other on the means of safeguarding the status quo.[129] Such an obligation could not in Grey's estimate be entered into without revealing it to parliament, and that, he thought, would entail the most 'searching questions' as to whether the engagement covered Gibraltar. Faced with this problem, Hardinge recommended, and Grey accepted, the idea of reducing the proposed agreement to a simple exchange of notes between Britain and Spain. Grey assumed that such notes could be published. He also thought that France might either supplement her existing agreement with Spain with a similar note, or that Britain might assure France that she would consult with her at the same time as with Spain.[130]

This course was hardly compatible with that which Jules and Paul Cambon had recommended. But at the beginning of April, when Grey was planning to have Hardinge convey his latest ideas to Spain, the two brothers were poorly placed to influence events. Jules had already left Madrid for Berlin, Paul was on the point of departing from England for a holiday in Sicily, and Pichon, who was fast earning for himself the reputation of an absentee landlord at the Quai d'Orsay, was about to leave Paris to spend Easter in the

Jura. Moreover, Clemenceau, the political future of whose government was in question, seems to have been as anxious as Grey to avoid awakening German susceptibilities by the publication of a tripartite agreement.[131] Neither he, nor Pichon, were therefore in any mood to quibble over what was essentially a matter of form, and on 6 April they consented to the mode of procedure that Grey proposed.[132] The Spanish ministers, devoted to safeguarding Spain's dignity and status, were also heedful of a warning from Jules Cambon that if they abandoned the idea of a tripartite agreement, France would compel Britain to begin the negotiations afresh.[133] Thus Hardinge, who from 8 to 10 April accompanied Edward VII on a semi-official visit to Alfonso XIII at Cartagena, found it difficult to persuade Maura and Allendesalazar to accept his suggestion for a simultaneous exchange of identic notes with Britain and France. Only after Maura learned of Clemenceau's decision did he agree to forego a tripartite treaty.[134] Nevertheless, the understanding reached at Cartagena caused the French chargé d'affaires at Madrid to wonder if the British and Spanish governments were intending to use an exchange of notes to extend their agreement to cover points exclusive to themselves.[135] From Berlin Jules Cambon wrote on 13 April to urge on Georges Louis, the political director of the Quai d'Orsay, the capital importance of Britain, France, and Spain being linked by a single instrument. Circumstances could change; France's relations with Spain might be modified.[136] Another alternative was put forward by Camille Barrère, the French ambassador at Rome, who after discussions with Paul Cambon advised Pichon that if notes were to be exchanged with Spain, they should also be exchanged between Britain and France.[137]

Pichon had in the meanwhile begun to regret his acceptance of an exchange of notes. But faced with Britain's opposition to anything that smacked of a tripartite treaty, Pichon had little scope for diplomatic manoeuvre. On 17 April he, Paul Cambon, and Clemenceau reviewed the situation, and Pichon then sought Grey's agreement to a procedure whereby the British and French governments would communicate to each other the notes which they exchanged with Spain, and then complement these with an engagement to concert with each other at the same time as with Spain if the eventuality foreseen in the notes should arise.[138] This, Hardinge pointed out, was a 'much more direct and emphatic' commitment than the obligation contained in the projected British note to

Spain. 'It presents', he minuted, 'the disadvantages of a tripartite agreement and the impression of an unfriendly coalition.'[139]

Grey seems to have shared this view. Despite Pichon's desire to keep his proposed Anglo-French agreement a secret, both Grey and Campbell-Bannerman felt that if it became necessary to communicate the Anglo-Spanish notes to parliament, then any complementary understanding with France would also have to be made public.[140] Bertie alone amongst Grey's officials saw some value in an Anglo-French exchange of notes. Having reconciled himself to France being a party to an arrangement with Spain, he advised Grey that a separate accord with France would be useful, this insofar as in the event of the defeat of France by Germany in a war in which Britain was not engaged: 'it would give us a locus standi to object to the transfer to Germany of any of the French possessions covered by the engagement between France and England.' Hardinge thought otherwise. If France were defeated he felt that Britain would only be able to prevent the cession of French territory by force of arms. Grey agreed, but conscious of the need to think in terms of public usage, he observed that 'a "locus standi" makes it easier for us to put our case before the public and that is something.'[141] For the moment Grey told the French ambassador that he thought that it would be 'much better to make a simple communication to each other of the text of the Notes which we had exchanged with Spain, and to express our views upon them in conversation'.[142]

Pichon finally acquiesced in the course that Grey advised. But he was far from pleased to learn from León y Castillo that Grey intended to publish the notes which Britain was to exchange with Spain. This, Pichon thought, would compel the French government to make public the Franco-Spanish notes; otherwise he would be criticised for neglecting France's interests. Grey was prepared to delay publication until the matter was raised in parliament, and with a view to easing French fears about the effect of this upon Germany, he assented to the elimination from the notes of any reference to a third power threatening the status quo.[143] Not that the accords were to remain a secret long. Edward VII's visit to Cartagena and Hardinge's talks with the Spanish ministers had already led to reports of an impending Anglo-Spanish naval alliance, and Paul Cambon suggested to Grey that in order to guard themselves against German ill-will, it might be wise to settle on how the notes might be made known to the German government.[144] Pichon agreed with this idea, and when towards the end of May it became apparent to the Quai d'Orsay that the French press might already know the substance of the notes, Paul Cambon was requested to talk with Grey about their possible communication to the other great Powers.[145]

The issue of how and when their communication should be made was considered on 1 June by Pichon and the French ambassadors at London, Madrid, and Rome. Always the opportunist, Barrère suggested, and Pichon agreed, that they might profit from this occasion 'pour revenir sur certains engagements moraux et les faire renouveler'.[146] What this amounted to was made clear by Paul Cambon when on 6 June he reminded Grey that the Moroccan crisis had turned the Anglo-French agreement into 'something like an alliance', and enquired of him 'whether, if Germany brought pressure to bear on France or Spain in consequence of the Spanish notes, English support would be forthcoming'. In response to this Grey, without questioning Cambon's assertion, gave the assurance that he would 'regard the spirit of the Agreement of 1904' as applying to the provisions of the exchange of notes: a phrase which could be interpreted as meaning that he would be prepared to contemplate Britain giving military and naval assistance to France and Spain in the event of their being menaced by Germany because of their participation in the accords.[147]

The form taken by the Mediterranean agreements of 1907 could hardly have satisfied Jules Cambon. He had made it plain to Pichon that he still thought that an Anglo-French exchange of notes should accompany those exchanged with Spain.[148] Nevertheless, the texts of the notes met with his approval. Thus, despite the absence from them of any explicit reference to diplomatic support such as he had originally proposed, they did foresee the possibility of the parties concerting together, and this he considered to be the point 'ou l'entente devient un commencement d'alliance'. Clearly in his opinion the Spanish notes were a means of maintaining the territorial status quo against what he conceived to be an expansionist Germany.

Similar views were held by Grey and some of his officials. Ever since January the British foreign secretary had seen in an accord with Spain a means of countering German pressure upon the government at Madrid, and Bertie had repeatedly laid stress upon the importance of preventing Germany from acquiring a foothold in the Spanish islands. Much as they, like the French, may have desired to avoid giving Germany any cause for complaint, there can be little doubt that those in the Foreign Office and diplomatic service who were most closely concerned with the exchange of notes considered Germany to constitute the greatest immediate threat to Britain's interests in Spain. In this respect their search for an Anglo-Spanish agreement was far from being even 'practically the same' policy as that pursued by Salisbury in 1887. Salisbury had endeavoured to maintain the status quo in the lands bordering the eastern Mediterranean by associating Britain with the Triple Alliance. He had distinguished between the 'hungry' and the 'satisfied' Powers, and had, at least insofar as Austria-Hungary and Germany were concerned, sought to work with the latter. But in the twenty years since 1887 circumstances had changed. British acquiescence had been purchased in the professed ambitions of France in Morocco and, more significantly, Germany had joined the ranks of the dissatisfied.

Britain's participation in the exchange of notes with Spain cannot, however, be solely attributed to British fears of Germany. The efforts of a Germany company to obtain cable landing rights in the Canaries had certainly stimulated Grey's apprehensions with regard to the role being played by Radowitz at Madrid, and the Foreign Office had readily supported the formation of an Anglo-French cable consortium. Grey had also been prepared to back French wishes in this matter, and to give such assistance as the Spaniards might desire in resisting German demands. Yet he was reluctant to appear to be acting simply in the interests of a British commercial enterprise, even when that enterprise constituted a valuable strategic asset. Indeed, the struggle over the German cable concession proved in the end to be not so much a cause of, as a means towards, the achievement of the accords with Spain.[149] The cable issue also provided the Cambon brothers with the opportunity to raise the subject of a tripartite agreement with Pichon, and Jules Cambon's initiative both precipitated the negotiations for an accord, and ensured that France would be included in the eventual arrangements. Prior to his intervention the British had thought in terms of a bilateral agreement with Spain which might include provision for the defence of the Spanish islands, the non-alienation of these and Spain's extant and prospective possessions on the northern littoral of Morocco, and the future security of Gibraltar from land-based attack. France was not judged to have a permanent interest in Britain's continued possession of Gibraltar, and the Foreign Office was as much concerned with preventing France from acquiring a position on the northern coastline of Morocco as with excluding Germany from the region. Moreover, the British government had not sought, and did not require the assistance of another great Power in the area covered by the notes. If Spain were pledged not to concede any of its maritime possessions to another Power, then Britain could always rely upon its superior naval strength to defend them against a foreign rival.

After the communication of Jules Cambon's project to Perez Caballero it had become increasingly difficult for Grey to contemplate a bilateral agreement with Spain such as Bertie had recommended. The Spanish government was attracted by an accord *à trois,* and the French were anxious to be a party to anything that might be settled between London and Madrid. While a British guarantee of Spain's possessions could be explained away as payment for fresh Spanish pledges on Gibraltar, a tripartite agreement on the lines suggested by Jules Cambon could not be justified in such terms. Grey chose therefore to work for an exchange of notes based upon respect for the territorial status quo and a commitment to engage in consultations. In pursuing this course both he and his officials were keenly aware that their diplomacy might be interpreted as directed towards the encirclement of Germany. Even Eyre Crowe was moved in April to suggest that it might be worth considering whether France 'might not be asked to stand out of the Spanish negotiations altogether for the present and to come in only if and when Germany did likewise'.[150] This would not only have conflicted with the initial desire of the French for a tripartite agreement, but also with the wishes of Barrère and the Cambon brothers for a quadruple arrangement which would eventually include Italy in a new Mediterranean alignment.[151] Grey had not been ill-disposed towards the idea of Italy being associated with the Mediterranean accords through an exchange of notes between herself and Spain.[152] When in November 1907 Barrère suggested to Bertie that Italy should be instigated to make with England an agreement analogous to the Anglo-Spanish exchange of notes, he was curtly informed that this course would be 'an unnecessary offence to Germany'. Spain, Bertie explained, had possessions with which she might be persuaded to part, but there was no likelihood of Italy behaving in that fashion. Grey agreed with this analysis.[153] His intention had been neither to isolate Germany, nor to effect a realignment of the Mediterranean Powers, but simply to strengthen the resolve of Spain to resist such inducements as might be offered to her to part with any of her maritime possessions.

The French too had wanted to exclude other Powers from the Spanish islands. But French diplomacy at Madrid was also a function of French imperialism in the Maghreb. The Cambon brothers and Barrére were all exponents of a policy which they hoped would win for France a pre-eminent position in the western Mediterranean, and a protectorate over the greater part of the Shereefian empire. And the Moroccan crisis of 1905 had made Jules Cambon all the more aware of the value of having British assistance in keeping Spain in check. He was equally conscious of the danger to France of allowing England to pursue a separate understanding with Spain. Like the officials of the Foreign Office he recognized that the *entente cordiale* might prove to be a purely transient feature of international politics, and just as they were anxious to ensure that a potentially hostile France should not be able to threaten Britain's position at Gibraltar, so he wished to guard against Britain achieving any advantage at Madrid. Indeed, although the notes exchanged with Spain had the appearance of a hardening of the lines of diplomatic confrontation in Europe, those who were responsible for them fully appreciated the flexibility of the international system. Fear of Germany's intentions may have been uppermost in their minds, but the shape and form which they gave to the accords of May 1907 were in part determined by mutual suspicion and the memory of earlier Franco-British rivalries.

Acknowledgement

I should like to thank the British Academy for the award which it made to me from its Small Grants Research Fund in the Humanities for the purpose of consulting the French archival sources cited in this paper.

NOTES

1. One of the best accounts of the negotiations which preceded the conclusion of the accords of 1907 is to be found in G. Monger, *The End of Isolation: British Foreign Policy 1900-1907* (London, 1963), pp. 318-322.

2. G. Chklaver (ed.), *Au Service de la Russie: Alexandre Iswolsky. Correspondance Diplomatique, 1906-1911* (Paris, 1937), pp. 161-162. Jules Cambon MSS. (Ministere des Affaires Etrangeres, Paris), 14, Bompard to Jules Cambon, 15 June and 29 June 1907. (Hereafter cited as 'M.A.E.' All French foreign ministry correspondence cited in this paper is drawn from the Nouvelle séries.)
3. G. P. Gooch and H. W. V. Temperley, *British Documents on the Origins of the War 1898-1914* (London, 1928), Vol. VII, nos. 39, 40, 41, 42, 43, and 44. (Hereafter cited as 'B.D.')
4. *B.D.*, Vol. VII, no. 50.
5. F.O. (Foreign Office Archives, Public Records Office, London), 371/364, despt. 300, memo by Lord Granley enclosed in de Salis to Grey, 21 June 1907.
6. F.O. 371/364, despt. 82, Goschen to Grey, 18 June 1907.
7. *B.D.*, Vol. VII, no. 49.
8. See for example Salisbury MSS. (Hatfield House, Hertfordshire), A/131/4 and A/131/7, Drummond Wolff to Salisbury, 29 July and 11 August 1895.
9. F.O. 72/2098, despt. 112, Drummond Wolff to Kimberley, 30 March 1894.
10. For a contemporary assessment of the strategic importance of Spain's geographical position see F.O. 72/2161, despt. 30, 'Remarks on naval strategic conditions with reference to the Iberian Peninsula and Morocco' by Capt. E. T. Troubridge, enclosed in Durand to Lansdowne, 13 April 1902.
11. Salisbury MSS., A/114/34 and A/114/37, Dufferin to Salisbury, 28 February and 12 March 1896. Salisbury MSS., A/133/23, Drummond Wolff to Salisbury, 18 July 1898. A. J. Marder, *The Anatomy of British Sea Power* (London, 1964), pp. 218 and 274-275.
12. Salisbury MSS., A/131/28, memo enclosed in Drummond Wolff to Salisbury, 20 February 1896; D.M.I. to Sanderson, 22 February 1894; F.O. 72/2098, Admiralty to F.O., 31 March 1894.
13. Marder, *Anatomy of British Sea Power*, pp. 216-218.
14. The whole episode is recounted in R. G. Neale, *Britain and American Imperialism, 1898-1900* (Brisbane, 1965), pp. 58-74.
15. Salisbury MSS., A/133/25, Drummond Wolff to Salisbury, 30 July 1898; A/133/29, Drummond Wolff to Balfour, 25 August 1898. F.O. 72/2100, tel. 102, Salisbury to Drummond Wolff, 12 August 1898. As Drummond Wolff recognized, the choice of Paris for the Hispano-American peace negotiations established for the moment 'the supremacy of French influences in Spain', F.O. 72/2100, despt, 283, Drummond Wolff to Salisbury, 14 August 1898. Adagh MSS., (Public Records Office, London), memo by Sir John Adagh, 18 August 1898.
16. F.O. 72/2098, tel. 114, Balfour to Drummond Wolff, 29 August 1898.
17. Balfour MSS. (British Library, London), Add. MS. 49691, Balfour to Salisbury, 30 August 1898; Salisbury to Balfour, 31 August 1898. F.O. 72/2100, despt. 194, Salisbury to Drummond Wolff, 6 August 1898. F.O. 72/2100, tel. 328, Drummond Wolff to Balfour, 31 August 1898. F.O. 72/2099, Drummond Wolff to Balfour, 14 September 1898. F.O. 72/2100, tel. 118, Balfour to Drummond Wolff, 1 September 1898. C. Howard, *Britain and the Casus Belli, 1822-1902* (London, 1974), pp. 115-116.

18. Salisbury MSS., A/133/32, Drummond Wolff to Salisbury, 8 September 1898.
19. Moret had already suggested to Drummond Wolff in March 1898 that there might be scope for an Anglo-Spanish understanding. F.O. 72/2098, Drummond Wolff to Kimberley, 14 March 1894. F.O. 72/2099, tel. 344, despt. 320, tels. 354 and 355, despt. 340, Drummond Wolff to Salisbury, 11 September, 14 September, and 26 September 1898. F.O. 72/2099, undated note in the handwritting of Dufferin and seen by Salisbury. The office of minister of state in Spain was equivalent to that of foreign minister in other European countries.
20. F.O. 72/2099, tels. 122 and 123, Salisbury to Drummond Wolff, 16 September 1898. F.O. 72/2099, despt. 322, Drummond Wolff to Salisbury, 17 September 1898. Cab. (Cabinet Papers, Public Records Office, London) 41/24/43, Salisbury to Queen Victoria, 27 October 1898.
21. F.O. 425/235, despt. 387, Drummond Wolff to Salisbury, 5 November 1898.
22. F.O. 425/235, despt. 390, Drummond Wolff to Salisbury, 7 November 1898.
23. F.O. 425/235, despt. 286, Salisbury to Drummond Wolff, 26 November 1898.
24. F.O. 425/235, tels. 138P and 140P, Salisbury to Drummond Wolff, 11 November and 14 November 1898.
25. F.O. 425/235, despt. 280, Salisbury to Drummond Wolff, 26 November 1898.
26. Cab. 41/24/45, Salisbury to Queen Victoria, 21 November 1898. F.O. 425/242, tel. 148P, Salisbury to Drummond Wolff, 7 December 1898.
27. F.O. 425/242, despt. 21, Drummond Wolff to Salisbury, 4 February 1899.
28. F.O. 425/242, despt. 64, Drummond Wolff to Salisbury, 17 March 1899.
29. *Die Grosse Politik der Europäische Kabinette*, Vol. XV, 4205 and 4206. Spain's diplomatic position at the turn of the century is considered in G. B. Bledsoe, 'Spanish Foreign Policy 1898–1936', in *Spain in the Twentieth Century World: Essays on Spanish Diplomacy 1898–1978*, ed. V. W. Cortade (London, 1980), pp. 3–40.
30. C. Andrew, *Théophile Delcassé and the Making of the Entente Cordiale* (London, 1968), pp. 147–148.
31. M.A.E. Espagne 15, Reverseaux to Hanotaux, 16 May 1896. M.A.E. Espagne 15, despt. 29, Patenôtre to Delcassé, 15 March 1901. F.O. 72/2161, Durand to Sanderson, 17 November 1902.
32. F.O. 72/2100, tel. 295, Drummond Wolff to Salisbury, 18 August 1898. de Margerie MSS. (M.A.E.) J. Cambon to de Margerie, 15 March 1906. On Jules Cambon's attitudes towards the Hispano-American war see J. F. MacDonald, 'Jules Cambon et la ménace de l'impérialisme americain (1898–1899)', *Revue d'histoire diplomatique* (1972): 247–255.
33. M.A.E. Espagne 15, despt. 87. Delcassé to Lefaire, 15 July 1901.
34. Andrew, *Théophile Delcassé*, pp. 149–151 and 191–194.
35. *Documents Diplomatiques Francais, 2nd series*, Vol. III, nos. 53, 58, 60, 81, and 113; Vol. IV, no. 78. (Hereafter cited as *D.D.F.2.*) Delcassé MSS. (M.A.E.), 2, J. Cambon to Delcassé, 14 February and 28 February 1903.
36. *D.D.F.2*, Vol. III, no. 162. Andrew, *Théophile Delcassé*, p. 217.
37. Delcassé MSS., 2, J. Cambon to Delcassé, 24 May 1903. M.A.E. Espagne 15, J. Cambon to Delcassé. *D.D.F.2*, Vol. III, no. 259.

38. M.A.E. Espagne 38, despt. 71, J. Cambon to Delcassé, 5 June 1903. Delcassé MSS., 2, J. Cambon to Delcassé, 6 June 1903.
39. M.A.E. Espagne 38, despt. 182, Delcassé to Bompard, 26 June 1903. Andrew, *Théophile Delcassé*, pp. 218-219.
40. Ibid., pp. 201-215.
41. *D.D.F.2*, Vol. III, no. 364. Delcassé MSS., 2, J. Cambon to Delcassé, 11 August 1903.
42. Delcassé MSS., 2, J. Cambon to Delcassé, 10 December 1903 and 1 March
43. Lansdowne MSS., F.O. 800/142, Durand to Lansdowne, 30 July 1903 and 23 August 1903.
44. Lansdowne MSS., F.O. 800/126, memo by Louis Battenberg, 7 August 1903.
45. L. A. Mcgeoch, 'British Foreign Policy and the Spanish Corollary to the Anglo-French Agreement of 1904', in *Diplomacy in an Age of Nationalism. Essays in Honor of Lynn Marschall Case*, eds. H. N. Barker and M. L. Brown (The Hague, 1971), pp. 209-222. P. Guillon, *L'Allemagne et le Maroc de 1870 à 1905* (Paris, 1967), pp. 779-780.
46. M.A.E. Espagne 40, despt. 110, J. Cambon to Rouvier, 6 July 1905. *B.D.*, Vol. II, nos. 373, 376, 377, and 378. *D.D.F.2*, Vol. IV, nos. 98, 117, 119 and 120.
47. *D.D.F.2*, Vol. VI, no. 403; Vol. VII, no. 84.
48. M.A.E. Espagne 39, despt. 14, J. Cambon to Delcassé, 30 January 1904. Delcassé MSS., 2, J. Cambon to Delcassé, 1 March 1904.
49. *D.D.F.2*, Vol. VI, no. 54.
50. *D.D.F.2*, Vol. IV, no. 389.
51. Nicolson MSS., F.O. 800/337, Nicolson to Sanderson, 4 February 1905.
52. Nicolson MSS., F.O. 800/336, Sanderson to Nicolson, 15 February 1905.
53. Nicolson MSS., F.O. 800/337, Nicolson to Sanderson, 25 February 1905. Nicolson MSS., F.O. 800/336, Lansdowne to Nicolson, 19 April 1905.
54. Cecil MSS. (Hatfield House), S(4), 52/162, Bertie to Cranborne, 30 June 1903.
55. P. M. Kennedy, 'The Development of German Naval Operations Plans against England, 1896-1914', *English Historical Review*, lxxxix (1974): 48-76. Guillen, *L'Allemagne et la Maroc*, pp. 553-557 and 583-586.
56. F.O. 185/1004, despt. 120c(ommercial), memos by Dufferin enclosed in Lansdowne to Nicolson, 30 November 1905.
57. F.O. 185/844, tel. 22P, Lansdowne to Nicolson, 2 May 1905. F.O. 72/2209, despt. 86, Nicolson to Lansdowne, 5 May 1905. F.O. 72/2211, Lansdowne to Nicolson, 26 November 1905. F.O. 72/2219, despt. 3, Croker to Lansdowne, 5 December 1905. F.O. 368/48, despt. 3c, Nicolson to Grey, 3 January 1906. F.O. 368/51, despt. 133c, Acton to Grey, 29 August 1906 and minute by Dufferin. F.O. 371/116, Admiralty to F.O.
58. *D.D.F.2*, Vol. VI, no. 205.
59. Delcassé MSS., 2, J. Cambon to Delcassé, 8 April, 14 April, and 6 May 1905. *D.D.F.2*, Vol. VII, no. 229.
60. *D.D.F.2*, Vol. VIII, no. 223.
61. F.O. 72/2209, despts. 58 and 85, Nicolson to Lansdowne, 6 April and 5 May 1905. *B.D.*, Vol. III, no. 87. F.O. 27/3703, despt. 279, Lansdowne to Bertie, 8 May 1905. Bertie MSS., A, F.O. 800/179, Bertie to Lansdowne, 12 May 1905.
62. Nicolson MSS., F.O. 800/336, Lansdowne to Nicolson, 3 June 1903. *B.D.*, Vol. VII, no. 1.

63. Bertie MSS., A, F.O. 800/179, Bertie to Hardinge, 23 November 1905.
64. *B.D.*, Vol. VII, no. 7.
65. F.O. 72/2211, tel. 49, Nicolson to Lansdowne, 4 July 1905. Bertie MSS., A, F.O. 800/179, Bertie to Lansdowne, 8 July 1905: Barrington to Bertie, 11 July 1905. Lansdowne MSS., F.O. 800/127, Bertie to Barrington, 13 July 1905.
66. F.O. 72/2211, tel. 46, Lansdowne to Nicolson, 4 July 1905.
67. M.A.E. Espagne 40, despt. 110, J. Cambon to Rouvier, 6 July 1905.
68. F.O. 72/2209, despt. 126, Nicolson to Lansdowne, 29 June 1905. Editorial note, *B.D.*, Vol. VII, no. 1.
69. F.O. 371/135, 'Negotiations with the Spanish Government respecting a proposal that H.M. Govt. should undertake the defence of the Canary and Balearic Islands', F.O. memo, 9 March 1906, with minutes by Grey and Hardinge.
70. On 31 May 1906 King Alfonso XIII married Princess Victoria Eugenia of Battenberg. Jules Cambon MSS., 11, de Margerie to J. Cambon, 12 March 1906. *D.D.F.2*, Vol. IX, pt. ii, no. 453 and p. 934.
71. P.M. Kennedy, 'Imperial Cable Communications and Stategy, 1870-1914', *English Historical Review*, lxxxvi (1971): 728-752. J-C. Allain, *Agadir 1911* (Paris, 1976), pp. 133-35. F.O. 368/51, despt. 78c, Cartwright to Grey, 24 May 1906. F.O. 368/51, 'Memo respecting Cable Communications with the Canaries in relations to English, French, Spanish, and German Interests' by G. Young, 5 November 1906. F.O. 371/336, despt. 78, 'General Report on Spain for the Year 1906,' enclosed in de Bunsen to Grey, 27 April 1907.
72. F.O. 368/51, Admiralty to F.O., 30 June 1906.
73. F.O. 368/51, despt. 122c, Grey to de Bunsen, 2 August 1906. F.O. 368/51, Babington-Smith (G.P.O) to F.O., 2 July 1906; G.P.O. to F.O. 13 July 1906.
74. F.O. 368/51, tel. 23c, Grey to de Bunsen, 14 July 1906. F.O. 368/51, despt. 109c, de Bunsen to Grey, 17 July 1906.
75. M.A.E. Maroc 394, Berard to M.A.E., 22 December 1904; Berard to Rouvier, 10 July 1905.
76. *D.D.F.2*, Vol. X, no. 166.
77. F.O. 368/51, despts. 109c and 116c, de Bunsen to Grey, 17 July and 26 July 1906. M.A.E. Maroc 394, tel. 228, Bourgeois to J. Cambon, 10 July 1906. M.A.E. Maroc 394, tels. 266 and 268, J. Cambon to Bourgeois, 11 July and 12 July 1906.
78. F.O. 368/51, tel. 48c and despts. 116c and 118c, de Bunsen to Grey, 22 July, 26 July and 28 July 1906. F.O. 368/127, despt. 2c, de Bunsen to Grey, 5 January 1907. Grey MSS., F.O. 800/77, de Bunsen to Grey, 4 August 1906. M.A.E. Maroc 394, tel. 277, J. Cambon to Bourgeois, 22 July 1906. M.A.E. Espagne 15, J. Cambon to Bourgeois, 11 August 1906. *D.D.F.2*, Vol. X, nos. 125 and 166.
79. F.O. 368/51, note by Hardinge, 25 July 1906. F.O. 368/51, tel. 25c, Grey to de Bunsen, 25 July 1906. M.A.E. Maroc 394, tel. 228, Bourgeois to P. Cambon, 24 July 1906.
80. F.O. 368/51, despts. 128c and 130c, Acton to Grey, 9 August and 23 August 1906.
81. M.A.E. Maroc 394, Barthou to Pichon, 27 February 1907.
82. Ibid.

83. F.O. 368/51, despt. 197c and 204c, de Bunsen to Grey, 18 December and 28 December 1906. F.O. 368/127, 'Further Memo respecting Cable Communications with the Canaries in relation to English, French, German, and Spanish Interests' by G. Young, 10 January 1907.
84. F.O. 368/51, tel. 9c, Grey to Bertie, 22 December 1906.
85. Grey MSS., F.O. 800/77, Grey to de Bunsen, 28 December 1906.
86. F.O. 368/51, tel. 9c, Grey to Bertie, 22 December 1906.
87. Campbell-Bannerman MSS. (British Library), Add. MS. 52514, Grey to Campbell-Bannerman, 27 December 1906.
88. F.O. 368/51, tel. 83c, minute by Law on de Bunsen to Grey, 29 December 1906.
89. *B.D.*, Vol. II, pp. 397–420.
90. *B.D.*, Vol. VII, no. 8.
91. *D.D.F.2*, Vol. X, no. 380.
92. Paul Cambon MSS. (M.A.E.) 11, J. Cambon to P. Cambon, 2 January 1907.
93. *D.D.F.2*, Vol. X, no. 383.
94. F.O. 368/127, tel. 3c, Bertie to Grey, 5 January 1907, and minute by Villiers. F.O. 368/127, despt. 5c, Bertie to Grey, 5 January 1907.
95. F.O. 368/127, despt. 9c, de Bunsen to Grey, 18 January 1907, and minutes by Campbell, Hardinge and Grey.
96. F.O. 368/127, tel. 4c, Grey to de Bunsen, 10 January 1907.
97. The concession was finally granted to *Feltern und Guilleaume* by royal decree in June 1907.
98. M.A.E. Maroc 394, Barthou to Pichon, 27 February 1907.
99. de Margerie MSS, J. Cambon to de Margerie, 15 March 1906. Jules Cambon MSS., 11, J. Cambon to Louis, 29 March and 5 April 1906.
100. F.O. 371/94, tel, 106, de Bunsen to Grey, 14 November 1906. F.O. 371/94, tel. 112, de Bunsen to Grey, 22 November 1906 and minutes by Eyre Crowe, Hardinge and Grey. F.O. 371/94, despt. 213, de Bunsen to Grey, 25 November 1906. Jules Cambon MSS., 11, J. Cambon to Pichon, 14 November 1906. *D.D.F.2*, Vol. X nos. 246, 275 and 290. I. C. Barlow, *The Agadir Crisis* (Chapel Hill, 1940), pp. 44–67.
101. M.A.E. Espagne 41, despt. 74, J. Cambon to Bourgeois, 19 May 1906. According to Hardinge the French were also worried about the possibility of the German navy securing the use of the docks at Ferrol. But there is no indication in the French archives that this played any significant part in leading Jules Cambon to propose a new agreement with Spain. Hardinge of Penshurst, *Old Diplomacy* (London, 1947), pp. 134–135.
102. Paul Cambon MSS. 11, J. Cambon to P. Cambon, 2 January 1907. *D.D.F.2*, Vol. X, no. 384. *B.D.*, Vol. VII, no. 7.
103. F.O. 371/94, despt. 277, de Bunsen to Grey, 8 December 1906.
104. *B.D.*, Vol. VII, nos. 6 and 7. *D.D.F.2*, Vol. X, no. 390.
105. *B.D.*, Vol. VII, no. 3.
106. Cab. 38/12/58, minute by Grey, 12 December 1906. *B.D.*, Vol. VII, nos. 4 and 5.
107. Cab. 38/12/59, minutes of the 94th meeting of the C.I.D., 20 December 1906.

108. F.O. 371/364, 'Note on the Spanish Territory adjacent to Gibraltar' by Clarke, 16 December 1906. Cab. 38/12/62, 'Spanish territory which British interests required to be secured against alienation to another Power', note by Clarke, 28 December 1906. As de Bunsen pointed out Britain also had the Spanish pledge of March 1899 on Gibraltar. Grey MSS., F.O. 800/77, de Bunsen to Grey, 23 February 1907.
109. *B.D.*, Vol. VII, no. 8. Bertie MSS., A, F.O. 800/179, Grey to Bertie, 30 December 1906.
110. Balfour MSS., Add. MS. 49746, Bertie to Balfour, 14 September 1898.
111. *B.D.*, Vol. VII, no. 8.
112. *D.D.F.2*, Vol. X, no. 384.
113. *B.D.*, Vol. VII, no. 9.
114. F.O. 371/364, despt. 31, Grey to Bertie, 18 January 1907. F.O. 371/355, de Bunsen to Grey, 21 January 1907. *B.D.*, Vol. VII, no. 10.
115. F.O. 371/334, despts. 7 and 58, de Bunsen to Grey, 5 January and 16 March 1907. F.O. 371/366, despt. 78, 'General Report on Spain for the Year 1906', enclosed in de Bunsen to Grey, 27 April 1907. Grey MSS., F.O. 800/77, de Bunsen to Grey, 8 January 1907.
116. *B.D.*, Vol. VII, no. 9.
117. Bertie MSS., A, F.O. 800/179, Tyrrell to Bertie, 17 January 1907.
118. Bertie MSS., A. F.O. 800/179, Bertie to Hardinge, 19 January 1907.
119. Campbell-Bannerman MSS., Add. MS. 52514, Grey to Campbell-Bannerman, 11 January 1907.
120. Grey MSS., F.O. 800/100, Campbell-Bannerman to Grey, 14 January 1907.
121. F.O. 371/334, despt. 27, de Bunsen to Grey, 26 January 1907. M.A.E. Espagne 41, J. Cambon to Pichon, 5 February 1907. M.A.E. Espagne 41, tel. 44, J. Cambon to Pichon, 24 February 1907. Paul Cambon MSS., 11, memo by P. Cambon, 14 February 1907. *B.D.*, Vol. VII, no. 16.
122. *D.D.F.2*, Vol. X, no. 412.
123. *B.D.*, Vol. VII, no. 11.
124. *D.D.F.2*, Vol. X, no. 412.
125. *B.D.*, Vol. VII, no. 19.
126. Cab. 38/13/11, note by Admiralty, 25 February 1907.
127. Cab. 38/13/12, minutes of the 96th meeting of the C.I.D., 28 February 1907.
128. *D.D.F.2*, Vol. X, nos. 423 and 428. Grey MSS., F.O. 800/77, de Bunsen to Grey, 23 February 1907.
129. *B.D.*, Vol. VII, nos. 17 and 18.
130. *B.D.*, Vol. VII, nos. 20, 21, and 23.
131. *B.D.*, Vol. VII, no. 22. Bertie MSS., A., F.O. 800/164, Bertie to Grey, 30 March 1907.
132. *B.D.*, Vol. VII, no. 24.
133. Bertie MSS., A., F.O. 800/179, Hardinge to Bertie, 10 April 1907.
134. M.A.E. Espagne 41, despt. 147, P. Cambon to Pichon, 25 April 1907. *B.D.*, Vol. VII, nos. 25 and 26.
135. M.A.E. Espagne 41, Daeschner to Pichon, 13 April 1907.
136. *D.D.F.2*, Vol. X, no. 458.
137. M.A.E. Espagne 41, tel. 120, Barrère to Pichon, 14 April 1907.

138. M.A.E. Espagne 41, despt. 323, Pichon to P. Cambon, 17 April 1907. M.A.E. Espagne 41, tel. 85, Pichon to P. Cambon, 20 April 1907. M.A.E. Espagne 41, tel. 41, P. Cambon to Pichon, 22 April 1907. *B.D.*, Vol. VII, no. 30.
139. F.O. 371/364, note by Grey and minute by Hardinge (reg. 24 April 1907).
140. F.O. 371/364, despts. 249 and 252, Grey to Bertie, 25 April and 26 April 1907. M.A.E. Espagne 41, despt. 143, P. Cambon to Pichon, 24 April 1907.
141. F.O. 371/364, despt. 217, Bertie to Grey, 27 April 1907, and minutes by Hardinge and Grey.
142. F.O. 371/364, despt. 252, Grey to Bertie, 26 April 1907. Bertie MSS., B, F.O. 800/185, Hardinge to Bertie, 30 April 1907.
143. *B.D.*, Vol. VII, nos. 37 and 38. The British cabinet gave its approval to the notes on 3 May. Cab. 41/31/17, Campbell-Bannerman to Edward VII, 3 May 1907.
144. M.A.E. Espagne 41, despt. 149 and tel. 48, P. Cambon to Pichon, 26 April and 9 May 1907.
145. M.A.E. Espagne 41, tel. 71. Pichon to P. Cambon, 27 May 1907. F.O. 371/364, tel. 20, Bertie to Grey, 31 May 1907. *B.D.*, Vol. VII, no. 45.
146. M.A.E. Espagne 41, tel. 71, P. Cambon to Pichon, 6 June 1907. F.O. 371/364, tel. 21, Bertie to Grey, 1 June 1907.
147. *B.D.*, Vol. VII, no. 50.
148. *D.D.F.*2, Vol. X, no. 481.
149. F.O. 368/127, 'Further memo respecting Cable Communication with the Canaries' by Young, 10 January 1907.
150. *B.D.*, Vol. VII, no. 22.
151. *B.D.*, Vol. VII, no. 14. M.A.E. Espagne 41, J. Cambon to Pichon, 5 February 1907. M.A.E. Espagne 41, tel. 130, Barrère to Pichon, 19 April 1907.
152. *B.D.*, Vol. VII, no. 32.
153. *B.D.*, Vol. VII, no. 20. Bertie MSS., A, F.O. 800/177, Grey to Bertie, 6 November 1907.

KEITH E. NEILSON

Wishful Thinking: The Foreign Office and Russia 1907-1917

Few would doubt that a country needs to acquire information about the states with which it deals: it is largely for this reason that embassies, attaches, and intelligence services are maintained. The need for accurate information in order to pursue a rational foreign policy is so obvious as to rank as a truism, but there are ramifications involved in the process of foreign policy making which require closer examination.

Complications begin when it is considered how information is gathered and what happens to it once gathered. Those who gather, collate, and interpret information shape, in many ways, the answers which it provides. The questions they ask of the information gathered, the way they perceive the matter with which they are dealing, their preconceptions, and prejudices — their political 'taste' as it were: all of these things have a subtle yet profound influence upon the foreign policy decisions which are made.[1]

The difficulty for the historian is that this 'taste' is difficult to determine. Men rarely write down what James Joll has aptly termed their 'unspoken assumptions'.[2] The process of discovering what men thought about the countries with which they dealt, their institutions, and the individuals who ran them, involves piecing together small fragments often overlooked by diplomatic historians whose general interest is in determining other matters. Defining such attitudes is more the province of the biographer, but except in cases where the life of an individual has been intimately connected with a particular country, the focus of the biographer tends also to lie elsewhere.

For those interested in the 'why' of foreign policy, however, an interest in such matters is unavoidable. This is particularly relevant when dealing with British foreign policy in the period leading up to the Great War. Zara Steiner has shown in *Britain and the Origins of the First World War* that British policy prior to 1914 was shaped almost exclusively by the foreign secretary, ably assisted by his closest advisors at the Foreign Office.[3] This small group of men and the British representatives abroad made up an elite whose opinions and points of view affected substantially the policies which Britain pursued.[4]

What follows, then, is an attempt to determine just what that elite thought about Russia and Russian politics in the decade from 1907 to 1917. These two dates mark a natural beginning and end to a distinct period in Anglo-Russian relations. The first marks the signing of the Convention over Persia, an event which signalled a new phase in Anglo-Russian relations.[5] The second marks the end of Anglo-Russian relations as such and ushers in the new period of Anglo-Soviet relations, a change-over which was accompanied by the need for large-scale revisions in British thinking about Russia. While British attitudes were reasonably consistent during this period, the onset of the Great War changed the priorities of the British elite with respect to Russia in the period from 1914 to 1917. British concerns became dominated more and more by the need for an effective Russian war effort, often at the expense of pre-war considerations. For this reason, the periods from 1907 to 1914 and from 1914 to 1917 will be considered in two sections, although the continuity between them is substantial.

The most pervasive belief which existed at the Foreign Office about Russia was that the latter was a reactionary country. In many ways this reflected the wider beliefs of the average educated Englishman. There existed, as a legacy of the nineteenth century and Russia's clashes with England in both the European and colonial arena, a deep reservoir of Russophobia in Britain.[6] For those who made policy, the fact that Russia was held to be the most illiberal state in Europe was mainly important in the way that it had an impact upon Anglo-Russian affairs. Grey and the two men who served him as permanent under-secretary, successively Sir Charles (later Baron) Hardinge and Sir Arthur Nicolson, were quite aware that Russia's unsavoury reputation made any agreements with her difficult to justify to the British public. While Grey attempted to keep foreign affairs outside the realm of public opinion and could write to Nicolson (in the latter's capacity as ambassador to Russia from 1906 to 1910) in February 1908 that the tangible benefits of the Anglo-Russian Convention would soon silence widespread public criticism of it, the truth was that every effort was made to tailor the news from Russia to present the Russian government in the best possible light.[7]

The visit of Edward VII to Reval in 1908 to see the Russian Emperor was a case in point. When the trip was in the discussion stage, Hardinge wrote revealing to Nicolson that

> Grey is in favour of the idea and probably Asquith also, but they are both a little afraid of the extremists in their party and what they might say of the King's visit to Reval. If you agree with me in this I hope you will not be alarmist to Grey about Finland or the Duma. If the visit can take place we shall in my opinion have scored our success whatever may take place later....[8]

Nor was Grey above suggesting that news from Russia be laundered in order to avoid awkward discussions at home. A year later, just before the visit of Nicholas II to Cowes, Grey asked Nicolson to send a despatch to London which 'might show the progress and development of a constitutional government in Russia, and draw a comparison between the actual situation at the present moment and that of a few years ago'.[9]

It was clear at the Foreign Office that public acceptance of any arrangement with Russia depended to a great extent on how that country was perceived. While the French government advanced the view that the loose entente between the three countries could be maintained whatever government existed in Russia, the British did not agree. In May 1909, Hardinge wrote to Nicolson that the French view 'is an absurd mistake, since a reactionary Government in Russia would meet with no sympathy at all in this country, and it would be impossible to grow closer to Russia in any way while such a Government was in power'.[10] Such a view did not change prior to the war. When the possibility of a formal Anglo-Russian military alliance was discussed at the Foreign Office in 1914, Nicolson noted that such an arrangement was 'out of the question so long as the public in England remain in their present mind'.[11]

This was a constant obstacle to the foreign policy based on the belief that 'Britain's safety rested on a powerful fleet and on agreements with France and Russia', which Grey and his advisors wished to pursue.[12] Such an obstacle did not daunt their pursuit of Russia. It was believed—perhaps hoped is a better word—that Russia would gradually become a more acceptable partner for Britain. A combination of reform in Russia and awareness in Britain of the German threat would make a growing closeness with Russia more palatable. Hardinge put it clearly in a memorandum written in 1909:

> It must not be forgotten that although from time to time there may be a reactionary wave in Russia the Russia of the future will be liberal and not reactionary.... Moreover public opinion in this country which is in complete sympathy with the liberal and constitutional development of Russia does not yet sufficiently grasp the danger to Europe of German's ambitious designs.... [13]

Such a belief had several implications for the Foreign Office's view of Russia and her internal politics.

The first was that the Foreign Office identified its interests in Russia with those political elements which supported closer relations with Britain. Not coincidentally, these elements were also those which were acceptable to the British public. There were no doubts as to whom these individuals and parties were. As Nicolson wrote to Hardinge in February 1910, 'the sincere supporters of the entente are the Emperor, Stolypine, Iswolsky, the liberal press, and perhaps a large number of liberal and progressive deputies and others.'[14] A similar view was held by Hugh O'Beirne, the long-time counsellor at St Petersburg. In October of that same year, O'Beirne wrote that support for a pro-western orientation of Russia's foreign policy existed in 'politicians other than those of the Right, among the lower rank officials, in the so-called "intelligenzia", and, generally, in those circles which supply the strength of Liberalism in Russia.'[15]

A corollary of the British preference for the Russian liberals was a dislike of the 'reactionary' parties in Russia. Not coincidentally, these elements did not favour closer relations with Britain and were unacceptable to the mass of the British public. Again, the Foreign Office was well aware of whom this reactionary group entailed. In Nicolson's annual report on Russia for 1906, he noted that it was the 'military party' in Russia which did not favour closer Anglo-Russian relations.[16] After four years as ambassador, he was more specific. In February 1910, he informed Hardinge that 'the opponents [of the Anglo-Russian entente] are some members of the Cabinet, the Court circles in great measure, the Right parties, and very many in the Army, bureaucracy and elsewhere, and the "Right" press — a pretty formidable array.'[17] Two years later, O'Beirne echoed Nicolson's views, noting that those who favoured a Russo-German alliance were 'to be found chiefly in Court and military circles and among the higher class of officials'.[18]

The division of Russian politics into 'good' and 'bad', respectively 'liberal' and 'reactionary', elements led to a close eye being kept on the rise and fall of Russian ministers. These men were judged not so much by their competence as by their political leanings. As mentioned, two particular favourites of the British were P. A. Stolypin, the long-term prime minister, and A. P. Izvolsky, the foreign minister from 1906 to 1910. These two were thought to be the strongest backers of an entente with Britain, and their continued political ascendency was considered essential. Even relatively trivial events were scrutinized for their supposed political significance. Hardinge saw the awarding of a decoration to Stolypin shortly after the conclusion of the Balkan crisis of 1909 as a political statement. 'I cannot help feeling', Hardinge wrote, 'that there is an intentional demonstration on the part of the Emperor.... intended to show his confidence in Stolypin's Gov[ernmen]t and also in the loyalty of our policy.'[19]

If there were favourite Russian politicians, there were also those who were disliked. A particular *bête noir* was I. L. Goremykin, a former minister of the interior who had also served briefly as prime minister.[20] Goremykin was held to be typical of those who preferred a German alignment of Russian policy. Should Goremykin become foreign minister, Hardinge wrote in 1909, 'a foreign policy more in accordance than now with German aims in Europe would be gradually substituted for the policy recently pursued by Russia of cooperation with England and France.'[21] Another important individual who believed that it 'should be a fundamental principle of Russia's foreign policy to establish the closest possible relations with Germany' was S. Witte, the man who had overseen the industrialization of Russia and had served briefly as prime minister.[22] Others were categorized more simply. The minister of the interior from 1913 to 1915, N. A. Maklakov, was referred to as 'the reactionary Maklakow'.[23]

Those who made British policy made every effort to indicate to the Emperor the preferences of the British government for certain ministers. In an audience with Nicholas II in 1909, Nicolson 'touched on [Stolypin's] health, and praised him as far as I thought it was prudent to do so.'[24] Such a cautious approach was necessary, since it was important not to give the appearance of interfering in Russia's internal affairs. The sensitivity of the Emperor on this subject was well known and there was no desire to irritate him unnecessarily.

The attitudes of the Emperor introduced another complication for Anglo-Russian relations. While the Emperor was held to be a supporter of the entente, he often found Britain too radical politically. In a letter to Buchanan early in 1911, Nicolson put this point plainly:

> If our affairs at home develop in a direction which the Emperor may consider to be ultra-democratic and as indicating instability in our internal situation, he will most probably be disposed to seek comfort in more conservative quarters. There are many around him who strongly urge him to take such a course, and I am not sure that some of our friends in the Russian Cabinet would be so eager in supporting our understanding if they thought that we were embarking on an advanced political programme at home.[25]

The situation created by such an attitude bordered on the comic: the Foreign Office wished for Russian politics to become more liberal in order that Russia would be more acceptable as a British ally; at the same time they hoped that British politics would not become too liberal in order that Britain would be more acceptable as a Russian ally!

Closely connected with British hopes for reform in Russia was the position occupied by that country's parliament, the Duma. Created as a placatory gesture during the revolution of 1904–1905, the Duma was seen as the touchstone of liberal reform in Russia. When the Emperor had suspended the Duma briefly in 1906, the then British Prime Minister, Sir H. Campbell-Bannerman, uttered his famous 'La Duma est Morte; vive la Duma' speech to the inter-parliamentary union in order to underline the significance which the Duma held.[26] For British Liberals, the Duma was evidence that Russia was progressing in the path towards constitutional government, and its continued existence was necessary if the entente with Russia was to remain acceptable.

Because of such sentiment, public events often took on a greater symbolic significance than their actual importance would warrant. In the summer of 1909, the Emperor and a Duma delegation came to Cowes to return the visit of Edward VII to Reval a year earlier. This was hailed at the Foreign Office for two reasons. First, it was hoped that such a visit would help to cement the bonds of the Convention. Second, it was thought that such a meeting could only strengthen the liberal forces in Russia. As Nicolson wrote to Hardinge in June, Russian liberals believed 'that the oftener the Emperor saw the King the better it would be for the constitutional progress in Russia.'[27] After the conclusion of the visit, O'Beirne made it clear to Grey how closely such events were followed in Russia:

> The Cowes meeting has naturally been considered by Russian Liberals largely in its bearing on the internal politics of the country, and it has been interesting to note the intense satisfaction with which they learnt of the King's reference to the visit of the Duma members, and the Emperor's remarks in reply.[28]

O'Beirne went on to outline the general British belief that politics in Russia were growing more liberal. Such 'growth of constitutional ideas and of a liberal spirit among the governing classes', he opined, could best be encouraged by 'the development of Anglo Russian and Franco Russian relations'.[29]

A major problem for the Foreign Office was how the Anglo-Russian alliance was perceived in Russia. Because the British government was unable to give Russia a definite promise of support in the case of European hostilities, she did 'not inspire confidence', as Nicolson's handpicked successor as ambassador, Sir George Buchanan, pointed out, and was 'regarded as a very weak reed to lean on when serious troubles arise'.[30] The indefinite character of the British alliance was an obvious liability. Buchanan informed Grey in March 1914 that those in Russia who favoured a pro-German tilt to Russia's policy had suggested to the Emperor that 'as Russia cannot count on England's support in the event of war, an understanding with the latter country is of no practical value.'[31] Even the supporters of the entente, the ambassador continued, felt that its 'vague and undefined character' made it less valuable than it might be.

The inability of Britain to 'tighten up the ties with Russia' was a 'nightmare' for Nicolson.[32] The permanent under-secretary feared that Russia, denied firm support by Britain, would turn elsewhere for support. The July crisis of 1914 brought this fear to a head. Nicolson thought, as he wrote to Buchanan on 28 July, that the crisis might be taken by Russia as a 'test of friendship, and that were we to disappoint her all hope of a friendly and permanent understanding with her would disappear.'[33] While this could be dismissed as just another example of Nicolson's Russophile tendencies, such a view was shared by the influential assistant under-secretary at the Foreign Office, Eyre Crowe. The latter minuted on a telegram on 30 July that, while he wanted to ensure that Britain's actions did not precipitate a war, 'if and when, however, it is certain that France and Russia cannot avoid the war, and are going into it, my opinion, for what it is worth, is that British interests require us to take our place beside them as allies'.[34] Buchanan, working in the heated atmosphere caused by Russia's declaration of war, put his beliefs in more emotional terms on 3 August. 'I only pray', the ambassador wrote, 'that England will prove true to herself and to her friends, as if she deserts them in their hour of need she will find herself isolated after the war'.[35] This is not the product of war hysteria; in December 1912 Buchanan had noted that should a war break out between Russia and the Central Powers and should Britain remain 'aloof', the 'Entente will die a natural death and no power on earth will bring it to life again.'[36]

In the event, Britain did join Russia. It is easy to imagine that once the alliance was solidified by the signing of the Declaration of London in early September the pre-war concerns which the British held about the nature of the Anglo-Russian relationship would evaporate. This was not entirely the case. Instead, with the exigencies of war the concerns tended to change somewhat, but remained quite recognizable until at least 1916. It was only the over-riding concern about the effective prosecution of Russia's war effort which brought about fundamental changes in the Foreign Office's views of Russian internal affairs.

Although Russia became an ally, and a necessary one, with the outbreak of the war, there was still concern at the Foreign Office that British public opinion would find Russian methods repugnant. Of particular concern was the fear that 'Cossack outrages' would accompany the expected advance of Russian troops.[37] To counter any such charges, the Foreign Office sent the well-known Russian scholar and Russophile, Professor Bernard Pares, to Russia in 1914. Pares' mission was to gather material at the front to rebut charges of Russian brutality. Nor was the home front neglected. A special effort was made to place articles before British readers extolling the virtues of Russians. Much was made of the innate goodness of the Russian soldier: a simple, stalwart individual, motivated by an intense patriotism and deep religious feelings.[38]

Despite the patriotism displayed in Russia and the unexpectedly rapid mobilization of her army, British fears about the stability of Russia and her commitment to the entente were not easily dispelled. On 13 September, Buchanan pondered whether or not the Emperor would take the 'golden opportunity' which the newfound political solidarity in Russia gave him to satisfy the 'legitimate demands' for liberal reform in Russia.[39] By December, there were rumblings in Russia about the war. A 'considerable section' of the Russian public believed that the western allies were not doing their share and had left Russia to 'bear the brunt' of the fighting.[40] Combined with this were rumours of a separate peace. According to one report which reached the Foreign Office:

> the Russian Government is absolutely loyal to the Allies; but there are very powerful influences at work, both among the merchant and banking class and also among the official and military class, in favour of a speedy arrangement with German .... [they argue that] the whole weight of the war—both in

blood and money—has fallen upon Russia, that the Allies in the West are not playing their part, and that England has been very mean about her financial arrangements with Russia.[41]

While Nicolson could write about this report that 'I am not perturbed as to Russia', he did admit that much of the report 'we had heard before'.[42]

Despite Nicolson's optimism, British representatives continued to have misgivings about the internal situation in Russia. In February 1915 Buchanan spoke 'with absolute frankness about the internal situation', in an audience with Nicholas.[43] Concern was compounded by the political unrest which accompanied the Russian military reverses during the spring and summer of 1915.[44] On 10-11 June serious riots broke out in Moscow. The reports of these riots illustrated the continuation of pre-war beliefs among British observers. Buchanan was informed by M. V. Rodzianko, president of the Duma and a prominent liberal, of a suspicion that the riots were 'organized by German agents'.[45] R. H. B. Lockhart, the acting consul in Moscow, advanced the idea that the riots were due to 'strong' feelings against certain reactionary Tsarist ministers, including Maklakov.[46] The combination of German intrigue and reactionary ministers found ready acceptance at the Foreign Office and evoked the usual hopes for reform. George Clerk, the head of the newly-created War Department at the Foreign Office, noted that the riots were 'a healthy symptom, if only the Russian Gov't respond in a spirit of recognition.'[47] The dismissal of Maklakov on 18 June was greeted with approval. Buchanan felt that the 'removal of Maklakoff from office especially if it is followed by that of other unpopular ministers will go far towards allaying public dissent.'[48] Others agreed. Nicolson termed the removal 'fortunate' and hopes generally ran high that increased participation in the Russian government by liberals would result in a more effective Russian war effort.[49]

By August, the ongoing Russian defeats led to further charges of inaction against Britain and France. There were fears at the Foreign Office that Russia might regard Britain as an ally of doubtful value. Lancelot Oliphant, a Persian expert and an influential member of the War Department, minuted that 'some far reaching and effective steps' had to be taken to counteract such a belief.[50] One such was an effort to improve British propaganda in Russia. In addition, Buchanan gave an interview to leading Russian newspapers in mid-August, outlining the British contribution to the allies, while Lord Kitchener, the secretary of state for War, reassured Russian military authorities of British support.[51] Grey also informed Buchanan that the ambassador could make 'discreet use' of military information sent by Kitchener to 'impress on Russian Government that we are ready to do our part without delay.'[52]

In September 1915 there were two events which touched upon British sensitivites about Russia. On 5 September Nicholas assumed supreme command of the army, dismissing the pro-liberal Grand Duke Nicholas. On 16 September Nichols prorogued the Duma. For the British these two events were connected. Two explanations were advanced; both in line with the long-held British beliefs about Russian politics.[53] The first explanation, in Lockhart's words, was that the events of September were inspired by the pro-German element at Court and were designed 'to provoke a revolution and thus make peace.' The second interpretation, again according to Lockhart, was that it was 'a move of reactionaries to gain time and to put off the evil day [of governmental reform] as far as possible.'

There was mixed reaction to these events. Clerk was not convinced that Nicholas' assumption of command was wise. When rumours of the impending change reached the Foreign Office, Clerk noted that 'the Emperor would seem to be taking a big risk as regards H.[is] M.[ajesty]'s own position unless the result is to stem the German advance.'[54] Nicolson shared these sentiments initially, arguing to Hardinge that 'after the war there will have to be great constitutional changes in Russia if serious trouble is to be avoided' and that it would be best if Nicholas's personal prestige could avoid direct identification with any military disasters.[55] A fortnight later, Nicolson changed his mind. The assumption of command by the Emperor, he wrote, was 'by no means a bad idea, though opinions very [sic] widely in respect to it.'[56]

This change probably reflected responses to the prorogation of the Duma, which raised less concern at the Foreign Office than might have been expected given the pre-war sensitivities. This was due to the fact that the war was beginning to take precedence over the affairs of the Duma. While Buchanan reported that prorogation had led to a sympathy strike at the important Putilov munitions works and was 'sure to make a very unfavourable impression on the army', there were other considerations to examine.⁵⁷ On 17 September, Lockhart reported that M. V. Chelnokov, the mayor of Moscow and a man prominent in the liberal attempts to improve the war effort, had accepted the prorogation as a necessary step. Chelnokov, Lockhart reported, felt that some Russian political parties 'had not been able to rid themselves of their old fault of making speeches... without taking into consideration the possibility of putting into practice the measure that was being discussed.'⁵⁸ While Chelnokov thought prorogation was a 'reactionary coup', he rejected any idea that it was a preliminary to a separate peace, a view which no doubt was greeted with relief in London. By the end of September, Buchanan reported that the Duma had taken its dismissal in a patriotic spirit and was focussing its efforts on the war effort, eschewing any attempt to challenge the authority of the government.⁵⁹

What remained significant for the Foreign Office was the composition of the Council of Ministers and the energetic pursuit of the war. Nicolson noted that he had been informed by the Russian ambassador to London that 'the Duma itself w[oul]d not mind being prorogued *if* accompanied by a change in the Ministry.'⁶⁰ Throughout August and September there were hopes that the reactionary Goremykin would be replaced as prime minister by the minister of agriculture, A. M. Krivoshein, generally considered to be a liberal.⁶¹ Chelnokov argued that Goremykin's retention was due to the influence of the Empress and her coterie and the Foreign Office accepted this view, but with a sinister twist. Oliphant noted that Goremykin's staying in power 'looks like the handiwork of Ruspine [Rasputin], and until they both go, there is little hope of improvement'.⁶² Reports at the beginning of October of a weakening in the prime minister's position were greeted with pleasure. 'We can only hope', Oliphant minuted, 'that this forecast may prove correct'.⁶³

Buchanan's ongoing concern about Russia's internal situation and the war effort led the ambassador to request permission from London to ask for an audience to discuss such problems. British attitudes to Russia were evident from the discussions in London of this request.⁶⁴ Grey noted that an audience would be useful as Buchanan could ventilate 'the general internal situation, which is causing us much concern.' Goremykin's position as prime minister was a particular sore spot. Grey realized that the Emperor did not want to have a 'chief adviser forced on him' and would resent any efforts to 'impair his autocratic power', but added that keeping Goremykin in power 'is causing great mischief'. Nicolson was more blunt. The permanent under-secretary argued that, 'as we are allies in war', Buchanan was justified in speaking more plainly on domestic matters 'than would be possible or proper' otherwise. However, when Buchanan reported that he had been advised by Sazonov that the Emperor would resent such advice, Nicolson decided it would be 'imprudent' to offer it.[65]

By the beginning of November 1915, concerns about Russian internal politics were renewed by a false rumour that Sazonov was to be replaced as foreign minister by Goremykin.[66] This was greeted with dismay. Goremykin's 'age and temperament' were, in Oliphant's words, 'in no way suited to the present crisis.' His appointment would only have a 'sinister result'. Clerk put the matter in wider perspective. The head of the War Department stated that he 'look[ed] with grave misgivings on the situation that is developing in Russia' and put forward the opinion that Britain and France could 'not escape speaking very plainly at Petrograd on the delicate subject of Russia's internal affairs'. When it became clear that Sazonov was not to be replaced, the news engendered a mixture of relief and bewilderment. 'It is well nigh impossible to fathom these ministerial intrigues and reports in Russia', Oliphant wrote, 'we can only hope for the best.'[67] His concern was added to on 8 November when Krivoshein resigned. The loss of a prominent liberal minister, Oliphant pointed out, could only be viewed as 'a severe loss to the Allied cause'.[68] Nicolson's comment was similar. Krivoshein's fall was, the permanent under-secretary opined, 'not encouraging from the point of view of Russia's internal situation'. Only a report that A. A. Khvostov, the new minister of the interior, was more liberal than earlier thought, gave any cheer to those who read the auguries of Russian politics in the autumn of 1915.[69]

By the end of 1915 and the beginning of 1916 it was becoming clear that British hopes for internal reforms in Russia were unlikely to be realized. Lockhart's despatch of mid-December put the matter clearly. 'The gulf which divides the Government from the intellectual classes', the British consul wrote, 'seems wider than ever'.[70] The reactionary policies followed by the Emperor and his closest advisors had alienated the liberals with the consequence that the latter 'rely more than ever on the English and the French'. Faced with their own political impotence, Russian liberals pinned their hopes on the allies 'bring[ing] some influence to bear' on the Russian government concerning the internal situation. Such thinking was naive. The recovery of the Russian war effort was essential if the losses of 1915 were not to be repeated. This was not the time to raise the nettlesome issue of internal reform. An anonymous note on Lockhart's despatch made the point clear: 'we are', it said, 'as helpless as the Russian Liberals.'

This new phase in relations was evident by the end of January 1916. In his report on the situation in Moscow during the last six months of 1915, Lockhart wrote that the Russian government was more firmly in control than before. 'In this connection', he went on, 'it seems clear that the Russian Government puts itself and the interior question before everything else.'[71] While 'intellectual Russia... is in revolt against the Government... the peasantry are practically unaffected by the unrest which prevails in the large towns'. As a consequence of these observations, Lockhart concluded that 'it is with considerable confidence that one can say to-day that internal trouble of any serious nature during war-time is most unlikely, providing always that Russia suffers no further [military] disasters.'

Lockhart struck a pessimistic note about the future. 'It would be a great mistake', he opined, 'to presume the death of bureaucracy and the success of the Liberal movement as a foregone conclusion.' For the most part, Buchanan shared the views of his junior colleague. He also thought that political reaction was the order of the day in Russia. Nicholas II, Buchanan wrote, was attempting to combine 'efficiency in administration and support of autocratic rights' by means of his appointments in the government.[72] He departed, however, from Lockhart's assessment in that the ambassador believed that Nicholas put victory ahead of the internal situation, citing the events of the summer of 1915 as evidence. Buchanan's conclusion was a masterpiece of *realpolitik* which would have sent shivers down the spines of those Russian liberals who looked to Britain for political support against the autocracy. While the Emperor had missed a 'unique opportunity' for reform, Buchanan stated, 'the internal situation, unsatisfactory as it is, is not likely... to prejudice the course of the military operations.... [and] the question of efficiency is the only one that concerns us directly as Russia's ally'.

This did not mean that the long-standing British views of Russia were abandoned completely. Buchanan spoke frankly of British concerns about the internal situation during an audience with the Emperor early in February 1916. He made particular note that, in the post-war, British investment might be wary of coming to a country 'in which Revolution might break out at any moment.'[73] And changes of ministers still brought predictable remarks. A few days after his audience, Buchanan was able to report with satisfaction the dismissal of Goremykin and his replacement by B. V. Sturmer.[74] The remark of F. O. Lindley, the first secretary at Petrograd, on this event proved to be more prescient than Buchanan's satisfaction. 'The new Prime Minister', Lindley wrote, 'is better than the old, that is all one can say in his favour and it is not much.'[75] Having given up on the possibility of wide-ranging reform, Buchanan's hopes for Russia were more modest but still in line with pre-war beliefs. What the country really required, Buchanan informed the Foreign Office, was 'a man of the type of Peter the Great to stamp out the corruption and inefficiency which permeates the administrative machinery of this country'.[76] This being unlikely, the ambassador was willing to settle for 'the appointment of competent and liberal minded ministers' and an extension of the powers of the liberal-dominated public organizations which 'alone [had] given proof of efficiency and administrative capacity during the war'.

The position of the public organizations was a difficult one. Originally conceived to aid with the war effort, bodies like the Union of Towns, the Union of Zemstvos, and the War Industries Committees (WIC) had become suspect in the eyes of the autocracy.[77] The Emperor and his advisors thought that such extra-governmental agencies had become a threat to the existing ruling structure and treated them accordingly. The British were quite aware of this. In a summary of events sent to the Foreign Office in mid-April 1916, Lindley noted that A. I. Guchkov, founder of the Octobrist party and head of the WIC, had achieved 'remarkable' influence with working men.[78] 'Up to now', Lindley reported, 'he has always exercised that influence with the sole object of supplying the Army, but after the war it is thought by some that M. Guchkov may attempt to use the instrument which he controls for securing great political changes.' Cooperation with Guchkov was fatal to the reputation of Tsarist ministers. A. A. Polivanov, since 1915 the minister of war and a man of acknowledged ability, was dismissed from his post at the end of March 1916. His fault in the eyes of the Emperor was that he was *'trop parlementaire'* and Nicholas wanted a man 'he could trust to work in less close co-operation with non-official organisations'.[79]

Despite the natural sympathy of the British with the public organizations, there was doubt as to their efficacy in solving Russia's munitions problems. The military attaché, Colonel A. F. W. Knox, felt that the WIC had 'done little but talk' and that excessive funds had been chanelled 'wastefully' into small concerns.[80] Such a view was shared by French observers. In fact, as Buchanan pointed out in mid-June 1916, matters concerning the public organizations in general and the WIC in particular had become almost exclusively political: 'To support them is Liberal and to condemn them is reactionary.'[81] In the circumstances of the Great War, British support tended more and more to be on the side of efficiency and an improved war effort.

This had a natural effect on attitudes towards Russian politics. By the summer of 1916, with Russian armies generally victorious, the moderate Russian liberals seemed to have lost the chance of effecting reform which had seemed so likely a year earlier. The political setback which the Emperor had dealt them in September 1915 had led to what one historian has called 'a profound crisis of confidence'.[82] The Tsarist government made every effort to ensure that the 'crisis' was permanent. Lockhart's despatches from Moscow made the political counter-offensive of the government plain. After seeing a report compiled by the Russian director of police, General E. K. Klimovich, in which the public organizations were labelled 'highly dangerous and revolutionary organisations', Lockhart wrote two perceptive analyses of the situation.[83] In the second, dated 5 August 1916, Lockhart demonstrated just how far away from a complete acceptance of the liberal view of Russia he had moved:

> From the point of view of a bureaucrat, the report seems to me to be not unfair. The report, however, *does* show how difficult is the prospect of any compromise between the two parties in Russia. It also illustrates the difficulty of the Emperor's position, and throws some light, perhaps, on the reactionary constitution of the present Cabinet.
>
> At the present moment further comment is perhaps unnecessary. It is interesting to note, however, that the Government at any rate is well informed regarding the possible danger from

a movement which presents a new feature in Russian history. It is also interesting to note that this new movement, which is perhaps a far more powerful menace to the autocracy than the Duma, has its centre in Moscow.

Such reportage was a bitter pill in London. The minute which Harold Nicolson, the son of the permanent under-secretary and a junior member of the War Department, added to Lockhart's first despatch undoubtedly summed up the feeling at the Foreign Office towards such a political situation in Russia: 'This is all very depressing, hopeless.'

The final blow to liberal Russia for the Foreign Office was the dismissal of S.D. Sazonov as foreign minister in July 1916. Sazonov had been the hand-picked successor of Izvolsky when the latter left office in 1910 and was considered a firm supporter of Britain and the entente.[84] A further point in his favour was that, in Lockhart's words, he 'sought to work with the Duma and was trusted by the public organisations'.[85] To make matters worse, Sazonov was succeeded by Sturmer, a man whose reactionary nature was now evident to the British. To Oliphant, Sazonov's dismissal was just another example of the 'short sighted' policies of the 'reactionaries' in Russia.[86] Sazonov's departure, he argued, would lead to a further deterioration in the internal situation to the detriment of Russia's foreign policy.

From mid-1916 to the outbreak of the March revolution, British reports about Russia's internal affairs were generally gloomy. This was in marked contrast to their generally favourable assessment of the war effort and general attitudes towards the war. In November, Buchanan was able to report that the Emperor had assured him that a separate peace with Germany was out of the quesiton, and by the beginning of 1917 Russia had seemingly recovered from the shortages of munitions which had plagued her earlier in the war.[87] But not even the fall of Sturmer, 'a man whom I utterly despise', Buchanan informed Hardinge, was sufficient to end the gloom over Russian politics.[88] When the Duma sat in mid-November the Russian liberals were determined to reassert themselves against the government. P.N. Miliukov, the leader of the Cadet party, opened the session with his famous 'stupidity or treason' speech, castigating the government for its handling of the war. In a long letter to Grey, Buchanan described the political paralysis which resulted, as the parties of the extreme left and right turned to disruptive and obstructive tactics to express their views.[89]

By the beginning of 1917, it was clear to the British that the position of the Emperor and his government was uncertain. On 29 December 1916, Buchanan sent a despatch stating that 'there is no doubt' that within the Russian army 'the feeling has been steadily turning against the Imperial Family'.[90] A certain fatalistic attitude coloured British reports on Russia early in 1917. Reporting on the political events of the preceding month, Lindley put the views of the Embassy pointedly:

> I never hear anyone say a good word either for the Emperor or Empress, and their assassination is quite openly discussed by persons in responsible positions.... Nevertheless, it seems quite possible nothing will happen. There is no revolutionary organization in existence; the Grand Dukes are unlikely to assassinate anyone else themselves.... The army remains and, so long as the war lasts, it is to be hoped it will be too busy to be able to take an active part in politics.[91]

The British despondency was shared by many prominent Russians. Such feelings were magnified in January 1917 when Nicholas announced a major change in his cabinet. General A. A. Manikovskii, the head of the artillery department at the Russian war office, told Knox in despair that it was to be hoped that 'beloved Ally England would help Russia to settle her internal affairs'.[92] The British no longer believed that such intervention would have much effect, although Buchanan put his fears for the internal situation directly to the Emperor during an audience in January.

The British mission which came to Petrograd in late January 1917 was quick to pick up the political undertones in Russia. George Clerk, who accompanied the mission for the Foreign Office, had typical views. 'As a first impression', he wrote on 30 January, 'I think these people moved perhaps by an impulse they scarcely understand, and the army mean to go through with, and win, the war.... But what will happen politically, God knows'.[93] Clerk went on to deprecate 'the pathetic belief in the wonderful effect of plain speaking by the Allied mission'. Such action would be 'too late' and even Buchanan, while the ambassador 'undoubtedly has a great position here' was unable to 'shift the Emperor'. The optimism which Clerk expressed about the continuation of the war and the pessimism which he expressed about the political scene was echoed by Buchanan. Early in February, the ambassador reported to Hardinge that 'it is very difficult to say anything positive about the present internal situation', but added that there was no revolutionary organization capable of achieving much, 'unless it exists in the army', with the consequence that 'the day of reckoning is likely to be postponed till after the war.'[94]

While the British representatives in Russia were surprised by the timing of the March revolution, it is clear that such an occurrence was not unexpected. Lindley wrote to Clerk a week after the revolution and the former expressed hope that those at the Foreign Office would not consider the Embassy 'very blind' not to have foretold the end of the Romanovs more accurately.[95] Clerk's minute on this letter made it clear that the Foreign Office put the responsibility for the revolution on the 'folly and obstinacy' of the Tsarist regime and did not blame Buchanan and his subordinates for not predicting the actual date accurately. 'The real organizers', Clerk concluded, 'were waiting for the war to finish before starting a revolution, but the way they took hold of the situation when it arose deserves high praise.'

The composition of the Provisional Government should have found high praise at the Foreign Office. Its cast of ministers read like a list of the flower of Russian liberalism: those very elements which the British had long favoured. Nonetheless, concern about the economic chaos and disorganization which accompanied the revolution, and their effect upon the war effort tended to overshadow the pleasure which was due to the accession of a liberal government. General William Robertson, the chief of the Imperial General Staff, put such a view clearly, when he wrote of a revolution that 'the only thing one can hope for it is that it will not greatly affect the war'.[96] There is little doubt that such concern was shared at the Foreign Office. Buchanan was unable to obtain consistent views about the prosecution of the war from members of the Provisional Government, causing Oliphant to minute unhappily, 'it is impossible to form any opinion as to the future course of events in view of such contradictory opinions held by members of the same govt.'[97]

The Foreign Office was also very much concerned about the divergence of political allegiances and views within the revolutionary movement. On 23 March Lockhart pointed out that there were elements within the socialist camp in Russia which were 'at heart anti-war' and noted that if they were to become predominant this would pose a 'serious danger' to the war effort.[98] The way in which the new government came to power led to the fear that it would be replaced by a less stable and reliable regime, and this led to a curious ambivalence towards the Provisional Government. Knox's despatch dealing with the revolution expressed this feeling clearly:

> If the present cabinet had been appointed by the ex-Emperor of his own free will or under joint pressure of the Allies, the change from the old regime would have been all in favour of the more energetic prosecution of the war. The new Government has more brains, honesty and breadth of view than the old. It has the confidence of the vast majority of the Russian people and it is sound on the war.[99]

The key word in Knox's despatch was 'if'. The military attaché went on to point out his fear that extremist elements which favoured a separate peace might gain the upper hand. He concluded with atypical uncertainty: 'it is difficult to estimate the result which this upheaval will have on the conduct of the war.'

The inability of the Provisional Government to deal simultaneously with its political opposition and the war led to its being regarded with less enthusiasm than its liberal makeup would have suggested. When Buchanan reported that Miliukov, now the foreign minister in the new regime, had stated that the government 'was afraid apparently' of taking action against socialist anti-war propaganda, Oliphant minuted that 'this shows the impotence of the Govt. *vis à vis* of the Socialists, even more clearly than usual'.[100] As reports of a decline in the fighting capacity of the Russian army grew, so, too, did the British disillusionment with the Provisional Government. Buchanan wrote to Hardinge on 7 May, and the ambassador's dejection was evident: 'I try not to be too pessimistic about the military and naval outlook, but it is very difficult not to be so when one reads the reports of our officers.'[101] It was still difficult to find the Provisional Government speaking with one voice, and this led to confusion at the Foreign Office. Buchanan received conflicting reports daily, causing Oliphant to note on one telegram, 'with various Ministers each telling a different story to the Ambr. it is impossible to form an opinion except that the position is parlous.'[102]

The reorganization of the Provisional Government in mid-May, with a larger representation from the left, did not improve British opinions. While Buchanan felt on 15 June that with respect to the Russian army 'the outlook is more hopeful', it was equally clear that large elements in Russia 'are at heart bent on stopping the war as soon as possible and on almost any terms.'[103] An American traveller lately returned from Russia told the Foreign Office that Russia must be considered of 'no use' during the war, and this view was generally shared at the Foreign Office in late June.[104] As Oliphant noted on the American's report, it 'may be somewhat highly coloured in parts: but the general situation strikes me as accurately described'. Hardinge looked for silver linings, but was not sanguine: 'I hope he is unduly pessimistic. It is worth reading.'

The failure of the Russian July offensive ended any optimism which still existed about possible Russian military achievements in 1917. Despite this, a brief ray of hope flickered at the Foreign Office when the Provisional Government moved energetically to suppress the civic unrest of 17–19 July — the so-called 'July days'. It was widely believed that the disorder had been orchestrated by German agents, and Buchanan saw in the actions of the government a hopeful step backwards in the slow slide towards peace. 'I take', he wrote to Hardinge on 23 July, 'a more hopeful view of the situation as a whole than I have for some time past.'[105]

The hope of the Foreign Office now rested upon the head of the new leader of the Provisional Government, A. F. Kerensky, and the hope that he would reintroduce discipline into the army. The appointment of General L. G. Kornilov, a noted disciplinarian, as commander in chief at the beginning of August was viewed as a positive step, but by the end of the month it was evident that Kornilov was not to be given sufficient authority to restore the army. Only Buchanan managed to maintain a semblance of optimism. On 15 August, he wrote to Hardinge that while 'I cannot look upon the situation as satisfactory.... I still believe that Russia will pull through, though the obstacles in her path... are appalling'.[106] By the end of the month opinion at the Foreign Office was unanimous that Kerensky had 'played his part' and the possibility of a coup against him was anticipated with little regret.[107]

However, when such an attempt was made by Kornilov in September and resulted only in failure, the darkest gloom was everywhere at the Foreign Office. Although Buchanan could write in the immediate aftermath of the abortive coup that 'desperate as is the situation I do not abandon all hope', his was a voice in the wilderness.[108] Oliphant noted on this report that 'the future could not look worse than it does', and Ronald Graham, Hardinge's protegé and hoped-for successor, added that 'the only hopeful sign is the partial elimination of the extremist elements in the new Govt.' The events of October did not provide any cheer for those who hoped for an improved political situation. Buchanan was showered with reports of the threat which the Bolsheviks posed for Kerensky's government, shaking even the ambassador's perennial optimism.[109]

October saw a recrudescence of the Foreign Office's long-term belief in German influence in Russia. On the 23rd, Hardinge sent a message to Buchanan marked 'this must go in our most secret cypher', enquiring as to whether the ambassador felt Kerensky was a German agent.[110] While Buchanan replied that 'I do not believe there is a word of truth in these rumours', his rebuttal revived assumptions at the Foreign Office about the corruption of Russian politicians. The ambassador, while exonerating Kerensky, added that some Bolsheviks were German agents and that it might be worthwhile to bribe them. This proposal met with interest from Hardinge, but before the mechanics of such an idea could be investigated the Bolshevik revolution changed the situation irremediably.

The response of the Foreign Office to the Bolshevik takeover was predictable. It was hoped that their advent to power would be brief and that a way could be found to maintain a war effort in the interim.[111] By the beginning of December it was evident that the intention of the Bolsheviks to sign a separate peace with Germany was to be the determining factor in British policy. Any individual or group, even the 'old officers and upper classes who, thoroughly discredited under the old regime, have learned nothing and dream of a return to the old order', was to be supported provided it promised to maintain the eastern front.[112] The Foreign Office's dream of liberal Russia was dead.

Between 1907 and 1917 a small group of men at the Foreign Office, and the British representatives in Russia, built up a picture of that country which had two great flaws. This was not due to being misinformed about Russia. The British representatives in Russia had a remarkable grasp of the twists and turns of the political scene in that country. The accounts by Buchanan, Knox, and Lockhart for the period of the war square nicely with recent western and Soviet accounts of the same events.[113] The flaws resulted instead from the interpretations made of the reports from Russia and, too, from what was not reported from Russia.

The first flaw concerned the position and strength of the Russian liberal movement. There is little doubt that the British saw this movement and the men in it as the hope and future of Russia. As a consequence of such a belief, the British tended to overestimate both the actual and potential political significance of the Russian liberals, as well as their competence. Conversely they underestimated the reactionaries. The second flaw concerned the Emperor Nicholas II. The British quite correctly divined that he was an essential element in determination of Russian policy. They also were correct in their assumption that his loyalty to the entente with Britain was firm. Where they erred was in their assumption that the Emperor was in any way interested in or committed to a policy of reform which would favour the liberal elements in Russian politics. Not until late 1915 did it begin to penetrate British thinking that the Emperor and not merely those around him was a thoroughgoing reactionary, opposed to any schemes which would reduce his autocratic prerogatives.

There are several explanations for these misperceptions. The first stems from the diplomatic and military situation which prevailed around the turn of the century. The rise of a powerful Germany altered the balance of power on the Continent and made the British aware that they lacked the resources to take care of both their imperial and possible continental responsibilities. As a result, the Anglo-Japanese alliance was signed in 1902, followed by the creation of the Anglo-French entente two years later. The Anglo-Russian Convention can be seen as part of this trend; an attempt to reduce the possible areas of contention with Russia in order that the more immediate threat of a Germany bound upon European hegemony could be dealt with. While some have argued that the British leaning towards France and Russia prior to 1914 had little to do with the balance of power and 'a screen erected to conceal Britain's imperial vulnerability', this does not detract from the fact that some arrangement with Russia was essential to Grey's foreign policy.[114]

The need for a Russian alliance led to wishful thinking on the part of those at the Foreign Office. Liberal Russia solved several problems for the elite. First, Russian liberals favoured an alignment of Russian foreign policy with Britain and France; not with Germany. Second, the Russian liberal movement was the only political aspect of Russia which had widespread public acceptance in England and, more importantly, support within the Radical element of the British Liberal party. While, as Keith Robbins has noted, 'Grey was not immune from a general tendency among politicians to believe that public opinion corresponded with their own inclinations', it is clear that at the very least, a liberal ascendency in Russia, a lively Duma, and promises of governmental reform all would have made a closer alliance with Russia more acceptable in Britain.[115]

Another explanation for the elite's belief in liberal Russia lies in cultural chauvinism. Since Britain had moved towards constitutional government, it seems to have been assumed that such a trend was a universal one. This belief flew in the face of the Emperor's unwillingness to permit reform, an attitude which became evident to Russian liberals before it did to the British decision makers.[116] By the time that the British were convinced that Nicholas II intended to maintain his autocratic position at all costs, they were more concerned about Russia's war effort than political change.

A further reason for the British misperception of Russia lay in the sources of information which they had. The Russian liberals tended to be a cosmopolitan group, well versed in western European languages and steeped in western political thought. For these reasons alone, the British representatives in Russia found them a congenial lot. Lockhart, for example, was firmly enmeshed in the social life of Moscow's liberal elite.[117] Buchanan's circle of friends was similarly circumscribed, although the ambassador enjoyed good relations with the Emperor as well. Lacking personal relationships with the reactionary elements of official Russia, British officials tended to view Russia through the eyes of their liberal Russian friends. And while these friends were well informed, their ideological biases coloured their view of events. Although the elite always attempted to take a dispassionate view of Russia, the fact that they shared the political views of, and sympathized with, the Russian liberals meant that they gave more weight to liberal views than was justified.

British attitudes to Russia allow some remarks about whether or not the Anglo-Russian convention was signed due to a fear of Russia. Keith Wilson has advanced the theory that Eyre Crowe and Arthur Nicolson's preference for a Russian understanding was a product of Russophobia, rather than any Russophilia.[118] While it is evident that Britain certainly feared a Russian thrust in central Asia, there is little evidence that this generated any Russophobia among the elite. There seems to have been no thought that the interests of Britain and Russia were fundamentally inimicable, nor was there, as there was in the case of Germany, a belief that Russia was irrevocably committed to an anti-British policy. The major fear of Russia that did exist was that 'reactionary' Russia would gain the upper hand and promote an alliance with Germany. If there was any Russophobia in Nicolson and Crowe, it was directed not at Russia as such, but merely towards those Russians who favoured Germany. To take this a step further in the fashion of Wilson who sees Russophobia as triggering the appearance of Russophilia at the Foreign Office, it seems likely that any semblance of Russophobia was the product of Germanophobia.

The way in which Russia was regarded by the British in the period from 1907 to 1917 suggests some thoughts about historical continuity. Modern analysis of the Soviet Union has some intriguing parallels with the earlier British experience. Many Soviet specialists, 'Kremlinologists' as they are referred to, spend much time searching through appointment lists to Communist Party posts looking for the emergence of 'soft' and 'hard' line policies as reflected by the changes of personnel. The British fascination with the appointments of 'liberals' and 'reactionaries' shared with the Kremlinologists a belief that personalities are more important than ideology, a projection of the Western concept of a pluralistic society into one that is and was not. Similarly, the recent theory that the needs of a modern state will require a 'convergence' of Soviet and Western systems, seems no more than a restatement of the British belief of the inevitable emergence of a Russian liberal state. The events of 1907 to 1917 showed that the British assumptions were wishful thinking; the events of the future will show whether or not history repeats itself.

Acknowledgements

I wish to thank my colleague A. H. Ion and J. Neilson for their comments on an earlier version of this paper.

NOTES

1. I use the term 'taste' in the sense discussed by C. J. Lowe, *The Reluctant Imperialists*, 2 vols. (London, 1967), Vol. I, pp. 1–2.
2. J. Joll, *1914 The Unspoken Assumptions* (London, 1967).
3. Z. Steiner, *Britain and the Origins of the First World War* (London, 1977), pp. 128–214.
4. The concept of a foreign policy making elite is from D. C. Watt's seminal essay, 'The Nature of the Foreign-Policy-Making Elite in Britain', in D. C. Watt, *Personalities and Policies* (London, 1965), pp. 1–15, although I circumscribe the composition of the elite much tighter than does Watt.
5. The best introduction to the Convention is B. Williams, 'Great Britain and Russia, 1905 to the 1907 Convention', in F. H. Hinsley, ed., *British Foreign Policy Under Sir Edward Grey* (Cambridge, 1977), pp. 133–47.
6. J. H. Gleason, *The Genesis of Russophobia in Great Britain* (Cambridge Mass., 1950).
7. G. P. Gooch and H. W. V. Temperley, eds., *British Documents on the Origins of the War, 1898–1914*, 11 vols. in 13 (London, 1926–38), Vol. IV, doc. 550, Grey to Nicolson, 24 February 1908. (Hereafter cited as *B.D.*)
8. *B.D.*, Vol. V, doc. 194, Hardinge to Nicolson, private, 13 April 1908.
9. Grey to Nicolson, 8 June 1909, as cited in D. McLean, 'English Radicals, Russia and the Fate of Persia 1907–1913', *English Historical Review*, 93, 367(1978), 348.
10. *B.D.*, Vol. V, doc. 860, Hardinge to Nicolson, private, 10 May 1909.
11. *B.D.*, Vol. X, pt. 2, doc. 540, Nicolson to de Bunsen (British ambassador to Vienna), private, 27 April 1914.
12. Z. Steiner, 'The Foreign Office under Sir Edward Grey, 1905–1914', in Hinsley, ed., *Grey*, p. 24.
13. *B.D.*, Vol. V, appendix III, 'Memorandum by Sir Charles Hardinge on the Possibility of War', April 1909.
14. *B.D.*, Vol. IX pt. 1, doc. 115, Nicolson to Hardinge, 23 February 1910. I have made no effort to standardize the transliteration of proper Russian names found in direct quotations. In the text I have used a modified form of the Library of Congress system.
15. Ibid., doc. 187, O'Beirne to Grey, 5 October 1910.
16. *B.D.*, Vol. IV, doc. 243, 'Annual Report from Russia for 1906', 2 January 1907.
17. *B.D.*, Vol. IX, pt. 1, doc. 115, Nicolson to Hardinge, 23 February 1910.
18. Ibid., doc. 583, O'Beirne to Grey, 5 July 1912.
19. *B.D.*, Vol. V, doc. 834, Hardinge to Nicolson, private, 12 April 1909.
20. For Nicolson's view of Goremykin, see H. G. Nicolson, *Sir Arthur Nicolson Bart. First Lord Carnock. A Study in the Old Diplomacy* (London, 1930), p. 211.

21. *B.D.*, Vol. V, appendix III, 'Memorandum by Sir Charles Hardinge on the Possibility of War', April 1909.
22. *B.D.*, Vol. X, pt. 2, doc. 536, Buchanan to Grey, 31 March 1914.
23. Ibid., doc. 528, Buchanan to Grey, 18 March 1914.
24. *B.D.*, Vol. V, doc. 835, Nicolson to Grey, 14 April 1909.
25. *B.D.*, Vol. X, pt. 1, doc. 637, Nicolson to Buchanan, private, 3 January 1911.
26. See J. A. Spender, *The Life of the Right Hon. Sir Henry Campbell-Bannerman*, 2 vols. (London, 1923), Vol. II, pp. 260–64, for the Duma incident.
27. *B.D.*, Vol. IX, pt. 1, doc. 13, Nicolson to Hardinge, private, 6 June 1909.
28. *B.D.*, Vol. V, doc. 865, O'Beirne to Grey, 7 August 1909.
29. Ibid.
30. *B.D.*, Vol. IX, pt. 2, doc. 303, Buchanan to Nicolson, private, 28 December 1912. On Buchanan's appointment, see Goschen diary entry, 9 July 1910, in C. H. D. Howard, ed., *The Diary of Edward Goschen 1900–1914* (London, 1980), pp. 207–8.
31. *B.D.*, Vol. X, pt. 2, doc. 536, Buchanan to Grey, 31 March 1914.
32. Ibid., doc. 540, Nicolson to de Bunsen, private, 27 April 1914.
33. *B.D.*, Vol. XI, doc. 101, Nicolson's minute on Buchanan to Grey, 24 July 1914.
34. Ibid., doc. 318, Crowe's minute on Bertie (British ambassador at Paris) to Grey, 30 July 1914.
35. Ibid., doc. 665, Buchanan to Nicolson, private, 3 August 1914.
36. *B.D.*, Vol. IX, pt. 2, doc. 303, Buchanan to Nicolson, private, 28 December 1912.
37. See the discussion in K. Neilson, '"Joy Rides"?: British Intelligence and Propaganda in Russia, 1914–1917', *Historical Journal*, 24, 4(1981): 890–92.
38. H. W. Koch, 'Das Britische Russlandbild im Spiegel Der Britischen Propaganda 1914–1918', *Zeitschrift für Politik*, 27, 1 (1980): 71–96.
39. F.O. (Foreign Office Archives, Public Record Office, London), 800/375, Buchanan to Nicolson, 13 September 1914, Nicolson papers.
40. F.O. 371/2095/78627, Buchanan to Grey, private and secret, 4 December 1914.
41. Balfour papers (British Library), ADD MSS 49748, Vol. LXVI, Balfour to Nicolson, 21 December 1914.
42. Ibid., Nicolson to Balfour, 24 December 1914.
43. F.O. 800/75, Buchanan to Drummond (Asquith's private secretary), 3 February 1915, Grey papers.
44. The political events of 1915 can be found in R. Pearson, *The Russian Moderates and the Crisis of Tsarism* (London, 1977), pp. 39–64.
45. F.O. 371/2452/77011, Buchanan to F.O., 12 June 1915.
46. F.O. 371/2452/77065, Buchanan to F.O., 13 June 1915.
47. Ibid., Clerk's minute, 14 June 1915.
48. F.O. 371/2452/80972, Buchanan to F.O., 19 June 1915.
49. Ibid., Nicolson's minute, 21 June 1915.
50. F.O. 371/2454/106237, Oliphant's minute, 4 August 1915, on Buchanan to F.O., 3 August 1915.
51. F.O. 371/2456/121797, Buchanan to F.O., 17 August 1915.
52. F.O. 371/2450/116873, F.O. to Buchanan, 20 August 1915.

53. Lockhart diary entry, 16 September 1915, as cited in K. Young, ed., *The Diaries of Sir Robert Bruce Lockhart* (New York, 1973), pp. 24-25.
54. F.O. 371/2455/119748, Clerk's minute, 26 August 1915, on Buchanan to F.O., 25 August 1915.
55. F.O. 800/379, Nicolson to Hardinge, 1 September 1915, Nicolson papers.
56. Ibid., Nicolson to Hardinge, 15 September 1915.
57. F.O. 371/2454/133004, Buchanan to F.O., 16 September 1915.
58. F.O. 371/2455/149853, Lockhart's despatch 44, 17 September 1915.
59. F.O. 371/2455/143056, Buchanan's despatch 144, 24 September 1915.
60. F.O. 371/2454/133004, Nicolson's minute, 17 September 1915, on Buchanan to F.O., 16 September 1915, original emphasis.
61. See F.O. 371/2455/119748, Clerk's minute, 26 August 1915, on Buchanan to F.O., 25 August 1915; F.O. 371/2455/149853, Lockhart's despatch 44, 17 September 1915.
62. F.O. 371/2454/140516, Buchanan to F.O., 28 September 1915; and Oliphant's minute, 29 September 1915.
63. F.O. 371/2454/141732, Oliphant's minute, 1 October 1915, on Buchanan to F.O., 1 October 1915.
64. F.O. 800/75, Grey to Buchanan, private and secret, 15 October 1915, Grey papers; ibid., Nicolson to Grey, 18 October 1915.
65. Ibid. Buchanan to Grey, private and secret, 19 October 1915 and Nicolson to Drummond, 20 October 1915.
66. F.O. 371/2457/161488, minutes by Clerk and Oliphant, both 1 November 1915 on Buchanan to F.O., 31 October 1915.
67. F.O. 371/2457/163880, Oliphant's minute, 4 November 1915, on Buchanan to F.O., 3 November 1915.
68. F.O. 371/2457/167888, minutes by Oliphant and Nicolson, both 10 November 1915, on Buchanan to F.O., 9 November 1915.
69. See F.O. 371/2457/179991, Lockhart's despatch 65, 29 October 1915 and minutes.
70. F.O. 371/2745/5724, Lockhart's despatch 77, 15 December 1915 and minutes.
71. F.O. 371/2745/25836, Lockhart's despatch 2, 22 January 1916.
72. Ibid., Buchanan's despatch 19, 28 January 1916.
73. F.O. 371/2743/22897, Buchanan to Nicolson, personal, 4 February 1916.
74. F.O. 800/75, Buchanan to Grey, 8 February 1916, Grey papers.
75. Ibid., Lindley to Drummond, 15 February 1916.
76. Ibid., Buchanan to Grey, 8 February 1916.
77. For positive views of the public organizations, see P. P. Gronsky and N. J. Astrov, *The War and the Russian Government* (New Haven, 1929), pp. 171-97 and S. O. Zagorsky, *State Control of Industry in Russia during the War* (New Haven, 1928), pp. 97-106. Critical views of them focussing on their political involvement and inefficiency are T. Fellows, 'Politics and the War Effort in Russia: The Union of Zemstvos and the Organization of Food Supplies', *Slavic Review*, 37, 1 (1978): 70-90; L. H. Siegelbaum, 'Moscow Industrialists and the War-Industries Committees During World War I', *Russian History*, 5, 1(1978): 64-83, and T. D. Krupina, 'Politicheskii krizis 1915 g. i

sozdanie osobogo sobeshchaniia po oborone', *Istoricheskie zapiski*, 83 (1969): 58-75.
78. F.O. 371/2745/77191, Lindley's summary in Buchanan's despatch 78, 13 April 1916.
79. W.O. (War Office Series, Public Records Office, London), 106/1076, Knox's despatch L 2, 30 April 1916.
80. Ibid.
81. F.O. 371/2745/122244, Buchanan's despatch 138, 15 June 1916.
82. Pearson, *Russian Moderates*, p. 98.
83. F.O. 371/2745/148198 and 174254, Lockhart's despatches 33 and 38, 11 July and 5 August 1916 and minutes.
84. See, for example, *B.D.*, Vol. IX. pt. 1, doc. 107, Nicolson to Grey, 9 February 1910.
85. R. H. B. Lockhart, *British Agent* (New York, 1933), p. 153.
86. F.O. 371/2750/144394, Oliphant's minute, 23 July 1916, on Buchanan to F.O., 20 July 1916.
87. F.O. 371/2752/224528, Buchanan to F.O., 6 November 1916. On Russia's improved military and munitions situation, see N. Stone, *The Eastern Front 1914-1917* (London, 1975), p. 282.
88. Hardinge papers (University Library, Cambridge), Buchanan to Hardinge, 5 December 1916, p. 28.
89. For the background, see Pearson, *Russian Moderates*, pp. 99-123. On the political paralysis, see CAB (Cabinet Papers, Public Records Office, London), 1/21/33, Buchanan to Grey, 5 December 1916.
90. F.O. 371/2995/9759, Buchanan's despatch 279, 29 December 1916.
91. F.O. 371/2995/23644, Lindley's summary in Buchanan's despatch 15, 18 January 1917.
92. F.O. 371/3004/16785, Buchanan to F.O., 21 January 1917.
93. F.O. 800/383, Clerk to T. Russell (Balfour's diplomatic secretary), 30 January 1917.
94. Hardinge papers, 29, Buchanan to Hardinge, 8 February 1917.
95. F.O. 371/2996/72662, Lindley to Clerk, 20 March 1917 and Clerk's minute of 7 April 1917.
96. Robertson-Murray correspondence, (British Museum), ADD MSS 52462, Robertson to Murray (British commander Egypt), 14 March 1917.
97. F.O. 371/2995/58125, Oliphant's minute, 20 March 1917, on Buchanan to F.O., 19 March 1917.
98. F.O. 371/2996/74117, Lockhart's despatch 36, 23 March 1917.
99. W.O. 106/1090, Knox's despatch Z 2, 31 March 1917.
100. F.O. 371/2996/73018, Oliphant's undated minute on Buchanan to F.O., 8 April 1917.
101. Hardinge papers, 32, Buchanan to Hardinge, 7 May 1917.
102. F.O. 371/3011/93586, Oliphant's minute, 9 May 1917, on Buchanan to F.O., 8 May 1917.
103. Hardinge papers, 33, Buchanan to Hardinge, 15 June 1917.
104. See F.O. 371/2996/124895, the account dated 21 June 1917 and the minutes of Oliphant and Hardinge.

105. Hardinge papers, 33, Buchanan to Hardinge, 23 July 1917.
106. Hardinge papers, 34, Buchanan to Hardinge, 15 August 1917.
107. See F.O. 371/2998/170957, the minutes of Clerk (1 September) and Hardinge (undated) on Buchanan to F.O., 30 August 1917. Concerning a coup, see F.O. 371/3015/174458, Hardinge's undated minute on Buchanan to F.O., 5 September 1917.
108. F.O. 371/2999/178508, Buchanan to F.O., 12 September 1917 and undated minutes by Oliphant and Graham.
109. See W.O. 106/5128, Knox to Buckley (M.I. 3), 15 October 1917.
110. F.O. 371/2999/201697A, F.O. to Buchanan, 23 October 1917; and Buchanan to Hardinge, personal and secret, 25 October 1917.
111. See F.O. 371/2999/221684, the minutes on Buchanan to F.O., 19 November 1917; F.O. 371/2999/224855, minutes.
112. Lloyd George papers (House of Lords Records Office), F/59/1/27, Lindley to Balfour, personal and confidential, 6 December 1917.
113. Compare with Pearson, *Russian Moderates,* and the best Soviet account, V. S. Diakin, *Russkaia burzhuazia i tsarism v gody pervoi mirovoi voiny* (Leningrad, 1967).
114. K. Wilson, 'British Power in the European Balance, 1906–14', in D. Dilks, ed., *Retreat from Power,* 2 vols. (London, 1981), Vol. I, pp. 40–41.
115. K. Robbins, 'Public opinion, the press and pressure groups', in Hinsley, ed., *Grey,* p. 71.
116. See the views of Chelnokov and Lvov (the first head of the Provisional Government) as reported by Lockhart early in 1916: 'the Emperor is by no means stupid, talks well and to the point, and is fully aware of what he is doing.... he is obstinate and vindictive, and quite obsessed with the idea that autocracy is his and his children's by Divine right'. F.O. 371/2745/25836, Lockhart's despatch 2, 22 January 1916.
117. See Lockhart's own account, *British Agent,* pp. 120–21.
118. Triggered by Paul Kennedy's remarks in a review of *Retreat from Power* in the *Times Literary Supplement,* 20 March 1981, and developed in a series of letters to the editor by Wilson and others in April-June 1981.

DAVID DILKS

The British Foreign Office Between the Wars

The very name of the Foreign Office conjures up images of solidity and amplitude; the massive shape of the building seen across the Horseguards Parade or the lake in St. James's Park, the convenient proximity to 10 Downing Street, the high reputation of the Office for competence, the distinction of secretaries of state from Castlereagh and Canning, Palmerston and Salisbury, Lansdowne and Grey, to Curzon, Austen Chamberlain and Eden. Yet until the middle of the twentieth century it was a much smaller Office than we might imagine. An industrious secretary of state of the nineteenth cenury, in Palmerston's day and even later, could be master of almost all the business. Managing Britain's foreign policy with cautious wisdom in the later nineteenth century, Lord Salisbury sought little advice about policy even from the leading officials, and knew the principal ambassadors of foreign countries so well that he often refrained from keeping written records of the conversations, that they should confide in him the more freely.[1] At the time when the British were adjusting their habits to the changes in the franchise, Salisbury became deeply conscious of the risks posed by electoral fashion; it might be taken as an axiom, he once wrote, that no act of British foreign policy could succeed unless it could be completed within one beat of the pendulum.[2] He remarked that the frequent failure of ministers in foreign policy must be viewed with indulgence, for they were fated to make bricks without straw; and on another occasion, during the Near Eastern crisis of 1877, that it was British policy to float lazily downstream, occasionally putting out a diplomatic boathook to avoid collisions.[3]

181

Only 142 'home civil servants', in all grades from the humblest door-keeper to the most elevated under-secretary, were employed in the Office when Salisbury ceased to be secretary of state at the turn of the century. By the outbreak of the First World War, that number had climbed to 187; after the war, when the Foreign Office and the Diplomatic Service were combined and the Office itself had taken on new functions, the staff had increased fourfold. Then during the 1920s, as some of those tasks diminished, the staff was reduced to 730; but by 1938, the figure had risen again, to 902. In the days when the Foreign Office and the Diplomatic Service stood separate, all the senior men serving in London knew each other well. Even after the amalgamation, those likely to become ambassadors or heads of British legations were generally acquainted with, and sometimes related to, each other. The overwhelming majority had been educated at public schools and the old universities, especially Oxford. Some were the sons of distinguished diplomatists; for example, the father of Sir Eric Phipps, ambassador in Paris, had been British minister at Brussels; the father of Sir Ronald Campbell, who succeeded Phipps in Paris, had been under-secretary of state for Foreign Affairs; the father of Sir Horace Rumbold, who preceded Phipps in Berlin, had been British ambassador at Vienna. For good measure, Rumbold's mother was the daughter of the United States minister at Berne.

The old system of recruitment required some social standing, since a letter of testimonial to the foreign secretary was needed before a candidate could present himself; and, more importantly, a high standard in languages, which usually entailed a period of study abroad before the stiff examination could be passed. Until well after 1945, women were not admitted to those parts of the service which might lead to the senior posts in the Foreign Office or in missions abroad. Indeed, there had been a deep reluctance to admit ladies to the Office even as typists. All candidates before the First World War had to take a test in handwriting; and Sir Alexander Cadogan, permanent under-secretary from 1938 to 1946, contemplating acreages of barely-legible minutes upon Foreign Office papers, more than once lamented the abolition of the handwriting test and on one occasion threatened to reintroduce it. Surprisingly, it was a place of little formality within. The more deferential members would occasionally address the permanent under-secretary as 'Sir', though that was not expected. For many years, entry into the

Foreign Office or the Diplomatic Service had been virtually restricted to men with some private means.

It was widely believed, and with justice, that in point of the general level of ability, the Foreign Office would compare well with any department in Whitehall, except perhaps the Treasury. The very nature of diplomats' business, their social connections, the need to master sometimes obscure languages, periods of service in exotic places, the persistent belief that foreign affairs constituted an area of the Government's business so arcane and delicate that it should be left to a small band of discreet experts, all contributed to a marked feeling of separation between the Office and the rest of the civil service. 'The Foreign Office manner' was supposed to spring from a mingling of disdain at the lack of suavity and decorum experienced in lesser departments and that tranquil consciousness of effortless superiority alleged to characterise young men from the more distinguished colleges of Oxford. Even in 1950, the permanent under-secretary told new recruits that this blend was not 'much liked in Whitehall', though he thought it 'rather a myth nowadays'; he remarked that the relations of the Office with the home civil service were 'now pretty good, thanks to care on both sides; but be on the watch to avoid causes of reproach'.[4] The wits said that like the fountains in Trafalgar Square, the young men of the Foreign Office played from ten till four.

As a measure of the increase in business, we may take the number of papers, telegrams, and despatches received at the Foreign Office. In the last complete year before the outbreak of the First World War, the total amounted to 68,119; by 1935, that figure had more than doubled, to 169,249; and in successive years thereafter, it rose to 187,878; then to 201,323; and in the last year before the outbreak of the Second World War, to no less than 223,879. In 1919, Britain maintained only eight embassies abroad. Five were in Europe, including the embassy in Moscow, and the other three were in Brazil, Japan, and the United States. By 1930, embassies in the Argentine, Belgium, Poland, Spain, and Turkey had been established. By the outbreak of war, four more missions had been converted into embassies, those in Chile, China, Egypt, and Iraq.

These may seem modest numbers, given Britain's international position; she had more widely scattered territories, interests, responsibilities, and, therefore, risks than any other great Power. But we must not assume that the British were for all practical purposes a part of Europe and so regarded themselves. It is not always easy to remember that Europe was the only continent in which the British did not have territory to defend. Before the First World War, most British ministers reflected far more seriously, and apprehensively, about the defence of India than about Belgium or France, at least while a rough equilibrium in Europe seemed secure. It may be thought that the events of the First World War, the virtual collapse of the central tenet of British strategy—that the largest empire in the world could afford to muster modest strength on land so long as it enjoyed a good margin at sea—would have wrought a revolution in British thinking. It was hardly so. To be sure, there was a partial movement. But the refusal of the British to offer what the French regarded as an adequate guarantee after the Anglo-American guarantee had broken down, the unwillingness of successive governments to give serious military meaning to Locarno despite the warnings of the chiefs of staff, the barely-concealed British impatience with the policy of France during the 1920s and much of the 1930s, and the rejection until February 1939 of the notion that Britain should build up a continental army, tell their own story. Only in 1934, and then not by unanimous consent, was Germany identified as the ultimate potential enemy. Here was the core of Britain's problem; if the British Empire were to be lost, much of that loss would take place in the Middle East, Egypt, and Asia, at the hands of Japan and to a lesser degree Italy. Britain's position as a great Power, at least in the minds of her ministers and leading civil servants, rested to such a degree upon the possession of Empire that the notion of treating parts of it as disposable seemed too dire to contemplate. Important as overseas possessions were to France or Italy, their significance to Britain was far greater. To adapt a saying of Lord Curzon, the British felt that if they once lost India and Australasia, they would sink at once to the rank of a third class Power, but the only continent from which the heart of the Empire could be pierced was Europe. Whether the British liked it or not, therefore, whether they read the lessons of 1914 correctly or not, they were drawn during the 1930s by an inexorable process to place their relations with the countries of Europe, and their preparations for warfare in Europe, even higher in the scale of priorities.

In the 1930s, we can already discern some of those pressures which since the Second World War have enforced the reduction of British obligations and the narrowing of British horizons. The chancellor of the Exchequer, Neville Chamberlain, had come firmly to the conclusion after 1934 that the British could not afford to fight Germany at one end of the world and Japan at the other. Regarding Germany as the greater danger, in which belief he struck up a little-noticed concordance with the permanent under-secretary at the Foreign Office, Vansittart, he concluded that Britain must seek to reach tolerable relations with Japan and alter the balance of her defence spending in favour of the Royal Air Force, tilting it against the Army and the Royal Navy.[5] At one moment, he even proposed that work upon the Singapore base should be slowed down. In effect he was saying that the British would not find it possible to deploy in the Far East a large fleet of capital ships. This was a strand of thinking altogether too radical because without this fleet no deterrent against Japan could be effective. The secretary of the Cabinet and of the Committee of Imperial Defence, Sir Maurice Hankey, was about to set off on a tour to the Dominions, chiefly to explain the purposes of the impending British rearmament. He refused to go unless he could obtain a clear and authoritative statement of Britain's commitment to the defence of her vast interests east of Suez. This was given by the prime minister, Ramsay MacDonald, and the lord president of the Council, Baldwin. The first lord of the Admiralty said with indignation that the policy suggested by Mr. Chamberlain was not even advocated by the Communist Party of Great Britain.[6] Nevertheless, what happened in the later 1930s and after the outbreak of war with Japan in 1941 shows that Chamberlain's fears had a good deal of substance.

Just as there was no other great Power to which overseas possessions meant so much, so was there no other Power which had so complicated a system for managing its foreign relations. Until Stalin discovered in 1939 and again in 1941 that the doctrine may become inconvenient, he used to say 'peace is indivisible'. A well-conducted foreign policy is not easily divisible between countries or themes, and least of all when conducted by a Power which has to weigh the interlocking fortunes of the continents; yet at no time in the later nineteenth century or the first half of the twentieth did the foreign secretary and his Office hold undivided responsibility for British foreign policy. India, the most important of all British possessions, the only one which provided Britain with a large army, was administered by a complicated set of arrangements within India; and the foreign policy of the government of India was superintended by the India Office. No neat dividing line could be drawn. Although policy towards Persia emanated from the Foreign Office, the essence of British interest in Persia stemmed from the possession of the Indian sub-continent and most of the force needed to sustain any vigorous policy in Persia or the Persian Gulf would have to be supplied by India. For powerful internal reasons, the government of India was sensitive to its own Muslim opinion, and to questions which might inflame Muslim opinion elsewhere. The view of the world which the viceroy and his colleagues conceived in Delhi or Simla could not always be reconciled with the judgement formed in London. Lord Curzon, as viceroy, had faced disagreeable differences of policy with the government at home; and Lord Curzon as foreign secretary found himself so seriously at odds with his colleague the secretary of state for India[7] that a damaging row erupted between them in public, after which the secretary for India had to resign.

The other British possessions abroad were all dealt with until 1925 by the Colonial Office. This arrangement felt increasingly anachronistic, since the four white Dominions (Canada, Australia, New Zealand, South Africa) had for practical purposes become independent Powers not only in their domestic affairs but on the international stage. In 1914, they had all been committed to war by the declaration of the king. By 1919, each was acknowledged to have a separate international personality, and each accordingly signed the Versailles Treaty. The British Empire had ceased to be a unit, even in matters of war and peace. The Locarno Treaty of 1925 had been so drafted that any of the Dominions might sign; the British government made plain its hope that some of them would. None did.

After 1925, a separate Dominions Office conducted Britain's official relations with those four countries. In addition, each preserved and used the right of direct communication with the prime minister in London. There took place before 1939 only limited contact and exchange of staff between the Foreign Office and the Dominions Office. The purpose of the latter's existence was to exemplify the different intensity, quality, and texture which the British desired to characterise their relations with the Dominons. The secretary of state for the Dominions, who generally held the Colonial Office as well, saw the four Dominion High Commissioners in London regularly, while staff of the Dominions Office were expected to serve by rotation in London and then in the British High Commission in one of the Dominion capitals.[8] Only a continuous effort of imagination could enable a later generation to capture the significance which the Empire-Commonwealth held for ministers and their leading advisers in those days. The force of the feeling varied, inevitably; but it would scarcely be fanciful to call it the dominant political instinct of such figures, so diverse in every other respect, as Balfour, Chatfield, Hankey, Halifax, Lothian, and Hoare. While it would exaggerate to say that the Dominions, with their known aversion to war with Germany in 1938 over the issue of the Sudetenland, determined British policy, every leading minister of the 1930s would have regarded it as a setback of the first order if Britain had to fight while several of the Dominions remained neutral. That this did not happen in 1939 may perhaps be regarded as a substantial achievement of British policy, and testifies to the readily-forgotten fact that in time of crisis the call of the blood and the surge of emotion commonly count for more than any nice calculation of interests.

In the management of Britain's relations with other countries (the term 'foreign countries' would not have been accepted), the India Office, the Colonial Office, and the Dominions Office all played a substantial role. The territories with which they dealt covered a good quarter of the earth's habitable surface, and included a quarter of its population. Moreover, there were other limitations upon the competence and primacy of the Foreign Office in the field of foreign relations. It would be hard to separate overseas trade from other important aspects of foreign policy; but the Board of Trade was for most purposes independent of the somewhat shadowy suzerainty which the Foreign Office was supposed to exercise over its activities. Those parts of the Treasury which dealt with the international finance—a subject the import of which needs little emphasis when we think of reparations, the debt settlement with the United States of 1923, the Dawes Plan, the Young Plan, the suspension of reparations, the default on the debt to the United States, the Neutrality Acts—stood always outside the control of the foreign secretary. From time to time, the Bank of England played an independent role.

Nor should we neglect the influence of the Admiralty, the Air Ministry, and the War Office. The armed services naturally provided the naval, air, and military attachés at the main embassies.

Their reports reached their parent departments through the head of the mission and the Foreign Office. In practice, their advice, and the views formed by the service departments in London, had a powerful bearing upon foreign policy. 'In wartime,' as Eden once remarked, 'diplomacy is strategy's twin';[9] and in a time of nominal peace or armed truce, when war may easily be the outcome of foreign policy, the relationship is hardly different. Indeed, strategy or military advice may become the elder brother. An assessment of the military prospects was by far the weightiest single reason for Britain's Far Eastern policy between 1931 and 1941,[10] and, if Chamberlain's diary and private explanations to French ministers are accepted, in the British Government's decision of March 1938 not to give a guarantee to Czechoslovakia, or to France in connection with her obligations to that country.[11]

The main duties of the Foreign Office and Diplomatic Service, as the amalgamated organism was known between the wars, were to collect information, from public and private sources; to assess it in the light of an expert knowledge; to advise about action; and to execute diligently the policy laid down by the foreign secretary, or in the more important and complicated matters, by a committee of ministers or the Cabinet itself. The influence which the Office, and by extension the missions abroad, could exercise in the process of policy-making varied according to time and circumstances. For all his intellectual gifts, power of lucid expression, personal charm, and political prestige, Balfour had neither the energy nor the will to do continuous battle with Lloyd George on behalf of his own position or his department's, and the foreign secretary then had no place in the War Cabinet. Neither Chamberlain nor Churchill repeated this error in the War Cabinet of 1939–1945. Without doubt, the Office and the foreign secretary preserved their position far better in the Second World War than in the First, or in the four years of Lloyd George's ascendancy which followed it. This fact derived in part from Eden's close friendship with Churchill and his toughness in standing up to the prime minister. Even Eden, however, had to accept that Churchill would keep some of the most important business in his own hands.[12] Balfour, and Curzon who succeeded him in 1919, had much to endure from Lloyd George. That was not uniformly true over the whole field of foreign policy. In much of it, including issues of the first order, the prime minister hardly intervened at all; but there were areas in which he not only insisted upon making policy, but concealed some of its essentials from the foreign secretary and other colleagues. This was especially true of his dealings with Greek emissaries in 1921-1922. It does not seem to have occurred to the prime minister that the telegrams reporting his clandestine meetings would be intercepted, deciphered, and placed before the foreign secretary. The collapse of Lloyd George's government in the autumn of 1922 reflected the disenchantment of a Conservative party which had the parliamentary battalions. Another event at that time that had a momentous consequence was a revolt of small beginnings by two junior members of the Cabinet against the foreign policy being pursued by the prime minister, Churchill, and Birkenhead.

The new administration under Bonar Law came to power determined to undo many practices of Lloyd George's regime. Continuing at the Foreign Office, Curzon regained effective control of foreign policy, and restored the country's international standing by his remarkable performance during the Lausanne conference, which in its combination of finesse, detailed knowledge and tactical adroitness could not have been excelled by any foreign secretary of the inter-war period.[13] Only one prime minister, MacDonald, held the Foreign Office, as Lord Salisbury had done in more leisurely times. MacDonald had a marked talent for diplomacy, and a special interest in everything which concerned relations with the United States; a subject which he kept largely in his own hands during his second government (1929-1931), and even to some degree in the national government after 1931. His habits in this respect caused a good deal of distress to his Labour colleague Henderson, and to Sir John Simon, foreign secretary from November 1931.[14] During Baldwin's three spells as prime minister, successive foreign secretaries enjoyed greater freedom and only a limited general support from the prime minister, punctuated very occasionally by something more vigorous. The most serious difficulties between Eden and Chamberlain were confined to a period of a few months towards the end of 1937 and in the first weeks of 1938. 'This letter on the last day of 1937 is really to say thank you to you for your unvarying kindness and help to me this year' Eden wrote to Chamberlain. 'I really find it hard to express how much I have appreciated your readiness at all times to listen to my problems and help in their solution, despite your many other preoccupations.'[15] Chamberlain had always intended to take a more active part in foreign affairs than Baldwin, and had been at pains to explain this to Eden in the spring of 1937.[16] Even if he had not intended it, the rapid onrush of events would have left him little choice; for since a prime minister is in a very real sense answerable for the actions of all his colleagues, almost every prime minister holding office in critical times finds it necessary to take the closest interest in foreign affairs. It could hardly be otherwise; before the war, Britain grew no more than half her food, still depended upon overseas investments to avoid an adverse balance of trade, had to import almost all raw materials except coal, and relied on exports to finance the process.

It is a mark of the professional expertise in the Diplomatic Service that appointments to embassies from outside were relatively rare. Paris and Washington were recognised as providing some exception to the rule. In Paris, a Conservative politician in the shape of Lord Derby occupied the embassy for two years from 1918 to 1920, and a Liberal in the person of the Marquess of Crewe from 1922 to 1928. Otherwise the ambassador was a professional diplomat until Duff Cooper, Lord Norwich, went there in the wake of the liberation in 1944. Washington was held by Sir Auckland Geddes, who in his varied life had previously been a professor of anatomy, director of Military Recruiting at the War Office and head of the Department of National Service; and then by career diplomats until Lord Lothian was appointed on the eve of the war, after ministers had considered a number of other candidates,[17] including Admiral Lord Chatfield (First Sea Lord, 1933–1938), Lord Lytton (Governor of Bengal, 1922–1927), Sir E. Grigg (Governor of Kenya, 1925–1931), and John Buchan, first Lord Tweedsmuir, then Governor-General of Canada. Berlin was held throughout by a professional diplomat except in the time of Lord D'Abernon; Rome by a diplomat for the whole period, and Tokyo likewise; the same was true with one brief exception for the embassy at Moscow, until the arrival of Sir S. Cripps in 1940.

The Foreign Office never suffered the indignity of having a permanent under-secretary brought in from another department, though that fate seemed possible at one stage in 1936 and 1937. The post was not always regarded as the pinnacle of a career. Those who had served extensively abroad sometimes wished to return to an embassy; for example, Lord Hardinge went to Paris after his spell as permanent under-secretary; Lord Tyrrell also went to Paris; and Sir Ronald Lindsay to the Embassy at Washington for the abnormally long tenure of nine years. Sojourns of three or four years, often interrupted by substantial leave, which have been normal in more recent times, were between the wars somewhat exceptional. To hold a post for five or six years was not unusual; and when an envoy made a special mark, like Sir Ronald Graham in Rome, he might be left in the same post for a decade. Among the permanent under-secretaries, Crowe had spent his whole career in the Foreign Office, and Tyrrell, Vansittart, and Cadogan most of theirs; Vansittart served in Paris, Tehran, and Cairo, and then the Foreign Office for thirty years, while Cadogan had a long spell as head of the League of Nations Department. Vansittart and Cadogan each held this most onerous post for eight years. Cadogan was the more calm and competent administrator, though he troubled little about the machinery of the Office so long as it worked. No permanent undersecretary had a greater influence on its structure or its collective thinking than Crowe; an official of the first rank coming from a background not usual in the higher reaches of the Foreign Office, for he was born in Germany, educated there, and married a German. His father had been a celebrated journalist, author of books on Italian art and British commercial attaché in several European capitals. He held views then thought unorthodox:

> Crowe has informed us till we nod,
> That he does not believe in God;
> But what we really want to know
> Is whether God believes in Crowe.

Although the old division between the staff of the Foreign Office and the diplomats was breaking down between the wars, it had by no means disappeared; nor was it unknown for a diplomat of distinction, serving in a post of high sensitivity, to find his advice rejected and conduct criticised. Sir Robert Craigie, ambassador in Tokyo from 1937, is a case in point. The work of the Office was concentrated in departments, according to geography; thus, the Southern Department dealt with Italy, the Central Department with Germany, the Northern Department with Russia. Above each group of departments would be a superintending under-secretary; and above them the permanent under-secretary. In short, the structure resembled a pyramid, at the apex of which stood the secretary of state. In the 1920s, virtually all the ministerial work was done by one man.

Even in the 1930s, the complement normally consisted of the secretary of state, and one or two parliamentary under-secretaries. There was a brief unhappy phase from June to December, 1935, when two Cabinet ministers, Hoare and Eden, shared a responsibility for foreign affairs, though the general superintendence lay in theory and practice with Hoare, and Eden's particular duties in the League of Nations. Only once was there any disturbance of the normal arrangements at the level of the permanent under-secretary, when Vansittart was appointed in 1938 to the newly-created post of chief diplomatic adviser. Upon his own insistence, he retained the room hitherto given to the permanent head of the Office. He made an equally determined, but less successful, attempt to retain control of the Secret Intelligence Service, which had traditionally worked under the direction of the permanent under-secretary. Since Vansittart's successor Cadogan argued, with the support of two secretaries of state, Eden and Halifax, that he must execute all the duties normally attached to his post, the experiment was doomed to be unsatisfactory. Vansittart found himself with a grand title; but deprived of any opportunity to shape policy continuously; the papers did not normally pass through his hands until action had been decided. It need hardly be added that the days in which the secretary of state could exercise a continuous detailed control over policy, and even write many of his own despatches, were past. The role of the permanent under-secretary and of other civil servants within the Office therefore increased; and despite all that has been written about the diminished influence of ambassadors in the era of swift communications, an ambassador highly esteemed in the Foreign Office could affect not only the handling and execution of policy, but its framing, to a marked degree. In the 1920s, D'Abernon from Berlin and Crewe from Paris had both achieved a high influence; in the 1930s, Sir Ronald Lindsay in Washington, and Sir Percy Loraine at Ankara and later in Rome, had the ear of successive foreign secretaries.

From the turn of the century British governments had experimented with means of co-ordinating strategic and foreign policies. Beyond occasional *ad hoc* committees of ministers, the government had no machinery for this purpose, unbelievable as it now seems, until Balfour began to develop the Committee of Imperial Defence from 1902. It continued to work between the wars, spawning a multitude of sub-committees; but the C.I.D. became steadily less important in the formulation of policy at high level because the prime minister's other duties had become so heavy that he could not preside regularly over it. In practice, this meant that the decisions were sometimes made by the full Cabinet after a discussion in that forum, and sometimes by the Cabinet on the recommendation of a ministerial committee. In the conditions of the middle and later 1930s, these expedients were plainly inadequate. The Foreign Affairs Committee of the Cabinet was instituted in Baldwin's last phase as prime minister, and met intermittently in his time and Chamberlain's. As the threat of war became more obvious, two committees of special importance, Defence Plans (Policy), and the Strategical Appreciation Sub-Committee of the C.I.D., tried to bring British foreign policy and military capacity more nearly into line than they had been for some years.

In matters of strategy, the Foreign Office and secretaries of state there had to depend largely upon the advice of the service departments; and that advice in its turn was bound to influence the nature and conduct of foreign policy deeply. As Vansittart used to remark, time was the commodity which the Foreign Office was expected to supply.[18] The Office had little expertise in economic questions, though one of its more distinguished under-secretaries, Sir Victor Wellesley, averred that the root trouble in most international problems lay in economic causes.[19] The proposal that the Office should develop a substantial economic section of its own was never fully realised during the 1930s. Unquestionably, this was a serious gap in the Foreign Office's armoury. Broad questions of international and economic relations, and especially movements of capital and reparations, could not sensibly be detached from other questions of foreign policy. Co-ordination with the Treasury often left a good deal to be desired. In the second Labour government, Snowden did not collaborate happily with the Foreign Secretary Henderson, and insisted upon taking his own line in the conference at The Hague. When the effective suspension of reparations was agreed upon in 1932, the negotiations for that purpose took place at Lausanne, while the Disarmament Conference was meeting a few miles away in Geneva. Most business for the Disarmament Conference fell upon the Foreign Office, though there were frequent differences of policy with the service departments, especially the Air Ministry; the issue of reparations was handled with very little reference to the Foreign Office by the chancellor of the Exchequer, Neville Chamberlain, who went straight from that negotiation to the long awaited conference between Britain, the Dominions, and India, held at Ottawa. The agreements reached there, like the tariff introduced earlier in the year, had large implications for the patterns of Britain's international trade, and therefore on a long view for her foreign relations. Nevertheless, the British delegation at Ottawa included no minister or senior civil servant from the Foreign Office.

There is some evidence that the permanent head of the Treasury and head of the Civil Service, Sir Warren Fisher, found the Foreign Office inefficient and needing internal reform. On several occasions in MacDonald's time as prime minister, protests were uttered against the late circulation of papers from the Foreign Office to ministers. The unfortunate Hoare, who had a considerable experience of other departments and a keen interest in administrative efficiency, was, five years later, translated to the turbulent atmosphere of the British Embassy at Madrid. 'Between you and me,' he wrote to Chamberlain, 'I have no faith in the departmental Foreign Office, as I know it of old. The young men there imagine that everything goes along normally as it does in Whitehall, whereas in a place like this, everything is completely abnormal and upside down.'[20] Hoare's own experience at the Foreign Office had ended abruptly in an episode which did the Office, and its permanent under-secretary, much damage. Ministers rightly believed that Vansittart had played a large role, and by no means a passive one, in the framing of the Hoare-Laval terms. In many respects, they followed the line of three conversations between Grandi, the Italian ambassador, and Vansittart in the preceding week.[21] The notion, propagated by Vansittart himself, that his presence in Paris was fortuitous has no foundation. After the debacle, Vansittart's dismissal was seriously considered by ministers. The new foreign secretary, Eden, decided that this step would be improper; responsibility for policy must remain with ministers.[22] At intervals thereafter, Baldwin and Eden tried to persuade Vansittart to leave his post as permanent under-secretary in favour of the Embassy at Paris or some other post abroad. He declined; they felt they could not insist.

A picture has come down to history of Vansittart as an unbending opponent of concessions to dictators. In fact, he not only advocated large concessions to Italy in 1935, but also concessions to Germany, including the return of some of her colonies. This was one of the Foreign Office's unhappier periods; and to say, as the official history of British foreign policy in the Second World War is apt to do, that 'The Foreign Office believed this...' or 'The Foreign Office advised that...'[23] is an offence not only to constitutional propriety but almost always to accuracy. It is hard to imagine that even a comparatively small senior staff would be solidly united on large and contentious issues. At the official level, the principal responsibility rested with the permanent under-secretary; but since the foreign secretary, answerable to his colleagues and Parliament, could give orders even if they contradicted the advice tendered by his officials, and expect them to be loyally obeyed, it was also just that he should bear the responsibility for the advice tendered.

As the risks grew and the penalties for failures of foreign policy became more obvious, disagreements among the officials multiplied. Some felt a powerful emotional or intellectual attachment to the Covenant and the League; in the Abyssinian crisis, they therefore believed that Britain should go to all lengths, the blocking of the Suez Canal or even war, to thwart Italy. Oppressed by the greater power of Germany, Vansittart felt that Britain could not afford the luxury of an enemy straddling the short route from Europe to the Indian Ocean and Australasia. After Mussolini had taken Addis Ababa, some of the officials judged that Britain must regard the sad episode as closed, and mend her bridges with Italy. This was the policy openly favoured by Chamberlain, and accepted only in part and reluctantly by the new secretary of state, Eden. Sir Alexander Cadogan, brought back from China after only two years to become the senior deputy under-secretary, followed neither Vansittart's judgement of German intentions nor his recommendations about tactics. The foreign secretary, sharing with many of his generation a powerful attachment to the League as the exemplar of a new and saner method of conducting international affairs, could not credit that Mussolini's support would be worth much purchase. Moreover, though a staunch defender of non-intervention in the Spanish Civil War, Eden became increasingly incensed at the cynical violations by Germany and Italy of their agreements; and since the violations by Italy were the larger and more blatant, the effect was to concentrate his attention, and that of many others, upon Italy to a degree unwarranted by that country's power. Even the ambassador in Rome, Lord Perth, had to admit in the summer of 1937 that Mussolini might intend to go to war with Britain. Chamberlain's accession as prime minister gave an edge to questions which had been smoothed over or left unresolved; but events would have done that within a few months anyway.

There was no concealment about Chamberlain's opinion that Britain must seek Italian goodwill actively. The service departments, especially the Admiralty, had no intention of becoming embroiled in the Spanish Civil War; equally, with their gaze fixed upon Japan as well as Germany, and conscious of the lag in British rearmament, they pressed hard for a reduction in the number of actual or potential enemies. They had a powerful ally in the secretary of the Cabinet and of the Committee of Imperial Defence, Sir Maurice Hankey, who never hesitated to tender advice on strategic questions directly to his prime ministerial masters. Because Italy was the weaker partner in the Axis, and like Britain would presumably wish to preserve the independence of Austria, it seemed probable that terms could be more easily reached with her than with Germany or Japan. To Eden, outraged by what Italy had done in Abyssinia and was doing in Spain, this messsage was by no means welcome. According to Hankey's account, which is open to dispute, every conceivable pretext was seized to delay coming to grips with Germany or Italy. He judged Chamberlain 'incredibly patient — much too patient I thought — with Anthony.'[24]

During this period Chamberlain decided Vansittart must be replaced, a resolution which Eden did not contest. The foreign secretary had found Vansittart a relentless worker for his own views, with a wide circle of acquaintances in politics and journalism, 'seldom an official giving cool and disinterested advice based on study and experience. He was himself a sincere, almost fanatical, crusader, and much more a secretary of state in mentality than a permanent official.'[25] For his part, the prime minister thought Eden erratic, unable to keep consistently to the policy which the Cabinet had agreed upon. By December, it was decided that Vansittart be succeeded by Cadogan as permanent under-secretary: 'I think the change will make a great difference in the F.O.', the prime minister wrote to his sister, 'and that when Anthony can work out his ideas with a sane slow man like Alec Cadogan he will be much steadier. Van had the effect of multiplying the extent of Anthony's natural vibrations, and I am afraid his instincts were all against my policy, though he told me the other day that he had always been in favour of it but had been obstructed by others!'[26]

Whether the foreign secretary and his officials in the Foreign

Office would have been able to handle Britain's external relations better, had there been a prime minister of a different disposition, remains a matter for speculation. Eden had not been persuaded by the view of the service ministers that Britain's foreign policy must be dictated by the state of her defences, and he contested vigorously the view that Britain's position in that respect, particularly at sea, was worse than that of 1914.[27] Chamberlain replied tactfully that British foreign policy must be, if not dictated, at least limited, by the state of the national defences;[28] and Eden himself had to conclude in a Cabinet paper, only a few weeks later, that if Britain were too obviously outstripped in the race for material strength, the forces of diplomacy could not guarantee her safety except at the cost of deep national humiliation. As Sir Edward Grey had remarked before the First World War, 'You must not rely upon your foreign policy to protect the United Kingdom.'[29]

In sum, there were weighty issues at stake between Chamberlain and Eden, including their differing reactions to the initiative proposed by President Roosevelt in January 1938. On most matters of substance, the view of the new permanent under-secretary, Cadogan, coincided closely with the prime minister's. For example, he was nearer to Chamberlain's position than to Eden's on the Italian question, was wholly opposed to any attempt to thwart Germany in Austria, and advised firmly (amidst argument in the Foreign Office) against a guarantee to Czechoslovakia. Eden's replacement as foreign secretary, Halifax, was no cipher. He had long dwelt in agreement with Chamberlain on the main issues of foreign policy. Serious disputes between the two were rare but important. Having at first been inclined to accept, Halifax came down firmly against the Godesberg terms which Chamberlain brought back after his second meeting with Hitler. 'Your complete change of view since I saw you last night', Chamberlain wrote to Halifax at the Cabinet, 'is a horrible blow to me, but of course you must form your opinions for yourself.'[30] The notion that British foreign policy of those days is to be explained in terms of undue influence exercised by Sir Horace Wilson or Sir Joseph Ball is neither likely on the merits nor supported by the documents. This is not to say that the part played by Sir Horace Wilson had no importance; but the overwhelming probability is that in essentials British policy would have been the same if Sir Horace Wilson had never set foot in Downing Street. Nor is there any solid reason to believe that Sir Warren Fisher improperly used his position as head of the Civil Service to interfere with Foreign Office promotions or the circulation of Foreign Office papers; though it is true that Fisher, in his anxiety to see a different foreign policy pursued and keep Cadogan out of the post of permanent under-secretary, did seriously propose that he should take it himself, and the Treasury did in the 1930s exert a stricter financial control over the office.

Hitler, by seizing Austria and then pressing his demands upon Czechoslovakia under threat of general war, had deprived the British of that commodity which the Foreign Office was supposed to provide, time. However much they might lament the cause, and however differently many of them might have wished earlier policy conducted, the British ambassadors in every major European capital favoured 'appeasement' in 1938. This was true of most senior officials in the Foreign Office, including Cadogan. All the chiefs of staff supported the policy. By way of a wry footnote to these events, we may notice that shortly after Churchill became prime minister, those two strong proponents of appeasement Lord Halifax and Sir Alexander Cadogan stood out, almost alone but unavailingly in the summer of 1940, against Japan's demand that the Burma Road should be closed.[31] Churchill, now having to bear the responsibilities of being prime minister, joined Chamberlain in insisting that the demand be accepted, on the time-honoured grounds that Britain could not afford to fight three enemies at once.

In 1936, the General Consular Service, the Levant Consular Service, and the Far Eastern Consular Service were merged. Criticisms of the old Foreign Office and Diplomatic Service had gathered strength in the last years before the war. In Churchill's coalition government, the minister of Labour, Ernest Bevin, took a close interest in recruitment to the Foreign Office. The Diplomatic Service, he said, must have its future being in a new environment, and the 'Court Circular' society of the chanceries would never return. There must be a broadening of the curriculum and an easier entry into the Diplomatic Service. 'If a boy from the secondary school can save us in a Spitfire, the same brains can be turned to producing the new world. Democracy does not mean merely voting in an election; it means broad opportunity. Servants of the community should come from no narrow class.' Eden, whom Bevin was to succeed as foreign secretary, held similar views, and the White Paper which he put before Parliament in 1943 admitted that some of the criticisms had force. The conditions which the Diplomatic Service had originally been established to meet had changed. Economics and finance could not be separated from politics; an understanding of social problems and labour movements was indispensable to a properly balanced judgement of events; the modern diplomat needed a more intimate understanding of these questions, and therefore a wider training and experience. In practice, the foreign secretary had not been free to move a man from a post abroad to the Foreign Office without considering the different terms of service, which might impose financial hardship; and as the White Paper remarked, 'the efficiency of the Service has undoubtedly suffered in consequence'. The system of recruitment would be recast so as to 'facilitate the entry, from any social sphere, of candidates with suitable qualifications by enabling them to obtain the necessary vocational training at the expense of the State'. In future, the Foreign Office would be regarded as one of the posts, and as the headquarters of the Foreign Service, rather than as a department of the Home Civil Service; from which the new Foreign Service would be entirely distinct.[32] The Commercial Diplomatic Service, the Consular Services amalgamated a few years previously, the Foreign Office and the Diplomatic Service thus fused in one organisation. Those reforms certainly strengthened the position of the foreign secretary. Eden, with a unique experience of the old and the reformed Foreign Office, had no doubt that the changes were necessary and produced a better balanced Foreign Service at the period when Britain most needed it.[33]

After returning as foreign secretary in December 1940, Eden had written to Churchill:

> It should be made plain that the responsibility for advising you and the War Cabinet on the conduct of foreign policy is that of the Foreign Secretary alone. This responsibility extends, of course, to the whole sphere of foreign policy. It is essential that this should be everywhere understood... We can none of us wish to re-enter a period of divided responsibility for the conduct of foreign policy....[34]

This was easier said than achieved. In practice, the Foreign Office has never been able to secure control of increasingly important functions carried out by other departments in the sphere of credit guarantees for exports, or international economic negotiations. Fisheries, agriculture, the application of science, atomic power, the activities of the multi-national corporations, energy policy—all have a direct bearing upon Britain's foreign relations, and all are outside the control of the Foreign Office, though continuous efforts are made to harmonise policy between the departments by an elaborate network of official and ministerial committees. Looking at the position of the Foreign Office in the machinery of British government, we thus become conscious of a paradox. The agencies which proved resistant to control in the war—the Ministry of Economic Warfare, the Political Warfare Executive, the Ministry of Information, even the B.B.C. in some of its functions—had been reduced or abolished after 1945. The India Office disappeared with the independence of that sub-continent in 1947; the Colonial Office vanished with the liquidation of Empire; the Commonwealth Relations Office, successor to the old Dominions Office, was merged with the Foreign Office in the later 1960s.

At the modest price of a change of title, to 'Foreign and Commonwealth Office', a unified Office and Diplomatic Service had therefore achieved at last that position of primacy in the direction of Britain's foreign relations which many of its staff had sought; but it is relative, rather than absolute, strength which counts in international affairs, and even by the later 1960s it was manifest that Britain would not find it easy to maintain her position as a Power of the second rank.

NOTES

1. Curzon Papers (India Office Library, London), box 70, Lord Salisbury to the Hon. G. N. Curzon (then under-secretary at the Foreign Office), 23 March 1896.
2. Curzon papers, box 70, Salisbury to Curzon, 23 December 1897.
3. Lady Gwendolen Cecil, *Life of Robert Marquis of Salisbury* (London, 1932), Vol. IV, p. 3; (London, 1921), Vol. II, p. 130.
4. Lord Strang, *Home and Abroad* (London, 1956), pp. 310-1.
5. Chamberlain papers (University of Birmingham), Neville Chamberlain to Hilda Chamberlain, 28 July 1934.
6. These events are treated in detail in the Ph.D. thesis of Dr. I. Hamill, 'The Strategic Illusion: The Singapore Strategy and the Defence of Australia and New Zealand 1919-1942'. University of Leeds, 1975.
7. The Hon. E. S. Montagu, who left office in March 1922.

8. On the work of the Dominions Office, see the Ph.D. thesis of Dr. E. J. Adams, 'Commonwealth Collaboration in Foreign Affairs 1939-1947: The British Perspective'. University of Leeds, 1982.
9. The Earl of Avon, *The Eden Memoirs: The Reckoning* (London, 1965), Foreword.
10. For a summary of the military and naval position and prospects of Great Britain in the Far East at the time of the crisis of 1931-1932, see R. Butler, D. Dakin and M. E. Lambert, eds., *Documents on British Foreign Policy 1919-1939* (H.M.S.O., London, 1965), Series 2, Vol. IX, pp. 677-8.
11. K. G. Feiling, *The Life of Neville Chamberlain* (London, 1946), pp. 347-8; E. L. Woodward and R. Butler, eds., *Documents on British Foreign Policy 1919-1939* (H.M.S.O., London, 1949), Series 3, Vol. I, pp. 212ff.
12. Churchill as Prime Minister dealt directly with Roosevelt and Stalin by telegram and in meetings, at some of which he was not accompanied by the foreign secretary. He refused to let Eden or the permanent under-secretary of the Foreign Office see in advance the text of the broadcast of 22 June 1941, in which he promised all possible aid to invaded Russia; J. Colville in J. W. Wheeler-Bennett, ed., *Action This Day* (London, 1968), p. 89.
13. The style of Curzon's diplomacy at Lausanne can best be followed in W. N. Medlicott, D. Dakin and M. E. Lambert, *Documents on British Foreign Office 1919-1939* (H.M.S.O., London, 1972), Series I, Vol. XVIII.
14. Dr. D. Carlton's *MacDonald versus Henderson* (London, 1970), gives examples; see also Lord Simon, *Retrospect* (London, 1952), pp. 177-8.
15. F.O. (Foreign Office Archives, Public Record Office, London), 954/7, Eden to Chamberlain, 31 December 1937.
16. The Earl of Avon, *The Eden Memoirs: Facing the Dictators* (London, 1962), p. 445.
17. D. N. Dilks, ed., *The Diaries of Sir Alexander Cadogan* (London, 1971), p. 90.
18. Memorandum of 31 December 1936, cited by W. N. Medlicott, 'Britain and Germany: The Search for Agreement 1930-37' in D. N. Dilks, ed., *Retreat From Power* (London, 1981), Vol. I, p. 100.
19. *Documents on British Foreign Policy*, Series 2, Vol. IX, p. 374.
20. Templewood papers (Cambridge University Library), XIII: 20, Sir S. Hoare to Chamberlain, 6 June 1940.
21. *Documents on British Foreign Policy* (H.M.S.O. London, 1976), Series 2, Vol. XV, pp. 392-6; cf. Baron Pompeo Aloisi, *Journal (25 Juillet 1932 - 14 Juin 1936)* (Paris, n.d.), p. 327.
22. Eden to King George V, 8 January 1936; *Documents on British Foreign Policy*, Series 2, Vol. XV, pp. 548-9.
23. E. L. Woodward, *British Foreign Policy in the Second World War* (H.M.S.O., London, 1962), p. v.
24. Hankey papers (Churchill College, Cambridge), 3/43, Sir Maurice Hankey to his son R. M. A. Hankey, 1 March 1938.
25. The Earl of Avon, *The Eden Memoirs: Facing the Dictators*, p. 242.
26. Chamberlain papers, Neville Chamberlain to Ida Chamberlain, 12 December 1937.
27. F.O. 954/7, Eden to Chamberlain, 9 September 1937.

28. F.O. 954/7, O. S. Cleverly (private secretary to the prime minister) to F. R. Hoyer Millar, Foreign Office, 13 September 1937.
29. The Earl of Avon, *The Eden Memoirs: Facing the Dictators,* pp. 492–4.
30. The Earl of Birkenhead, *Halifax* (London, 1965), p. 400.
31. *The Diaries of Sir Alexander Cadogan,* pp. 310–4.
32. Bevin's speech to the T.U.C., reported in *The Times,* 10 October 1940; Cmd. 6420, 'Proposals for the Reform of the Foreign Service', January 1943.
33. The Earl of Avon, *The Eden Memoirs: The Reckoning,* p. 258.
34. F.O. 954/7, Eden to Chamberlain, 10 January 1941.

M. L. DOCKRILL

Britain, the United States, and France and the German Settlement 1918–1920

British hopes for a stable post-war Europe depended to a large degree on close Anglo-American collaboration during and after the peace negotiations.[1] A Foreign Office Political Intelligence Department memorandum of November 1918 stated bluntly: 'It is in our interest to work vigorously and honestly in co-operation with America on the general lines of the programme which President Wilson has put forward and to which we have given our adhesion.' British desiderata for the future were clear cut: a stable Europe and the avoidance of entanglements in future continental wars. 'What we want is peace and order with open facilities for trade.' However, Britain could not afford to neglect the balance of power and the security of the coastline opposite British shores. British policy had always sought to prevent the rise of a single power, or association of Powers, capable of extending its domination over Europe. 'To avert this, our interest now, as it always has been, is to maintain the full and complete independence, political, military, and economic, of the different States between which the Continent is divided.' The great gain now was that these States would be based upon the principle of national self-determination rather than 'merely accidental congeries of territories without internal cohesion'. 'The existence of a common nationality will be more durable and afford a firmer support against aggression....'[2]

Thus British self-interest and Wilsonian principles were happily united, at least as far as European security was concerned. However, it was soon clear that close Anglo-American relations at the

Conference would preclude an alignment with France, since French notions of the future European order were not such as to recommend themselves to British planners. French suggestions for Anglo-French talks to co-ordinate their policies at the Paris conference before Woodrow Wilson arrived in Europe were brushed aside.[3] French demands, such as an independent or autonomous Rhineland garrisoned by Allied troops,[4] were characterised as dangerous and short-sighted, likely to bring about a renewal of hostilities in the future. As one British observer put it, 'the end of a victorious war does not find the French in a mood for letting down the fallen enemy lightly or of allowing those who are out of his reach if he recovers to dictate the terms that shall be imposed on him',[5] while Arthur Balfour, the foreign secretary, complained that

> the French seem to me to be so greedy that even if America and Italy did not exist we might find some difficulty in swallowing their terms whole. Their deliberative effort to exclude the Americans from any effective share in the world settlement is, in my judgment, neither in our interest nor that of the French themselves.[6]

Indeed, anti-French feelings which tended to become exaggerated in the hot-house atmosphere of the Paris peace conference in 1919, ran high in the British delegation. Lord Hardinge, the permanent under-secretary at the Foreign Office, commented that 'the French are opening their mouths very wide and would like to reduce Germany to servitude for the next 50 years'.[7] Lord Curzon, the Lord President of the Council and in charge of the Foreign Office in London while Balfour was in Paris, believed that 'the two greatest bands of Chauvinists in Europe are France and Italy as Wilson has already found out'.[8] Hence the British were pleased by manifestations of American anxiety for co-operation with the British to restrain France. In November 1918, Colonel House, Wilson's aide, hoped for early meetings of the Anglo-American delegations to co-ordinate their arrangements at the Conference, and he informed the British ambassador to France, Lord Derby, that President Wilson was aghast at the extent of French (and Italian) territorial demands and wanted close relations with Britain.[9] Before the Conference met, Leo Amery, in what Colonel Hankey, the secretary of the British Delegation, described to Lloyd George as 'a useful paper', urged his superiors 'to place Anglo-American relations on a permanent footing of mutual understanding and co-operation' which would enable the Anglo-American fleets to deter 'any new development of materialistic ambition in Europe'.[10]

Of course not all British officials viewed relations with the United States in such friendly terms. There were underlying feelings of rancour, chiefly concerning her late entry into the war, and her determination to exercise what some thought a disproportionate influence at the peace conference. Some British high ranking army circles were bitter about American claims to be 'the deciding factor in the war, without having to do actually much of the fighting', and feared that the United States now sought to replace Britain as the world's leading Power.[11] Among those who were acutely suspicious of the United States was the First Lord of the Admiralty, Walter Long, who, echoing what he claimed to be back bench Tory opinion, told Curzon in January 1919 that

> my only consolation is in [the] belief that Clemenceau will stand firm for France [against Wilson] and that our PM will not consent to play second fiddle. But I don't like the prospect... I don't trust Wilson and I am very fearful that our cause will suffer.[12]

These not too latent suspicions were to surface when the United States opposed British policies at the Conference.

But initially there was close collaboration at the Conference between the British and American delegations. Derby reported to Curzon that 'antagonism between France and America grows every day and the feeling against Wilson is bitter and becoming very articulate. The fact that the relationship between England and America is improving every day still further exasperates the French.'[13] The French were also blamed for the delays in the proceedings at Paris: Woodrow Wilson was to return to the United States in February and the British suspected that the French were deliberately spinning out the discussion in the meantime, since in his absence they hoped to force through decisions favourable to their interests. In Lloyd George's picturesque phrase, 'the old tiger[14] wants the grizzly bear back in the Rocky Mountains before he starts tearing up the German hog.' The prime minister was very bitter about what he described as unscrupulous French behaviour at the Conference — 'bullying, cajoling, lying, sowing dissension....'[15]

The British were not entirely unsympathetic towards French demands for guarantees for her future security, especially since Britain would have to come to her rescue if she were again attacked by Germany. However, these demands must be satisfied with the minimum effort on Britain's part and with minimum interference with Germany's sovereignty in Western Europe. Philip Kerr, Lloyd George's private secretary at the conference and the prime minister's main channel of communication during his absence in London for part of February and March, explained to House Lloyd George's views on how European peace was to be maintained in the future. 'The habit of militarism' was to be broken by destroying armaments in Europe and by interrupting conscription for five to six years. But to assure peace the treaty must contain no new 'Alsace-Lorraines' in the form of a Rhineland detached from the rest of Germany. However, Kerr expressed his belief that France needed some tangible guarantee against a renewal of the struggle in eight or ten years' time. The French regarded the League as 'little more than a scrap of paper' and, in order to persuade them to abate their inflated claims against Germany and to accept the League as a security bastion, the British Empire and the United States should promise France that, if Germany increased the quota of arms allowed her under the treaty, and if League economic and financial pressure failed, the two countries would build ship for ship and raise division for division against her, confronting her with a 300% margin in favour of the principal members of the League. House argued that the League should maintain such a preponderance from the start so that, if Germany attempted to increase her strength, the League could attack her. Kerr believed that France should be offered real security in return for her agreement to ease the path of subsequent negotiations.[16] The British and American delegations worked closely together to thwart France's Rhenish ambitions and to promote the Anglo-American guarantee as a means of persuading the French to withdraw their more extreme demands.

Despite this apparent Anglo-American consensus, relations between the two Powers deteriorated as the Conference proceeded. They quarrelled about American naval expansion plans,[17] about the future of the former German colonies and about reparations and the debts owed to the United States by the Allies. The British pressed the United States to redistribute some of the wealth she had accumulated during the war in the form of reconstruction credits to aid European recovery—the Keynes plan being the most famous example. The British were caught on the one hand between the coalition's election pledges on reparations, the desire to secure a fair share of what was going and a feeling that Germany should make retribution for her crimes, and on the other, anxiety not to crush Germany utterly. If the United States cancelled the war debts owed to her by the Allies, the Allies for their part would be able to scale down their reparations demands. To cut reparations without escaping the burden of war debts would place the Allies in an invidious position and give Germany a decided financial advantage. Kerr wrote to the prime minister in late February:

> I am in favour of restricting our commitments abroad until we set our own country thoroughly in order. I think it is America's turn to take on some of the burden of developing and financing the backward parts of the earth. We must see she makes her money available for this.[18]

British delegates protested frequently about Woodrow Wilson's hostility towards Britain's reparations claims on Germany and contrasted this with his insistence on the repayment in full of Britain's war time debts to the United States—'the only nation which has made a profit out of the war'[19] or, as Long put it, 'making money hand over fist'.[20] The quarrel over the future of Germany's former colonies led Australian Prime Minister W. M. Hughes into making virulent attacks on Wilson and invidious comparisons between America's meagre war time sacrifices and Australia's heavy losses in men and money.

Not that irritation with the United States led the British to modify their hostility towards French policy, not only in the Rhineland but over French support for Poland's territorial claims, an issue that the United States and France tended to agree on. Lloyd George wrote to Bonar Law on 30 March that

> I have never cared for the handing over of two or three million Germans to Polish rule. The Poles have never shown themselves very competent or efficient administrators and the Ger-

mans naturally resent being put under their sway. We do not want another Alsace-Lorraine in Europe. The Germans would never accept permanently this transference [Danzig]. There would be trouble within the next twenty years. We should either have to wage war to enforce the treaty or accept its abrogation...[21]

Altogether, in the British view, the grasping nature of French demands threatened the conclusion of the treaty, with incalculable consequences for European peace. Kerr pressed Lloyd George

to insist on a sane policy towards Germany...I am all for imposing stiff terms on Germany, but they must be terms which give the German people some hope and some independence. If the French have their way they will give them neither, and we shall gradually be driven to occupy the country.[22]

Curzon wrote from London in early March that he

regarded the recent proceedings at Paris with some anxiety and the future almost with dismay. When the Peace Treaty is presented there will very likely... be no German Government to sign, and if there is, I fully expect that the signature will be refused. What then?[23]

While a Foreign Office official at Paris, James Headlam-Morley, wished the Germans 'to feel... that there can be no mistake about it that what they have to undergo is the necessary and just retribution for what they have done'. He added 'it seems to me all the more important that we should not in any way give them grievances which might appear to be just.'[24] But the French continued to press for the separation of the Rhineland from Germany, much to the exasperation of the British participants at the Conference. Derby commented that the French

are still in a mortal funk of Germany... The disparity between the populations of the two Countries is a perfect nightmare to them. They are... determined to get a big buffer State between them and Germany and I feel confident that they will sacrifice almost anything to secure our support for that.[25]

By the end of March the British delegates were growing increasingly alarmed at the extent of the territorial, financial, and military demands being made on Germany, which they feared would forever alienate Germany from Western Europe and leave her in an unsettled and potentially aggressive condition. In the British view the responsibility for this unwelcome prospect rested unequivocally on France's shoulders. Hankey's famous memorandum of 19 March warning Lloyd George of the dangers to future European peace unless the treaty was modified, the Fontainebleau visit between 22 and 24 March by Lloyd George, Hankey, Kerr, and Sir Henry Wilson, the Chief of the Imperial General Staff, to discuss the treaty, and Lloyd George's Fontainebleau Memorandum of 26 March directed at Clemenceau, urging a peace of moderation and justice and brandishing the threat of a Bolshevik Germany as an otherwise likely outcome, were the manifestations of Britain's anxiety. This appeal cut very little ice with Clemenceau, who noted sarcastically the British Empire's insistence on securing the bulk of Germany's former colonies and her clamour for a large percentage of German reparations payments. Nor was he much impressed by the alleged Bolshevik threat.[26] Later Lloyd George was to complain that 'the French have been extraordinarily greedy'.[27]

The ensuing deadlock drove British statesmen to despair. Bonar Law wrote anxiously from London doubting that 'any German Government can accept such terms as will satisfy the Allies and if they do not what next?'[28] General Jan Christian Smuts, the South African statesman, opened the first salvo in what was to be a sustained campaign against what he regarded as the harsh measures which were to be imposed on Germany. Most of his complaints were concerned with the eastern settlement, and particularly with Poland's proposed borders with Germany, a concern shared by Lloyd George. In his letter Smuts pointed out that

1. We cannot destroy Germany without destroying Europe.
2. We cannot save Europe without the co-operation of Germany.
   Yet we are now preparing a peace which must destroy Germany, and yet we think we shall save Europe by so doing! The fact is that, the Germans are, have been and will continue to be *the dominant factor* on the Continent of Europe

and no permanent peace is possible which is not based on that fact... My fear is that the Peace Conference may prove to be one of the historic failures of the world; that the statesmen connected with it will return to their countries broken, discredited men and that the Bolshevists will reap where they have sown... Her appeasement now may have the effect of turning her into a bulwark against the oncoming Bolshevism of eastern Europe.[29]

British fears about the future stability of Europe were not the only reasons for British misgivings about the treaty. A German refusal to sign the treaty would necessitate an Allied invasion of Germany, and the British were reluctant, to say the least, to contemplate a renewal of hostilities. Marshal Foch, commander of the Allied forces, on the other hand, seemed positively to welcome the prospect that 'we are bound to begin war in a very short time'.[30] In early April, when approached by Hankey for information about Allied strategy in the event of a German refusal to sign the treaty, or of chaos leading to there being no legal German government to execute the document, Foch was anxious that, if the conflict was renewed, it should be sooner rather than later while 'we still possess sufficient forces to undertake operations which might be necessary to overcome all difficulties likely to arise'. He feared that rapid Allied demobilisation would prejudice the likelihood of successful Allied operations against Germany in the future. If Germany refused to sign, the Allies would march on Berlin. If, on the other hand, ordered government in Germany collapsed, the Allies would occupy Bavaria and seize the sources of German wealth such as the Ruhr coal-mines in order to achieve the economic ends set out in the treaty.[31]

By early April the Rhineland issue was moving towards a compromise, while reparations had become the main source of disagreement at Paris. Now not only the Powers but the British Empire delegation were bitterly divided over the issue. Lloyd George was desperately seeking a compromise which would prevent a final breach with Woodrow Wilson, who threatened to abandon the conference on 7 April unless the Allies adopted a more moderate line. But the prime minister continued to insist that Britain should obtain a fairly large proportion of what could eventually be extracted from Germany. Eventually Lloyd George threw his support behind a scheme put up to the Council of Four, to leave the determination of the total sum to the deliberations of an Allied reparations commission, which would report its findings in May 1921, when the prime minister hoped that passions might have calmed sufficiently for the Allies to agree to a more reasonable sum. The Australian prime minister, W. M. Hughes, opposed this compromise, and clamoured for Allied acceptance of the principle that Germany should be made liable for the whole costs of the war.

The British Empire delegation met in Paris on 11 April to decide the question and Hughes found himself in a minority of one. Lloyd George warned Hughes that inflated reparations claims would wreck the conference and would necessitate Britain's keeping 1,500,000 men permanently under arms. Louis Botha, the South African prime minister, in a letter to Lloyd George after the meeting, summed up the views of the majority in the delegation on the dire consequences that would follow from the imposition of vast demands on Germany. The result would be 'further embarrassment, danger and possibly—ruin'. The United States would withdraw from the conference, sign a separate peace with Germany, who would then refuse to sign peace with the other Allies, leading to the renewal of the war, with Anglo-American relations strained to breaking point, Bolshevism in Europe, and the possible collapse of the British Empire. The prospect of these dire consequences ensuing was averted at the meeting when Hughes backed down and accepted Lloyd George's proposal to support the Council of Four compromise.[32]

The draft treaty, which was presented to the German delegation at Versailles on 7 May 1919, had been hastily put together at the last moment, and the contents of the entire document further appalled those in the British delegation who had already protested about individual clauses. They now put pressure on Lloyd George to secure major modifications in the draft treaty to meet German criticisms. Headlam-Morley felt 'convinced that if any responsible person had read through the whole at leisure, he would have felt that the cumulative effect would be such that a thorough revision must be made'.[33] Smuts led the protestors, followed by George Barnes, a member of the war cabinet, H. A. L. Fisher, president of the Board of Education (on the grounds, according to E. R. Bevan,[34] that 'as a historian he feels strong dislike to the undoing of the work of Frederick the Great'[35]), Lord Robert Cecil, Bonar Law, and Lord Milner, the colonial secretary.

Smuts attacked virtually every article in the treaty and, in particular, the dangers of the guarantee to France which 'may at any time bring the British Empire into the fire'.[36] Botha supported him: 'the probability of wars has to be contemplated, wars which France may hold — not without some show of justice — to be unprovoked aggression, but which really have their roots in the Peace Treaty and the spirit in which France is going to carry them out'.[37] From London Winston Churchill, secretary of state for war, added his forebodings to those of his colleagues, urging Lloyd George to secure compromises which would induce Germany to sign the treaty. He feared that an Allied advance into Germany would be attended by logistical difficulties with every move forward. Furthermore, a long occupation of Germany would strain British resources to the utmost. 'I consider that we shall commit a political error of the first order if we are drawn into the heart of Germany.' He reminded the prime minister of Napoleon's experiences in Spain and asked him what would happen in India, the Middle East and Turkey if Britain's already inadequate forces were sucked into Germany. Britain should not follow 'too far Latin ambitions and hatreds', but should 'settle now while we have the power'.[38] The entire question was debated by the British Empire delegation in Paris on 30 May and 1 June 1919. This resulted in Lloyd George being authorised to press Clemenceau for concessions. But the delegation decided that the British army and navy would not join in hostilities designed to force Germany to sign the existing treaty.[39]

Lloyd George informed the Council of Four of the British Empire delegation's decision on 2 June. However, Clemenceau was not to be blackmailed by Germany's threat not to sign the treaty or by Britain's refusal to assist France militarily if she did not. It was Woodrow Wilson who took the lead in opposing any concession to the British view. All his disgust with Germany's wartime behaviour and with Britain's seemingly inconsistent policy at the peace conference welled up during a meeting of the American commission on 3 June and he refused to be swayed either by the feeling in favour of changes in his own commission, a personal appeal from Smuts or by threats by the British prime minister:

Well, I don't want to seem to be unreasonable, but my feeling is this: that we ought not, with the object of getting it signed, make changes in the treaty, if we think that it embodies what we were contending for; that the time to consider all these questions was when we were writing the Treaty, and that it makes me a little tired for people to come and say now that they are afraid the Germans won't sign, and their fear is based upon things that they insisted upon at the time of writing the treaty; that makes me very sick... Here is a British group made of every kind of British opinion, from Winston Churchill to Fisher. From the reasonable to the unreasonable, all the way round, they are all unanimous, if you please, in their funk. Now that makes me very tired. They ought to have been rational to begin with and then they would not have needed to have funked at the end... Though we tried to keep them from putting irrational things in the treaty, we got very serious modifications out of them. If we had written the treaty the way they wanted it, the Germans would have gone home the minute they read it.
Well, the Lord be with us.[40]

So much for Lloyd George's hopes for close Anglo-American collaboration at the peace conference. Eventually, after a series of quarrels with Woodrow Wilson, Lloyd George managed to secure a few minor concessions in the draft treaty, including the promise of a plebiscite in Upper Silesia. After Clemenceau had complained bitterly about France's continuing need for security, he accepted the revisions, although these made little difference to the treaty as a whole. Germany's decision to sign the treaty at Versailles on 28 June 1919 was a relief to all those in the British delegation who feared a renewal of the war.

Although Britain had secured the bulk of her demands in the treaty, many regarded it with disillusionment and despair — 'the moral bankruptcy of the Entente', as Lord Robert Cecil put it.[41] This feeling was reinforced by the outspoken attacks on the treaty by John Maynard Keynes and other intellectuals, who regarded the settlement as a betrayal of the promises made by Woodrow Wilson during the war. Repeated German protests about the harsh nature of the treaty kept the issue alive during the 1920s and beyond. The future would not bear out Kerr's optimistic assumption that

> Militarism is, I think, dead in Europe in the sense that it can no longer achieve anything. The economic necessity is becoming so pressing that no Government can stand which does not demobilise and organise all national armies for the purpose of economic production.[42]

Lloyd George and his associates could at least congratulate themselves on having defended Germany from the more extreme demands of the French and for having even secured last minute adjustments in the treaty in Germany's favour. However, the British Government also believed that Germany, by her conduct during and after 1914, justly deserved all the other impositions in the treaty, and rejected the call for its general reconstruction by Smuts. Punishment was a key feature in Britain's policy towards the defeated powers. While right wing *enragés* like Hardinge insisted that 'the big stick is what bullies like them understand better than anything else',[43] a recent writer has commented that 'the punitive overtones of the moralism of the moderate left have to be taken seriously'.[44] Both Lloyd George and Woodrow Wilson shared the conviction that the aggressor must make amends for his wrong-doing, and their attitudes corresponded to that of broad cross-sections of public opinion.

However satisfactory the gains made by Britain at the conference may have been, the future seemed fraught with uncertainty. Relations with France continued to deteriorate: the two quarrelled in the summer over the formulation of the peace treaties with the other defeated powers and Lloyd George showed little disposition to follow the French lead in taking a harsh stand against alleged German violations of the treaty during the autumn and winter of 1919. The nature of the Anglo-American connection remained ambiguous as Woodrow Wilson struggled, against increasing ill-health, to secure the passage of the treaty through the Senate. The British remained anxious to collaborate closely with the United States in the post-war world. Lord Grey of Fallodon, the former foreign secretary, was reluctantly conscripted as 'Special Ambassador' to the United States in the autumn in a desperate attempt to mend fences with President Wilson. He urged on London the need for a clear pro-American policy to strengthen relations between the two countries.⁴⁵ Curzon, who became foreign secretary in October, was anxious to comply—he replied that Britain intended to make the League 'a reality', would not consider the United States a possible enemy when she drew up her naval estimates, and promised that, while independence for Ireland was impossible, the British government intended to do all in its power to satisfy Irish demands.⁴⁶ On 6 October, Grey reported his increasingly isolated position in Washington: 'The President's illness has left me in the air and I do not know when I can be received by him. And it is of no use my doing things with anybody else.'⁴⁷ A Foreign Office official, William Tyrrell, sent to help Grey, complained in October 1919 that 'here we are faced with all the evils of a one-man regime with the one man on the shelf and party politics run mad.'⁴⁸

The Senate's subsequent rejection of the treaty of Versailles removed one of the central planks of British policy during and after the conference—the assumption of Anglo-American close and cordial co-operation to keep the peace. With the American rejection of the treaty went her defection from the League, and the end of Wilson's hopes that it would gradually mitigate the harsher aspects of the post-war settlement.⁴⁹ British leaders already regarded the League with the United States as a shaky enough enterprise: without the United States Lloyd George and his advisers wondered whether to withdraw Britain from participation in its counsels also. While evident public support for the League compelled the government to continue to uphold it, Lloyd George's private attitude towards that organisation continued to be one of scepticism.

France and Britain, with haphazard support from Italy, were left to uphold the Paris settlements without either active American interference or support. With the defection of the United States, what was to be the fate of the British guarantee to France, which the British had thoughtfully tied in with the American guarantee? To Clemenceau the guarantee was of limited value without the certainty of prompt Anglo-American assistance in the event of German aggression, but at least it held out the prospect of an Allied victory in the long run, and provided the promise of British support. Curzon toyed with the prospect of maintaining the British guarantee as a lever to secure French good behaviour in Europe and in the Near and Middle East, because of 'the immense importance in which she holds this guarantee treaty, and the unceasing terror in which she lives concerning her eastern border.'⁵⁰ Derby noted in his diary on 27 November 1919 that he had assured a French journalist who had expressed doubts about Britain's continued allegiance to the guarantee in the event of an American withdrawal, that

> he completely misunderstood the English people. We had given our word and though we were sorry that America was not a participant in the agreement our word stood and would stand and that it would be well that France should recognise that such a decision meant an extraordinary proof of our loyalty to France and it would be as well if in minor matters France would show equal loyalty to us.[51]

Derby soon had to eat his words when the cabinet decided to abandon the guarantee. This action was regarded by French politicians as another example of British perfidy. In March 1920, Derby reported rising anti-British feeling in France, which he ascribed partly to the abandonment of the guarantee but also to the comparisions being made between France's enormous sacrifices during the war with their meagre gains thereafter, and with Britain's having secured the bulk of her war aims in 1919. While the French believed that Germany would try to crush France as soon as she had recovered, they saw Britain retreating into isolation and ignoring the latent peril to Europe. The French continued to hope that Britain would at least agree to some kind of pledge to France that would deter Germany in the future. Derby commented that 'the French are a funny people'.[52] Churchill suggested that Britain should offer France a defensive alliance if, in return, 'France loyally accepts a British policy of help and friendship towards Germany'.[53]

Anglo-French relations remained uneasy after 1919 as British suspicions of France and her policy tended to increase. In December 1919, Lloyd George complained of 'the defection of Americans, [the] resistance of Germans and [the] uncompromising and at times exasperating attitude of France'.[54] In the following month Derby warned Curzon that

> unless we take a perfectly strong line that we will keep to the spirit and letter of the Treaty, we shall be in endless difficulties afterwards in these many points when the French and Italian Governments will try to secure something more out of Germany and perhaps out of us, than is contained in the Treaty.[55]

The French had good reason to be irritated by Britain's behaviour. At Paris Britain had led the way in insisting on a very high level of reparations. Later, however, she gave little or no support to French efforts to extract them. She had played a leading role in thwarting French security demands at Paris but showed no disposition thereafter to help her to uphold what was left. Lloyd George hoped that Germany would settle down within her new frontiers and concentrate on economic reconstruction. When she showed no signs of so doing, he began to champion a more conciliatory approach, believing that the recovery of German (and Russian) economic life was essential for the revival of British trade and prosperity. Even the hard-line Hardinge agreed by 1920 that if Germany maintained her treaty obligations and 'the danger of militarism removed, there is no reason why we should not do our utmost to help them improve their economic position, for their prosperity is essential for the whole of Europe as well as for themselves'.[56] French insistence on extracting reparations from Germany threatened these British hopes and, in addition, kept alive German resentment about the treaty. By 1920 anti-German passions in Britain were beginning to subside: those in France had not.

The British argued that foreign policy must evolve in the light of changing circumstances, especially in the context of her economic and financial difficulties, and of the need to oversee a world-wide empire with inadequate military and naval forces. In November 1919 Walter Long complained that:

> Notwithstanding the general talk of peace, we are confronted with grave causes of unrest in more than one part of the world, which may easily lead to trouble if not war... the possession of a strong Navy is the only justification for our claim to be a First Class Power: and I think there are indications of a tendency to reduce [it] in this respect to a very dangerous condition.[57]

The French could not be expected to appreciate Britain's curious mixture of insularity and concentration on imperial problems.

Both Britain and France were more or less able to thwart each other's German policies in the 1920s but were unable individually to promote a coherent long term solution which the other would accept. The two Powers with most at stake in the peace settlement could neither agree to uphold the treaty nor to work together to find some means of modifying it. Because Britain had distrusted the nature of French war aims since 1916,[58] she had based her conference and post-war policies on collaboration with the United States, because she thought that Wilsonianism, after the freedom of the seas issue was buried, was more akin both to British ways of thinking and to post-war stability than anything the French could offer. British politicians ignored Foreign Office assistant under-secretary Sir Eyre Crowe's warning in December 1918 that 'we must remember that our friend America lives a long way off. France sits at our door.'[59]

The difficulty was that Britain had not seriously considered any alternative policy if that of Anglo-American co-operation proved to be a mirage. Differing perceptions of their national interests and of the future of Europe inhibited any real alignment between Britain and France except for a brief period after Locarno.

NOTES

1. See also George W. Egerton, 'Britain and the "Great Betrayal": Anglo-American Relations and the Struggle for United States Ratification of the Treaty of Versailles, 1919–1920' in *Historical Journal*, 21, 4(1978): 885-911.
2. F.O. (Foreign Office Archives, Public Records Office, London), 608/435, 'The Settlement', Political Intelligence Department, 18 November 1918.
3. Lloyd George papers (House of Lords Records Office, London), F/50/3, Lloyd George to Clemenceau, November 1918.
4. Walter A. McDougall, *France's Rhineland Diplomacy 1914–1924, The Last Bid for a Balance of Power in Europe* (Princeton University Press, 1978) p. 38.
5. F.O. 608/173, General Radcliffe to Lord Hardinge, 20 January 1919, communicating a memorandum by Lt Col R. H. Beadon, 'Note on America and the Peace Conference', 17 January 1919.
6. Lloyd George papers, F/3/4/45, Balfour to Lloyd George, 29 November 1918.
7. Hardinge papers (Cambridge University Library), Vol. 39, Hardinge to Rodd, 6 December 1919.
8. Curzon papers (India Office Library, London), F/2/2 R-W, Curzon to Rodd, 24 January 1919.
9. Lloyd George papers, F/52/2/50, Memorandum by Ian Malcolm, Paris, 23 November 1918; F/3/3/45, Derby to Balfour, 20 December 1918.
10. Lloyd George papers, F/23/3/32, Memorandum by Col L. S. Amery, 'United States and the Occupied Enemy Territories', 20 December 1918; Minute by Hankey.
11. F.O. 608/173, General Radcliffe to Lord Hardinge, 20 January 1919, com-

municating a memorandum by Lt Col R. H. Beadon, 'Note on America and the Peace Conference', 17 January 1919.
12. Curzon papers, EUR F111 F/2/2, Long to Curzon, 3 January 1919.
13. Curzon papers, box 65, F/6/2(f), Derby to Curzon, 10 February 1919.
14. Georges Clemenceau, the French prime minister.
15. Lloyd George papers, F/89/2/8, Lloyd George to Kerr, 12 February 1919. For other examples of British anti-French feelings in 1919, see also John C. Cairns, 'A Nation of Shopkeepers in Search of a Suitable France', *American Historical Review,* 79, no. 3 (June 1974): 710–15.
16. Lloyd George papers, F/89/2/23, Kerr to Lloyd George, 18 February 1919.
17. For details see A. J. Marder, *From the Dreadnought to Scapa Flow: The Royal Navy in the Fisher Era, 1904–19,* 5 vols. (London, 1961–1970), Vol. 5, pp. 224–238.
18. Lloyd George papers, F/23/4/19, Kerr to Lloyd George, 21 February 1919.
19. Lloyd George papers, F/89/2/38, Kerr to Lloyd George, 3 March 1919.
20. Lloyd George papers, F/33/2/22, Long to Lloyd George, 7 March 1919.
21. Lloyd George papers, F/30/3/40, Lloyd George to Bonar Law, 30 March 1919.
22. Lloyd George papers, F/89/2/38, Kerr to Lloyd George, 3 March 1919.
23. F.O. 800/153, Curzon to Derby, 4 March 1919.
24. Political Intelligence Department, Foreign Office, Headlam-Morley to E. R. Bevan, 5 March 1919.
25. Curzon papers, F/6/2(f), Derby to Curzon, 7 March 1919.
26. See Michael L. Dockrill and J. Douglas Goold, *Peace without Promise: Britain and the Peace Conferences, 1919–1923* (London, 1981), pp. 28–9.
27. Lloyd George papers, F/30/3/40, Lloyd George to Bonar Law, 30 March 1919.
28. Lloyd George papers, F/30/3/37, Bonar Law to Lloyd George, 27 March 1919.
29. Lloyd George papers, F/45/9/29, Smuts to Lloyd George, 26 March 1919.
30. Balfour papers (British Library), 49744, extract from Derby's diary, 8 April 1919, in Derby to Balfour, 9 April 1919.
31. Lloyd George papers, F/23/4/50, Note by Foch, 8 April 1919.
32. Lloyd George papers, F/5/5/7, Botha to Lloyd George, 11 April 1919. See also Dockrill and Goold, *Peace without Promise,* pp. 54–6.
33. Headlam-Morley to Smuts, 19 May 1919, cited in Sir James Headlam-Morley, *A Memoir of the Paris Peace Conference, 1919,* edited by Agnes Headlam-Morley (London, 1972), p. 118.
34. A member of the Political Intelligence Department at the Foreign Office.
35. Headlam-Morley papers (University of Coleraine), E. R. Bevan to Headlam-Morley, 7 June 1919.
36. Lloyd George papers, F/45/9/34, Smuts to Lloyd George, 14 May 1919.
37. Lloyd George papers, F/5/5/9, Botha to Lloyd George, 15 May 1919.
38. Lloyd George papers, F/8/3/55, Churchill to Lloyd George, 20 May 1919.
39. See Dockrill and Goold, *Peace without Promise,* pp. 71–6.
40. Quoted in Howard Elcock, *Portrait of a Decision: The Council of Four and the Treaty of Versailles* (London, 1972), p. 276.

41. Lloyd George papers, F/6/6/47, Cecil to Lloyd George, 27 May 1919.
42. Lloyd George papers, F/89/3/11, Kerr to Lloyd George, July 1919.
43. Hardinge papers, Vol. 39, Hardinge to Wingate, 28 November 1918.
44. Marc Trachtenburg, 'Reparation at the Paris Peace Conference', *Journal of Modern History* (January 1979): 25.
45. Egerton, 'Britain and the "Great Betrayal"', 890.
46. Curzon papers, EUR F/2/2, Memorandum by Grey, September 1919; and Curzon to Grey, 9 September 1919.
47. Curzon papers, GF/2/2, Grey to Curzon, 6 October 1919. Wilson suffered a stroke on 20 October 1919.
48. Curzon papers, F/3/1, Tyrrell, Washington, to Curzon.
49. For Britain's reaction to the Lodge reservations to the treaty and the League, see Egerton, 'Britain and the "Great Betrayal"', 891ff.
50. Curzon papers, F/2/2, Curzon to Grey, 22 November 1919.
51. Curzon papers, F/6/2(f), extract from Derby's diary, 27 November 1919.
52. Curzon papers, F/6/2(f), Derby to Curzon, 5 March 1920.
53. Lloyd George papers, F/9/2/20, Churchill to Lloyd George, 24 March 1920.
54. Curzon papers, F/3/1, Curzon to Crowe, Paris (tel), 4 December 1919.
55. Curzon papers, F/6/2, Derby to Curzon, 3 January 1920.
56. Hardinge papers, Vol. 42, Hardinge to Harcourt Butler, 22 June 1920.
57. Curzon papers, K-L F/2/2, Long to Curzon, 28 November 1919.
58. McDougall, *France's Rhineland Diplomacy*, p. 23.
59. Minute by Crowe, 7 December 1918, cited in V. H. Rothwell, *British War Aims and Peace Diplomacy, 1914–1918* (Oxford, 1971).

B. J. C. McKERCHER

The British Diplomatic Service in the United States and the Chamberlain Foreign Office's Perceptions of Domestic America, 1924–1927: Images, Reality, and Diplomacy

During the last two years of the second Baldwin government, especially after the diplomatic crisis fostered by the ill-timed announcement of the Anglo-French disarmament compromise in July 1928, the American question came to dominate the diplomacy of Austen Chamberlain, the foreign secretary. During Chamberlain's tenure at the Foreign Office—from November 1924 to June 1929—several senior members of that ministry recognised that the United States presented some unique foreign policy problems. The Great War had paved the way for an American challenge to Britain's position as the only truly 'world Power'; Robert Craigie, the head of the Foreign Office American Department after February 1928, put the matter clearly to the Cabinet:

> Great Britain is faced in the United States of America with a phenomenon for which there is no parallel in our modern history—a State twenty-five times as large, five times as wealthy, three times as populous, twice as ambitious, almost invulnerable, and at least our equal in prosperity, vital energy, techni-

cal equipment and industrial science. This State has risen to its present state of development at a time when Great Britain is still staggering from the effects of the superhuman effort made during the war, is loaded with a great burden of debt and is crippled by the evil of unemployment.[1]

Two contradictory ideas under-pinned American foreign policy in the decade after the Paris Peace Conference which, reaching an acute phase in the late 1920s, the Chamberlain Foreign Office had to handle. The first was the avowal of the Harding, Coolidge, and Hoover administrations to involve the United States government in the efforts of American firms to compete for overseas markets in which, coincidentally, Britain was traditionally strong.[2] More important to British diplomacy, the second concerned the determination of American leaders to remain isolated from the political side of international politics.[3] This American abdication of political responsibility forced Chamberlain to pursue an interventionist diplomacy in various areas of the world where Britain and the United States each had a substantial economic stake and where the threat to international peace and security was most critical, most notably in western Europe.[4]

Suffusing British efforts to come to grips with the contradictions in American diplomacy was an American determination to achieve naval parity with Britain. A strong United States Navy could protect maritime trade routes and in the event of war in Europe or elsewhere, in which the Americans assumed they would be neutral because of their isolation, safeguard those routes from belligerent interference. This lay at the heart of Anglo-American differences in the late 1920s. By mid-1927 the Chamberlain Foreign Office[5] believed it understood the official, governmental foreign-policy-making process in the Republican United States and how to exploit it to Britain's advantage.[6] What needs examination is the image of domestic America that arose in the Foreign Office in the same period, since the official, foreign-policy-making process was susceptible to pressures brought to bear upon it by American public opinion.

The connection between the quality of information reaching the Foreign Office and the policies and strategies thus derived has always been crucial. In the 1920s whilst other ministries whose work centred chiefly on domestic affairs could test first-hand Britain's economic, political, and social climate before implementing policy, the Foreign Office relied heavily on a mass of second-hand information that came by despatch bag and telegram from abroad and, less often, by personal interview with British diplomats at home on leave and with the foreign diplomatic corps and others at London. But as all of this amounted to impressions of reality, some of it contradictory, it follows that the Foreign Office was to some extent cocooned from that reality. The key to any Foreign Office success resided with the diplomatic service abroad; the clearer and more distinct the images sent by the diplomats, the closer the Foreign Office was to international politics, and the better able it was to make policy and co-ordinate strategy.

What was true of most countries in general was especially so concerning the United States. That country was both distant and large, and possessed a heterogeneous population whose loyalties did not necessarily support the comity of English-speaking peoples; hence the British Embassy at Washington had to have assistance in assessing the domestic hubris that influenced the course of American foreign policy. Interestingly this help did not come from the various consulates spread throughout the United States;[7] instead, it came from the British Library of Information at New York (BLINY) which as part of its mandate analysed national press opinion to determine general American attitudes. The Chamberlain Foreign Office accordingly had two diplomatic sources in the United States working together that supplied it with an American image that helped to produce the diplomacy necessary to meet the American challenge of the 1920s.

Esme Howard, the ambassador to the United States from 1924 to 1930, recognised that he and his staff tended to get an unrepresentative view of American opinion.[8] The social and political circles in which they functioned daily were not only confined to the northeast portion of the country, they were dominated by politicians, civil servants, and the 'eastern establishment'. For instance, Embassy officials were really part of the swirl of Washington's political life; they could not dissociate themselves from it since their work entailed monitoring the debate and progress of legislation that touched on British interests, especially when it involved the White House or the State Department or important congressional bodies like the Senate Foreign Relations Committee and the House Committee of Naval Affairs. Realising that his Embassy was isolated to a great extent from the currents of opinion in the South and west of the Mississippi Valley, Howard encouraged senior members of his staff to travel to these regions whenever he could and, in the Spring of 1927, he even made an extended tour of the country.[9] But it remained that regular and constant contact with the regions outside of the Washington-New York-Philadelphia triangle could not occur. The exigencies of Embassy work and the problems involved with rail travel militated against this.

It was the limitations of the Embassy that underscored BLINY's importance. BLINY was established in 1920 as a successor to the New York-based British Bureau of Information, the propaganda arm of the British government in the United States that had been created during the Great War.[10] After the American rejection of the Treaty of Versailles, the Foreign Office decided that whilst the Bureau of Information should continue, it would be more effective if its propaganda work was balanced with helping the Washington Embassy supply the Foreign Office with appraisals of United States domestic opinion. Rechristened the Library of Information, its new dual purpose was made explicit: 'to serve as a clearing house, where information on British affairs is made available to the American public, while information is secured from American sources on various matters of interest to the Foreign Office and other departments'.[11]

BLINY acquired information primarily through subscription to a wide variety of regional newspapers and magazines. Robert Wilberforce and Angus Fletcher, the two principal BLINY staff during the 1920s, would analyse the leading articles and news reports of these publications, compile topical summaries, and despatch them to the Foreign Office News Department, the political section to which it was responsible. Because of Sir Arthur Willert, a senior member of the News Department after 1920 and later, in 1925, its head, the Foreign Office tended to equate American press opinion with public opinion. Willert had served as a *Times'* correspondent and a British government propagandist in the United States from 1910 to 1920,[12] so that his word on the American press was rarely questioned. It followed that BLINY's assessments of regional press opinion could be a valuable supplement to the purely political exegesis of Howard and the Embassy in presenting the Foreign Office with as accurate an image of the United States as possible.

The Embassy at Washington and BLINY did not work in isolation from one another. Howard established a close relationship with Wilberforce and Fletcher after he took up his ambassadorial appointment in February 1924. Before the end of that year Howard and Wilberforce devised a strategy by which BLINY would send advance copies of important speeches Howard was to make to a large circle of regional newspapers.[13] This had never been done before, and it had the double advantage of not only ensuring a wide distribution of the official British viewpoint on a range of issues affecting Anglo-American relations, it provided 'a good opportunity for opening up relations' with newspaper editors whom the Embassy and BLINY might later be able to exploit to Britain's advantage. In addition, when the Foreign Office American Department, which was responsible for monitoring the United States, would request special Embassy analyses of American press opinion to determine domestic attitudes toward particular diplomatic problems, the Embassy tended to turn to BLINY to conduct this work. Ascertaining the mood of domestic America in 1928 to the negotiation of the multilateral treaty to renounce the use of war in national policy—the so-called Kellogg-Briand pact—was a case in point.[14]

One problem dogged BLINY throughout the 1920s—the lack of adequate funding to maintain its operations and keep its staff. Of course the impact of government retrenchment in Britain throughout the inter-war years was felt in every ministry, but Howard and Willert were aware that BLINY's success was proportional to the money it could spend to acquire information and analyse it. Howard explained this to Chamberlain when, in the immediate aftermath of the abortive Coolidge naval conference of June-August 1927, Anglo-American relations were beginning to feel the strain imposed by the naval question.[15] Since the Embassy had contact chiefly with the Washington correspondents of the major American newspapers—'they do not really amount to much for they have to send what their bosses want to publish'—BLINY remained essential to the British diplomatic establishment in the United States. Howard argued that 'the Library of Information is doing quite good work at New York and has established really valuable work [sic] there', but the problem was that it did not have enough money to fulfill completely its mandate or to transfer its senior members from the temporary to the permanent civil service list. According to Howard, this second problem led to the situation where 'having no future prospects [the senior men] stay at the Library for a couple of years or three years at most and then go into some business'. At the time Howard wrote this, Wilberforce had left BLINY and would not be enticed back until August 1928. Howard implored that 'anything that will help increase the efficiency of the Library will be worthwhile'. Although efforts were made to improve BLINY's conditions as it continued to complete an immense amount of work, adequate funding was never realised in the 1920s.[16]

The course of Anglo-American relations during Chamberlain's tenure at the Foreign Office divides neatly into two parts, with the median formed by the Coolidge naval conference. In the first part the American question was unimportant and remained in the second rank of British foreign policy considerations; in the second, with the onset of Anglo-American naval deadlock over cruiser limitation, the American question became a matter of the first importance and gradually, by the winter of 1928-1929, dominated the foreign policy deliberations of Chamberlain and the second Baldwin government. In this way the image of the United States that had formed in the Chamberlain Foreign Office between November 1924 and the summer of 1927 was critical. By mid-1927 the foreign secretary and his advisers had definite views on domestic America and its probable impact on official, governmental foreign-policy-making. As Anglo-American relations came under increasing strain after mid-1927, the image of domestic America as perceived in the Foreign Office, an image which evolved in the almost two years after Chamberlain became foreign secretary, was crucial in framing British American policy. The Embassy at Washington and BLINY were the fundamental link between events in the United States and the Chamberlain Foreign Office; their image of domestic America had to be clear and distinct.

For the Embassy, BLINY, and the Foreign Office the key to understanding domestic America hinged on acquiring a balanced and objective view of its political make-up. The complete ascendancy of the Republican Party at the national level, controlling as it did the White House and the two houses of Congress, set the tone for political developments in the United States. Coolidge came to power on his own less than one week after Baldwin, Chamberlain, and the Conservative Party triumphed in the British general election of 29 October 1924. In almost his first official despatch from Howard, Chamberlain was told that Coolidge and the Republicans had succeeded because they stood for 'clear-cut Conservative principles and the average American voter at least knew what he was out for'.[17] Howard was certain that: 'In the future Republicanism will probably mean Conservatism as it is understood all over the world.' By this the ambassador implied that the Coolidge Administration would be careful and cautious in its handling of a wide range of domestic matters, such as controlling dissident groups like the Ku Klux Klan, and in adhering to the principle that 'the business of America is business'. In terms of foreign policy he was more explicit. There could be no chance of the American public permitting Coolidge to allow the United States to combine with other Powers in interventionist diplomacy. Coolidge's presidential opponent, John W. Davis of the Democratic Party, had supported an American connection with the League of Nations, a stance that cost him dearly at the polls. As Howard told the Foreign Office:

> ... in the face of the fear of 'foreign entanglements' and of being dominated by a European super-State, as the League has been declared to be, many Democrats probably preferred to vote for 'Coolidge and Common Sense', or choose not to vote at all.

But despite the isolationist tendencies of the new Administration and its electoral support, and the problems this engendered diplomatically, the Foreign Office saw in the complete Republican victory a suggestion that at least there would be some consistency of purpose at the upper levels of American political life until after the next presidential election in 1928.[18]

The lower levels of political life, however, were a different matter. The British were aware that a strong under-current of xenophobia existed in the United States, a situation that had to be weighed carefully in any diplomatic strategy touching the American question. Chamberlain's first exposure to this occurred in May 1925 when Henry Chilton, the counsellor at the Washington Embassy, reported that the United States Supreme Court upheld California legislation which precluded United States citizens from transferring land to a Japanese.[19] Within a month a number of other decisions limiting the rights of East Asians in the United States were also upheld by the Supreme Court.[20] These decisions played havoc with Coolidge Administration foreign policy in that Japanese-American relations were strained just at the moment when Frank Kellogg, Coolidge's secretary of state, was moving to convene a naval limitation conference which was to include Japan.[21] The lesson was clear that the course of American foreign policy could be diverted by the efforts of state governments.

Although there was a racist element in this sort of xenophobia, other manifestations were directed with equal force against 'White' nations and their citizens. Britain was noticeably vulnerable, this deriving from the fact that the original American colonies had won their independence from England in the late eighteenth century and, in the decade after 1914, Anglo-American relations had been subjected to the pressures brought about by the war and the subsequent post-war readjustment.[22] British susceptibility to American xenophobia was demonstrated clearly to the Chamberlain Foreign Office after the death in July 1925 of William Jennings Bryan, the former American secretary of state and presidential aspirant who had recently prosecuted a Tennessee teacher for suggesting in the classroom that Darwin's theory of evolution had some validity. The British press was less than kind in their assessment of Bryan's career — he was portrayed as a political failure — and, as the Washington Embassy reported, there had been 'considerable resentment' in the American press to the attitude taken by its British counterpart.[23]

Chilton observed that the newspaper chain owned by William Randolph Hearst, an extremely nationalistic organisation with nationwide coverage, was particularly incensed. For instance in noting that British newspapers had spoken disparagingly of Bryan's Midwest rural origins, Chilton reported that the Hearst newspaper responded with editorials saying that: 'Alongside England's rotten titled class, which now stands in line at the divorce court, dripping with slime, the farmers of the United States look like lilies of culture.' Foreign Office officials recognised that Hearst regarded 'everything with cynical indifference, but it pays him to indulge in tirades against this country'.[24] But they were also aware that the course of Anglo-American relations could be damaged if a trans-Atlantic press war was allowed to develop, especially over issues which the Foreign Office and the diplomats in the United States had no control. In working to resolve subsequent Anglo-American differences, Chamberlain and his advisers remained cognisant of the power of the American press.[25]

Indeed, when the opportunity arose after this, the Foreign Office through Willert and the News Department took every opportunity to cultivate the American press. In one instance, in June 1927, the London District of the Institute of Journalists was to host a meeting of United States newspaper editors who were travelling through Europe on a tour arranged by the Carnegie Endowment for International Peace, an influential domestic American foreign policy association.[26] The British organisers of the London meeting asked Arthur Balfour, a former prime minister and foreign secretary with decided pro-American sympathies, to speak at its luncheon. When Balfour's private secretary enquired if the Foreign Office thought this might benefit Anglo-American relations, the News Department was unequivocal in endorsing Balfour's attendance:

> ...these American Editors, who are mostly bringing their wives and making atrip [sic] of it, are a representative lot and are drawn from a considerable area of the more distant U.S.A. We cannot be entirely unconcerned about the impressions they may carry away with them.[27]

Balfour thus spoke to these American editors.

The Foreign Office felt that these under-currents of xenophobia, as important as they were—and Chamberlain and his advisers through the Embassy and BLINY saw them as a danger only if aroused by unscrupulous men like Hearst—represented half the reason the Coolidge Administration pursued a diplomacy of political isolation. The other half resided with a general American disillusionment with European politics after the peace settlement of 1919–1920. Despite the efforts of American leaders at the Paris Peace Conference, so the argument ran in the United States, that peace settlement had revived the jaded and decrepit system of secret diplomacy, the balance of power, and all of the other 'European' diplomatic practices that had been discredited by the outbreak of general war on the continent in 1914. The Foreign Office was kept abreast of such feelings in the United States, especially since the focus of domestic American disgruntlement with European diplomacy was the League of Nations.

The difficulty for Chamberlain in all of this was that his foreign policy was based both on the maintenance of the balance of power in Europe and the League of Nations. After the peace settlement, France and Germany had been at odds continually over how best to ensure peace and security on the continent. A succession of British leaders had been powerless to stem Franco-German animosities which most people, both in and out of government, saw as possessing the seeds of another world war.[28] Soon after taking the Foreign Office Chamberlain decided that it was in Britain's best interests to resolve European tensions by holding the pivotal position in the European balance of power.[29] By October 1925 he succeeded where his predecessors had failed when he arrogated for himself the key role in negotiating the Locarno accords, the treaties which among other things stabilised Germany's western border with an Anglo-Italian guarantee. Central to this entire process was Chamberlain's determination to bring Germany back into the community of great Powers, and he did this by working to secure German membership in the League of Nations.

The American response to Locarno and all it entailed, especially the prominent position given to the League, was a fundamental consideration for Chamberlain. Chamberlain was aware of American coolness toward the League when he took office. This emerged in the advice he gave one of his Cabinet colleagues, Robert, Viscount Cecil of Chelwood, who was one of the founders of the League and who was to travel to New York in December 1924 to receive the first Woodrow Wilson Foundation award. Cecil was advised that 'the true line of approach to the American fortress is not by the political work of the League but by its humanitarian achievements and practical usefulness'.[30] Over the next year and one-half, through the negotiation of Locarno and on to the Coolidge naval conference, this image of the United States' isolation from Europe and opposition to the League was re-enforced by Howard and BLINY.

In early January 1925 Howard reported on some conversations he had had with Charles Evans Hughes, Coolidge's departing secretary of state.[31] Hughes was especially concerned that the League might see fit to involve itself in the resolution of a dispute concerning one of its Latin American members or, worse, if one of those members called on the League to help it oppose measures which the United States might be forced to take to protect its interests in south or central America — Hughes made much of United States resolve to protect the Panama Canal. The basis of Hughes' argument, which Howard endorsed, was that League interference in Latin America would see 'an explosion of public opinion' in the United States in favour of strong measures to protect American interests. The League was obviously perceived as a potential American enemy.

Whilst Hughes' views could conceivably be construed as no more than the rhetoric of official Washington, Howard reported that they were shared by other Americans. Such feelings on the part of the Midwest were driven home to the Foreign Office later in the year after Howard completed a tour of Missouri and Illinois.[32] Invited to attend and speak before a dedication ceremony at the School of Journalism at the University of Missouri, he chose to speak on Britain, the League, and the United States. In this address, Howard acknowledged that United States membership in the League in 1920 would probably have been short-lived, a result of certain American disenchantment with the machinations of post-war European diplomacy. An American withdrawal would have been a 'deathblow' to the League, thus it was 'a blessing in disguise' that the Americans had rejected League membership. The consensus of the local press was that Howard had uttered the truth and the Foreign Office, though divided in its opinion about the ambassador making such frank statements, recognised the deep-seated antipathy a wide range of American opinion had for the League and its European members.[33]

The Foreign Office was also made aware that domestic American antipathy towards the League was tied to that contradiction in United States foreign policy that attempted to balance isolation in international politics, especially from Europe, with economic entanglements. BLINY put this in perspective in early 1926, just when the Locarno system was about to be initiated by German entry to the League. The Foreign Office American Department was aware that the Coolidge Administration was following an earlier Republican precedent to have the American underwriters of foreign loans supply information to both the State Department and the Department of Commerce about their activities.[34] In February 1926 R. I. Campbell, then a member of the Foreign Office American Department, observed that this was because: 'The U.S.G.[overnment] do however appear to seek to exercise some influence from the political point of view—and we have seen instances of this in connection with loans to France....'[35] Whilst eschewing a political role in Europe, Americans sought to protect their economic interests.

BLINY reported in that same month that some American commentators, who were not unsympathetic to the notion of greater

United States participation in international politics, were attempting through national periodicals to influence thinking Americans about the paradox of political isolation and economic commitments[36] — this coincided with the run-up to the 1926 mid-term Congressional elections scheduled for November. In one instance the Berlin correspondent of *The Chicago Daily News*, E. A. Mowrer, offered the persuasive argument that American foreign policy was unreal if its makers and American public opinion thought there was any difference between political and economic diplomacy in Europe.[37] Whether Americans realised it or not, 'the dominant section in America — the Wall Street element — has embarked on a policy of economic expansion in the world at large, which, for better or worse, has linked Europe and the United States together by strong financial ties.' The crux of Mowrer's argument was the League, as he believed American involvement, perhaps even membership, could resolve the inconsistency. But BLINY observed:

> The extraordinary ignorance of foreign affairs prevailing among public men of the United States is illustrated by the paradoxical position of those editors and senators who wish at all costs to keep America outside of the League of Nations. They argue that the United States must remain isolated if she is to remain safe. Participation in the League means, in their view, that America will be again involved in European nationalistic politics. But these same papers and senators are the most vociferous in demanding the full payment of War Debts.

The admonitions of Mowrer and those like him fell on deaf American ears.

By mid-1927, just before the American question was propelled into the first rank of British foreign policy problems, the Foreign Office had definite views on the United States, Europe, and the League. For Chamberlain, the best course was to keep the United States out of the international organisation. He outlined his views to Hugh Spender, the European correspondent of *The Christian Science Monitor*, a publication Willert characterised as 'important and friendly... the only American paper with a national circulation'.[38] Chamberlain did not mince his words when he told Spender: 'There are features of [American] public life and even of their constitution which make me doubt whether it would be on balance an advantage to the League that they should join until they have a clearer perception of conditions in the old world and of what is necessary for international cooperation.' The foreign secretary was convinced that the political conditions in the United States would preclude an effective American contribution to the work of the League, especially within the Council, its highest deliberative organ. League delegates had to be given 'a certain latitude' and a degree of independence to participate in its deliberations; Chamberlain understood this completely as he had attended every Council and Assembly as the principal British delegate since becoming foreign secretary. Any American representatives, he was convinced, would be denied such flexibility because the White House and State Department would have to square the actions, words, and bargaining positions of any American delegates to conform to the pressures exerted by Congress and the country at large. The various reports from Howard and BLINY had shown this, as had limited American participation in a few non-political League endeavours. In his letter to Spender, Chamberlain mentioned the difficulties caused by American involvement in a conference to control international opium traffic:[39]

> ... if an American delegate comes as, for instance, General Porter did to the Opium Conference with the announcement that he holds his instructions from Congress and snaps his fingers at the Government, that none but Congress can alter its resolutions, and that he can therefore make no concession to other parties, it is clear that the Council system would break down.

Aware of American public opinion's distrust and suspicion of foreigners, especially European Powers, and of the political necessity for leaders like Coolidge to cut and trim policy to meet the concerns of the electorate, Chamberlain opined that the certainty of American League membership would be almost continual 'deadlock'.

The Coolidge naval conference in the summer of 1927 showed Chamberlain and his advisers at London that the image of domestic America despatched to them by the Embassy at Washington and BLINY since November 1924 was accurate. The antecedents of that conference and of its deliberations have been analysed in detail before.[40] It was intimately connected with international arms limitation talks which had begun in March 1926 to provide a draft treaty for an eventual world disarmament conference—that such a conference did not meet until February 1932 suggests the difficulties that arose in arriving at a draft treaty aimed at restricting air, land, and sea weapons. The naval conference at Geneva broke down because the British and Americans could not agree on whether cruiser limitation should be at a figure convenient to Britain or to the United States; cruisers were at once the principal defenders of seaborne lines of communication and the chief means of imposing maritime belligerent rights. This important issue, as well as the course of the conference itself and the mutual Anglo-American recriminations brought to the surface in its aftermath, had a significant impact on domestic America—of course these same issues affected domestic Britain, though this is a different matter. As Chamberlain and his principal advisers worked to resolve the crisis in Anglo-American relations after mid-1927, their image of domestic America was crucial to the formulation and execution of their policy.

Given the sensitivity of the naval question on both sides of the Atlantic, especially on the American side as presented by Howard and BLINY over the years,[41] the British took the precaution of including in their delegation a member of the Foreign Office News Department whose job was to explain the official British position to the assembled newspapermen and answer their questions. This was a thoughtful piece of diplomacy in that Britain's case could be put in the best light; moreover, as such an official had rarely been included in formal delegations on the part of any Power at previous international conferences, it stole a march on the Americans and Japanese who did not send anyone in a similar capacity. George Steward, the News Department representative who possessed a short but distinguished record in diplomatic press liaison work—in 1922 the Belgian government made him a Chevalier de l'Ordre de la Couronne de la Belgique for helping good Anglo-Belgian relations —made extensive arrangements to publish the proceedings at Geneva.[42] He also set up interviews for senior British delegates with journalists, distributed important British speeches, and ensured that 'general information' concerning British proposals was placed quickly into the hands of the newspapermen.

The stumbling-block in British planning was that some American journalists unconnected with the American delegation and in no way representative of the American government went to Geneva determined to sabotage the conference. One was William Shearer, who had been hired by a number of United States steel and shipbuilding firms to influence American pressmen at Geneva against placing any limitations on United States naval strength. Whether Shearer was successful is a matter of dispute.[43] But it remains that as the Coolidge conference progressed, American pressmen at Geneva became inclined to see the cruiser limitation proposals fostered by Britain as ploys designed to hamstring American naval development whilst Britain's went on unimpeded. Shearer thought he succeeded, something that emerged two years later when he brought law suits in American courts to recoup monies he claimed companies like the Bethlehem Shipbuilding Corporation owed him for his disruptive work at Geneva.[44] More importantly, the Foreign Office believed Shearer had had a decided impact on the course of events, this emerging in a post-conference analysis of Shearer's 'vicious anti-British' propaganda conducted by Steward.[45]

During the conference, the Foreign Office worried about the way in which the domestic American press was reporting on the proceedings. For instance on 12 July John Steele, *The Chicago Tribune*'s London correspondent who had returned recently from a trip to the United States, was interviewed by Arthur Yencken, a News Department official.[46] Yencken wanted to discover why that newspaper had been engaged in 'cold blooded and deliberate lying'. He learned there would be no attempt on the part of the *Tribune* to reprimand its Geneva correspondent, a man named Wales. As Yencken was told: 'That's just Wales; he is very wild.' A week later Howard reported to Chamberlain that Chilton had returned from a tour of the West with the distressing news that public opinion there favoured expansion of American naval power.[47] The American press was clearly having a decided influence since, as Howard pointed out, this area had been one which supported less government spending above all else. As the distortions by American journalists became more pronounced, Howard was finally instructed to deliver a formal protest to the Coolidge Administration. He did so on 26 July,[48] but it had little effect. Official American opinion seemed to be hardening, the result of American domestic opinion displaying its anglophobia. The chance of a negotiated settlement was vanishing rapidly, something Howard was predicting as early as 21 July.[49] By this time as well, anti-Americans within the Baldwin Cabinet led principally by Winston Churchill, the chancellor of the

Exchequer, were themselves working to disrupt the conference by engineering the recall of the chief British delegates for consultations at a crucial moment in the negotiations.[50] In this atmosphere of aroused public opinion and the subversive machinations of naval hardliners, the conference ended with a whimper and no decisions on 4 August.

When the conference was less than two weeks old, BLINY had already concluded that despite the efforts of Steward the propaganda war had been lost in the United States.[51] John Bird, a junior BLINY official, offered an analysis of the domestic American situation that precipitated a heated debate within the Foreign Office about how best to consider that situation when making and implementing British American policy. He acknowledged that the American correspondents at Geneva were partly to blame, but the real problem was in not having someone with real knowledge of domestic America handling British press liaison. After undertaking a detailed assessment of a wide-range of American press coverage of the conference, he suggested that:

> The American public thinks that it understands the American proposals... Our proposals are understood only by the experts; therefore, the American public decides: 'Great Britain is trying to side-track a straightforward plan by means of technicalities and shilly-shallying.'

It was Bird's considered opinion that the domestic American reaction to the events at Geneva would have been markedly different if Willert had been there to handle the American press.

The debate within the Foreign Office occurred between the American and Western Departments. This was only natural. As the Western Department was responsible for advising on the government's disarmament policy, any criticism of the work of the British delegation amounted to criticism of Western Department counsel and of its members who accompanied the senior delegates in administrative capacities. Gerald Villiers, the Western Department head, laid the blame for the failure of the conference squarely on the American correspondents.[52] Even if Willert had been there, he opined, the result would have been the same. The American Department did not share Villier's pessimism.[53] Although acknowledging that Bird might have over-stated his argument about why British propaganda failed—"Mr Bird... whose thankless task it is to spend weary hours daily examining the United States press, has been submitted to the full force of the drubbing we have received during recent weeks'—the American Department felt his perception of domestic America reacting unfavourably to Britain was deadly accurate.

The American Department-Western Department rift was intensified by another report from Bird just as the conference was sputtering to a halt—the Foreign Office actually received it after the proceedings had ended.[54] Bird contended that despite the damage that had been done to naval limitation at Geneva, the damage done to domestic American opinion remained 'to a great extent potential'. American ill-feelings toward Britain were as much the result of the disfavour with which domestic America viewed the conference through the glasses of American correspondents, as it was at anger that the British press was seeking to lay the blame for failure almost totally on the United States. Bird indicated that British policy should be geared toward re-establishing 'the smooth course of Anglo-American relations', something that would not occur quickly if the Chamberlain Foreign Office took a hardline. After seeing this report, Villiers reacted by plumping for a harder line composed of 'more blunt and fewer mealy-mouthed words'.[55] Echoing Bird's concern, Craigie advocated the opposite tack: 'Unless we want to provide powder and shot for the "big navalists" in the U.S., the less we say about the failure of the Conference and its after-effects the better.'

Following additional reports from Howard, Chamberlain's initial reaction was to consider taking a stronger line toward the United States. The ambassador had indicated that immediately after the final plenary session at Geneva, news articles and editorial opinion in important organs of the American press argued that the conference had failed because the Baldwin government was imbued with 'the spirit of Tory reaction'.[56] This irked the foreign secretary, who immediately penned instructions to Howard to explain what the word 'Tory' meant when he met privately with influential Americans.[57] But the course of events in the United States from August to December 1927 impressed on Chamberlain the wisdom of American Department advice about the need to be cautious in pursuing British American policy.

Although neither Chamberlain nor the American Department

were about to be cowed by American pique,⁵⁸ they came to believe that there was a full-scale Anglo-American diplomatic crisis which, if not handled properly, could severely damage relations between the two countries. The corollary of continued strained relations, something Craigie had suggested after Bird's second report, was that a hardline would simply give more ammunition to American navalists who were intent on constructing 'a navy second to none'. Chamberlain and his senior advisers worried that if the Royal Navy ceased to be the most powerful in the world, it would mean the effective end of Britain as a Power of the first rank. Not only would Imperial defence be threatened and British maritime trade, the life line of the country, be imperilled, but Britain's ability to influence the course of international politics would decline markedly — Chamberlain's preoccupation with Locarno and the need for Britain to play a decisive role in maintaining the European balance of power was a major factor in this line of reasoning.

The perception in the collective Foreign Office mind of an Anglo-American diplomatic crisis was sharpened with the receipt of additional reports from Howard and BLINY. Most crucial was the official American view of the state of Anglo-American relations. Immediately after Geneva, a wide range of United States periodicals published articles that argued for the construction of a large navy to protect American sea-borne commerce from the future application of British maritime belligerent rights.⁵⁹ This argument was not the exclusive domain of shrill American jingoes, a fact driven home by Howard in August 1927. He had had a series of private, informal conversations with Herbert Hoover, the Republican secretary of commerce since 1920 who had pursued aggressive overseas trade policies.⁶⁰ In their conversations Howard and Hoover talked openly about the strain in Anglo-American relations that had resulted from the naval issue, the possibility of war breaking out as a result, the course of such a war, and the best way to obviate such a struggle. Although both deprecated the idea of Anglo-American war, they concurred that if it was fought the battles would occur at sea as each side would seek to blockade the merchant shipping of the other.⁶¹ As Howard observed privately to Chamberlain, the problem for Britain in fighting the United States, quite apart from the logistical problems of mobilising and engaging in combat, would be to preserve Imperial unity. Canada was the key. Given its small population and weak military posture, it would be forced into neutrality, and the impact of this on the other White Dominions as well as the colonies would be too terrible to contemplate.[62]

Roused to new heights of anglophobia in the wake of the Coolidge conference, the mood of domestic America seemed to support the endeavours of American navalists. BLINY's reports gave evidence of this throughout the autumn of 1927 in describing a phenomenon called '100% Americanism'. In the first week of October BLINY sent a detailed report which analysed the work of Frederick Bausman, a former member of the Washington State Supreme Court who dabbled in writing on foreign affairs.[63] Bausman was getting a good deal of attention because of a particularly anglophobic book he had just published. BLINY also informed the Foreign Office that Bausman had also published an article in the *American Mercury*, the paper of H. L. Mencken, the brilliant journalist who BLINY described as 'the scourge of 100% Americanism' but a man possessing 'animus against Great Britain'. Bausman's *Mercury* article was simply a *précis* of his book: 'It rings with all the charges: Britain's traditional unwillingness to brook a rival; bitterness over the debt dispute; petty evidences of anglophilism [in the United States]; alleged propaganda; the Rhodes Scholarships; naval rivalry at the Washington and Geneva Conferences; and so on.'

The Foreign Office recognised that Bausman lacked the prestige to sustain himself and his work in the national press in the United States for any length of time.[64] But there was a recognition that Bausman, despite his transitoriness, was probably representative of the '100% Americanism' gaining ground in the United States. James Headlam-Morley, the Foreign Office historical adviser, offered the comment that Bausman was arguing for defence of 'the principle called the freedom of the seas' and 'that war between America and Great Britain is almost inevitable and that America must prepare for it'.[65] The essential thing for the Foreign Office to know was if Bausman's view was 'a real indication of what is going on in America'.

Willert wrote to Fletcher to respond to Headlam-Morley's enquiry. The answer provided was that 'the American attitude towards Great Britain is taking quite a normal course'.[66] Fletcher observed:

> We are always slightly less popular when a Conservative Government is in power, simply because a Conservative Govern-

ment is known to be less yielding to American pretensions, or, to put it in the language of the American himself, because the Conservatives are 'Tories'.

Nonetheless Fletcher cautioned that the collapse of the Coolidge conference had 'hardened' domestic American opinion in favour of naval expansion. He was blunt in telling the Foreign Office: 'The immediate danger ahead seems to be the chance of a naval race.' London was cautioned to be 'cool' in its approach to the United States. The necessity to remain cool was accentuated by reports from other centres of '100% Americanism' which Howard and BLINY forwarded to the Foreign Office. Chicago was a good example. William Thompson, the mayor of that city, was charging the head of the local school board with insubordination because he had authorised the purchase of history books that were pro-British. Indeed, Thompson pictured the school board head as the 'stool pigeon of King George of England'.[67] When the *Chicago Tribune* published a series of articles suggesting that Britain contemplated an attack on the Panama Canal from British Honduras,[68] the need to avoid stridency in pursuit of British American policy became obvious.

Chamberlain became convinced that it was fundamental to British interests to approach the United States in a calm and prudent way. The views of Hoover had shown that official American opinion was distressed at the naval impasse and the reasons for it—the perception that the cruiser deadlock was actually a symptom of the deeper malady concerning belligerent rights versus the freedom of the seas. The impact of Hoover's words increased when, once it became clear that the naval conference at Geneva would fail, Coolidge suddenly announced his decision not to seek another full term as president; the secretary of commerce, the most dynamic member of the Administration, suddenly emerged as the front runner in the race to secure the Republican nomination for president.[69] However, the disaffection of domestic America towards Britain, despite Fletcher's observation that it was 'a normal course', remained an important consideration. '100% Americanism' was never dormant. Britain and the second Baldwin government and all of its 'Tory' works were the convenient focus of the America tendency to xenophobia. The Chamberlain Foreign Office became doubly concerned when this latter tendency was translated into a new United

States naval construction bill late in 1927. Prompted by the arguments of American navalists and the public clamour following the failure at Geneva, the Coolidge Administration asked Congress to provide funding for twenty-five light cruisers, nine destroyers, thirty-two submarines, and five naval aircraft carriers.[70] This bill was designed clearly with the Royal Navy in mind. Although there was no guarantee that such a sizeable increase in American naval forces would be sanctioned by Congress—indeed, as tempers cooled in the United States these proposed appropriations were reduced significantly—the image of domestic America channelled to London by the Embassy at Washington and BLINY was crucial in framing any British response.

In the almost three years between Chamberlain's selection as foreign secretary in November 1924—which occurred within days of Coolidge's election to his first full term as president—and the onset of naval deadlock in mid-1927, the Embassy at Washington and BLINY provided the Foreign Office with a clear image of domestic America. This suggested that care be taken in pursuit of any policies touching the United States. Of course the predilections of American leaders were fundamentally important in determining American foreign policy; but in another way, the mood of domestic America was just as significant. Domestic America was disinclined to look favourably on most political aspects of Chamberlain's foreign policy. To ensure that he and other British leaders would be influential in resolving European crises that might have the potential of unleashing another great war, Chamberlain took a prominent part in the negotiation of the Locarno accords. In general, domestic America favoured political isolation from international affairs, especially those of Europe. Moreover, a great part of Locarno and of the system of European peace and security stemming from it were based on active political involvement in the League of Nations. But the attitude of domestic America, an attitude confirmed by Coolidge's election and the posturing of Charles Evans Hughes over the 'Geneva Protocol', was that the League was a 'European super-State' that had the potential only of engaging the United States in 'foreign entanglements'. In all this there was a paradox in the United States approach to international affairs, a paradox shared by both the majority of political leaders and domestic America—the

241

desire to involve the United States heavily in international economic life, especially in Europe.

It was up to Chamberlain and his advisers to come to grips with the paradox in American foreign policy that was to a large extent fostered by domestic America. But during the first part of the second Baldwin government, there was one critical Anglo-American problem which Chamberlain and his advisers had to grasp — the nettled question of naval limitation. Reports from the Embassy at Washington and BLINY showed there to be widespread support for a powerful American navy. The image despatched to the Foreign Office, especially during the Coolidge conference and its immediate aftermath, was that the Royal Navy posed the greatest threat to United States security. This was part and parcel of a tendency of Americans to castigate foreigners on all manner of issues. Early in Coolidge's full term as president, American xenophobia had been directed against East Asians and enshrined in restrictive legislation. Anglophobia was never far from the surface, as that minor outburst over British press reaction to the death of William Jennings Bryan had shown. In the Summer of 1927 a severe case of anglophobia was whipped up by American journalists at Geneva who were caught in the wrangling over cruiser limitation. Again as the Embassy at Washington and BLINY had shown, an aroused domestic America could pressure its government to initiate, or at the least consider, policies which could threaten Britain's position as a Power of the first rank. Even if American leaders felt disinclined to pursue such policies, the political risks of ignoring the desires of domestic America might be too great to ignore.

The image of the United States despatched to London by the Embassy at Washington and BLINY between late 1924 and mid-1927 impressed on the Chamberlain Foreign Office the necessity of avoiding stridency in pursuing its American policy. It thus became a *sine qua non* of Chamberlain and his advisers to pursue this policy quietly and unobtrusively in order not to raise the ire of domestic America. It was up to those at London to come to grips with the paradoxes in American foreign policy, to pursue interventionist diplomacy in areas where British interests had to be protected, and to resolve the belligerent rights versus the freedom of the seas issue exposed by the naval deadlock. The Embassy at Washington and BLINY provided the Foreign Office with a clear and distinct image of domestic America around which British American policy was fashioned during the deepening Anglo-American crisis in 1928–1929. This image was fixed in the collective Foreign Office mind by mid-1927, so that the responsibility for policy towards the United States lay as much with the diplomatic service in the United States as it did with the Chamberlain Foreign Office.

NOTES

1. Memorandum on 'Outstanding Problems affecting Anglo-American Relations' by Craigie, 12 November 1928, *Documents of British Foreign Policy 1919–1939*, Ser. 1A, Vol. V, pp. 858–75 (hereafter *D.B.F.P.*).
2. For contemporary views, see J. B. Condliffe, 'The Economic and Social Movements Underlying Antagonisms in the Pacific', *International Affairs*, 9(1930): 519–530 (hereafter *I.A.*); J. Klein, 'Economic Rivalries in Latin America', *Foreign Affairs*, 3(1924): 236–243 (hereafter *F.A.*); A. Mond, 'International Cartels', *I.A.*, 6 (1927): 265–283: and W. O. Scroggs, 'The American Investment in Canada', *F.A.*, 11(1933): 716–919. Cf. F.O. 371/11183/562/95, memorandum by Department of Overseas Trade, 29 January 1926. For historical views, see F. C. Costigliola, 'Anglo-American Financial Rivalry in the 1920's, *Journal of Economic History*, 37(1977): 911–934; and M. J. Hogan, *Informal Entente: the private structure of cooperation in Anglo-American economic diplomacy 1918–1928* (Columbia, Missouri, 1977).
3. For an overview, see S. Adler, *The Isolationist Impulse: Its Twentieth Century Reaction* (New York, 1957); L. E. Ellis, *Frank B. Kellogg and American Foreign Relations, 1925–1929* (New Brunswick, New Jersey, 1961); and R. J. Maddox, *William E. Borah and American Foreign Policy* (Baton Rouge, 1969).
4. A. Chamberlain, 'Great Britain as a European Power', *I.A.* 9(1930): 180–188; and J. Jacobson, *Locarno Diplomacy: Germany and the West, 1925–1929* (Princeton, 1972), pp. 3–67 *et passim*.
5. B. J. C. McKercher, 'A British View of American Foreign Policy: The Settlement of Blockade Claims, 1924–1927', *International History Review*, 3(1981): 358–384.
6. For a more detailed study of the Baldwin government's efforts through the Foreign Office to resolve Anglo-American differences, see B. J. C. McKercher, *The Second Baldwin Government and the United States: Attitudes and Diplomacy* (Cambridge, 1984).
7. The consulates chief function seems to have been to report on the activities of the anglophobic efforts of Indian nationalists and Irish republicans, as well as to co-ordinate the visits of British dignitaries. For example, see F.O. 371/1249/1249, G. Campbell [consul-general, San Francisco] to Vansittart [head, F.O. American Department], 18 February 1925; and F.O. 371/12056/3161/1702, G. Campbell's despatch to Howard, 13 April 1927.
8. F.O. 371/12052/673/673, Howard's despatch to Chamberlain, 21 January 1927.

9. On Howard's tour, see Howard of Penrith, *Theatre of Life*, Vol. II: *Life Seen From the Stalls 1905-1936* (London, 1936), pp. 547-559 in which Howard errs inexplicably in his dating; and F.O. 371/12052/3487/673, Howard's despatch to Chamberlain, 3 June 1927. On the tour of Howard's counsellor in 1929, see F.O. 371/13551/3381/3381, R.I. Campbell's despatch to Howard, 29 April 1929; and Howard papers (Cumbria County Record Office) DHW 4/Personal/14, Campbell to Howard, 7 May 1929.
10. On BLINY's antecedents and origins, see P.M. Taylor, 'Publicity and Diplomacy: The Impact of the First World War upon Foreign Office Attitudes towards the Press', in D. Dilks, ed., *Retreat From Power. Studies in Britain's Foreign Policy of the Twentieth Century*, Vol. I: 1906-1939 (London, 1981), pp. 42-63; and P.M. Taylor, *The Projection of Britain. British Overseas Publicity and Propaganda 1919-1939* (Cambridge, 1981), pp. 68-74.
11. This mandate appeared on the first page of every BLINY annual report in this period; for example F.O. 395/420/284/58, 'British Library of Information. Annual Report. 1926'.
12. A. Willert, *Washington and Other Memories* (Boston, 1972), pp. 38-146.
13. Howard papers, DHW 5/12, Wilberforce to J. Balfour [2nd secretary, Washington Embassy], 1 December 1924; Wilberforce to Howard, 3 December 1924; and Howard to Wilberforce, 8 December 1924.
14. F.O. 371/12792/3418/1, Craigie to R.I. Campbell, 12 June 1928; and Fletcher to Craigie, 20 June 1928. F.O. 371/12795/4607/1, Fletcher to Craigie, 29 June 1928, enclosing BLINY memorandum, 29 June 1928; and Craigie minute, 12 July 1928.
15. F.O. 395/420/1271/75, Howard's despatch to Chamberlain, 25 November 1925.
16. In 1927, BLINY received 8,010 letters of enquiry from Americans and despatched 8,317 answers; it also examined 20,694 American newspapers and periodicals, sending 550 notes and 4,688 clippings to London. See F.O. 395/430/261/261, 'British Library of Information. Annual Report. 1927', 10 February 1928 [written by Fletcher]. This report pointed out that the 'outgoing circular material was drastically reduced owing to inadequacy of the staff'.
17. F.O. 371/9612/6455/218, Howard's despatch to Chamberlain, 6 November 1924.
18. Ibid., see R.I. Campbell minute, 19 November 1924; Vansittart minute, 20 November 1924; Chamberlain minute for Baldwin.
19. F.O. 371/10650/2685/2685, Chilton despatch to Chamberlain, 15 May 1925, with enclosure.
20. F.O. 371/10650/3313/2685, Chilton despatch to Chamberlain, 19 June 1925.
21. F.O. 371/10636/77/49, Howard despatch to Chamberlain, 22 December 1924.
22. For an overview, see S. Adler, 'The War Guilt Question and American Disillusionment 1918-1929', *Journal of Modern History*, 28(1956): 1-28; A. Marsden, 'The Blockade', in F.H. Hinsley, ed., *British Foreign Policy Under Sir Edward Grey* (Cambridge, 1977), pp. 488-515; C.M. Mason, 'Anglo-American Relations: Mediation and "Permanent Peace"', in Ibid. pp. 466-487; and

K. Middlemas and J. Barnes, *Baldwin: A Biography* (London, 1966), pp. 136–156.
23. F.O. 371/10651/4143/4057, Chilton despatch to Chamberlain, 6 August 1925.
24. Ibid., Craigie [F.O. American Department] minute, 19 August 1925; Wellesley [deputy under-secretary, F.O.], 20 August 1925.
25. For a case in point, see McKercher, 'Blockade Claims', 373–375.
26. On this organisation, see R. Savord [for the Council on Foreign Relations], *Directory of American Agencies Concerned with the Study of International Affairs* (New York, 1931), pp. 3–6.
27. F.O. 395/420/674/61, Bliss [Balfour's private secretary] to Willert, 30 June 1927; and Yencken [F.O. News Department] to Bliss.
28. For an indication, see S. Marks, *The Illusion of Peace. International Relations in Europe 1918–1939* (London, Basingstoke, 1976), pp. 1–54; and A. Orde, *Great Britain and International Security, 1920–1926* (London, 1976).
29. The rest of this paragraph is based on Jacobson, *Locarno Diplomacy*, pp. 3–67. Also see D. Johnson, 'Austen Chamberlain and the Locarno Agreements', *University of Birmingham Historical Journal*, 8 (1961): 62–81.
30. F.O. 800/256, Chamberlain to Cecil, 26 November 1924.
31. F.O. 800/257, Howard to Chamberlain, 9 January 1925.
32. F.O. 371/10652/6016/5302, Howard despatch to Chamberlain, 20 November 1925.
33. Ibid., cf. Vansittart minutes, 11 and 14 December 1925; Wellesley minute, 11 December 1925; and Tyrrell [permanent under-secretary, F.O.] minute, 12 December 1925.
34. The precedent was set by the Harding Administration; see the file of correspondence and minutes in F.O. 371/7307/5765/1913.
35. F.O. 371/11183/562/95, R. I. Campbell minute, 8 February 1926.
36. F.O. 371/11185/935/179, BLINY despatch to the F.O., 18 February 1926.
37. E. A. Mowrer, 'Our Imaginary Isolation', *The Forum* (February 1926), 186–195; a copy is contained in F.O. 371/11183/562/95.
38. F.O. 800/260, Chamberlain to Spender, 10 January 1927. Also see F.O. 395/418/1304/11, Willert minute, 15 December 1927.
39. On the opium conference, see F. P. Walters, *A History of the League of Nations* (London, New York, Toronto, 1969), pp. 184–186.
40. See M. J. Brode, 'Anglo-American Relations and the Geneva Naval Disarmament Conference of 1927' (unpublished Ph.D. dissertation, University of Alberta, 1972); Ellis, *Kellogg*, pp. 164–184; S. W. Roskill, *Naval Policy Between the Wars*, Vol. I: *The Period of Anglo-American Antagonism 1919–1929* (London, 1968), pp. 498–516.
41. F.O. 371/9619/6701/435, Howard despatch to Chamberlain, 21 November 1924; F.O. 371/10633/53/6, BLINY note on 'International Armaments', 13 December 1924; F.O. 371/11187/4382/268, BLINY despatch to F.O., 5 August 1926; and F.O. 371/12035/342/93, Howard despatch to Chamberlain, 7 January 1927 give indications of this.
42. This sentence and the next are based on F.O. 395/421/610/256, Steward to Willert, 21 June 1927.

43. See Brode, 'Anglo-American Relations', Appendix I.
44. Roskill, *Naval Policy*, Vol. I, p. 506.
45. F.O. 395/422/862/256, Steward 'Memorandum on Mr. W. B. Shearer', 15 August 1927.
46. F.O. 395/421/699/256, Yencken minute, 12 July 1927.
47. F.O. 800/261, Howard to Chamberlain, 21 July 1927.
48. This was reported on all the major wire services in the United States and Britain.
49. F.O. 800/261, Howard to Chamberlain, 21 July 1927.
50. Roskill, *Naval Policy*, Vol. I, p. 509; and BM Add MSS 51084, Cecil to Irwin [viceroy of India], 29 September 1927.
51. F.O. 395/421/720/256, Bird to Fletcher, 30 June 1927.
52. Ibid., Villiers minute, 19 July 1927.
53. Ibid., Thompson minute, 21 July 1927 and Craigie minute, 21 July 1927.
54. F.O. 395/422/839/256, Bird to Fletcher, 28 July 1927.
55. Ibid., Villiers minute, 17 August 1927 and Craigie minute, 19 August 1927.
56. F.O. 371/12040/4794/133, Howard despatch to Chamberlain, 5 August 1927.
57. Ibid., Chamberlain minute, 17 August 1927 and Chamberlain to Howard, 26 August 1927.
58. For example, see Ibid., Craigie minute, 17 August 1927.
59. For instance, J. Atkins, 'Between Geneva and the Deep Blue Sea', *Independent*, CXX(February 1928): 104-106; J. Carter, 'Where do we go from Geneva', *Independent*, CXIX(August 1927): 198-200; J. T. Gerould, 'Failure of the 3 Power Naval Conference', *Current History*, XXVI (September 1927); 'Great Britain's Opposition to the Freedom of the Seas', *Current History*, XXVII(October 1927): 112-115; and R. Smith, 'Breakdown of the Coolidge Conference', *Contemporary Review*, CXXXII(September 1927): 290-295.
60. For instance, see E. W. Hawley, 'Herbert Hoover, the Commerce Secretariat, and the Vision of an "Associated State", 1921-1928', *Journal of American History*, 61(1974-1975): 116-140. Cf. F.O. 371/11167/461/10, Howard despatch to Chamberlain, 15 January 1926.
61. This is fully analysed in McKercher, *Second Baldwin Government*, Chapter IV.
62. *D.B.F.P. 1A*, Vol. III. pp. 736-739, Howard to Chamberlain, 1 September 1927.
63. F.O. 395/420/1054/75, BLINY memorandum on 'Anti-British Propaganda in the United States', 7 October 1927. Enclosed in this memorandum are F. Bausman, *Facing Europe* (New York, 1926); and F. Bausman, 'Under Which Flag', *American Mercury* reprint (New York, 1927).
64. F.O. 395/420/1054/75, Willert minute, 21 October 1927; and Vansittart minute, 24 October 1927.
65. Ibid., Headlam Morley minute, 31 October 1927.
66. F.O. 395/420/1192/75, Fletcher to Willert, 18 November 1927.
67. F.O. 371/12039/6194/128, Howard despatch to Chamberlain, 10 October 1927.

68. F.O. 395/420/1255/75, Howard despatch to Chamberlain, 30 September 1927.
69. F.O. 371/12039/4793/128, Howard despatch to Chamberlain, 5 August 1927; and F.O. 371/12039/5583/128, Howard to Craigie, 14 September 1927.
70. F.O. 371/12036/7257/93, Howard telegram (524) to F.O., 15 December 1927, Thompson minute, 16 December 1927, Vansittart minute, 16 December 1927, and Chamberlain initials, 16 December 1927.

MICHAEL G. FRY

In Further Pursuit of Lloyd George: International History and the Social Sciences

The contributors to this volume would not readily concur in the view that they are, by writing diplomatic history, paddling in an intellectual backwater. Their admiration for Cedric Lowe's all too brief life's work underscores the point. Yet the tides seem to rise on other shores and the currents to flow in other channels. Periodically, historians examine themselves, their research and teaching, and the state of the discipline. The most recent outcome of this process of self-examination, of light-shedding without bloodletting, was unequivocal.[1] So much of the recent past and the challenging future lies with social history, the 'new political history', with fresh approaches to socio-economic phenomena, with the study of women, minorities, ethnic groups, and classes, with history from the bottom up, with local, community, and urban studies, with area and regional history, with comparative, integrated history, and with quantitative methodologies. Diplomatic history, as a subfield of political history, studying the external life of states, the formal relations between foreign offices and their equivalents, is not regarded as being on the exciting frontiers of inquiry. Devoted scholars and their seemingly diminishing band of apprentices are not at any critical point of intersection or departure. Journals shun their papers; conference organizers give them less space and time. The charge is oft repeated; diplomatic history is stagnant in terms of concepts, issues and methodologies.

Deprivation and displacement encourage people to talk to and write for themselves, to form separate groups and provide distinct outlets for their work. But such palliatives have limited benefits, and aphrodisiacs are positively dangerous if one courts one's kin. Neither languidity, born of accomplishment, nor resignation, the child of inertia, are appropriate responses to the predicament. One cannot simply mark time in the hope of a pendulum or two swinging back and bringing with them renewed centrality. What then can be done beyond exorcising the phrase diplomatic history from the vocabulary? What must be done to dismantle images and demonstrate that the caricatures developed about international history are, to some extent, just that?

First, historians of international relations, concerned primarily with the development and conduct of national foreign and defence policy, should reaffirm the relevance, the enduring significance of the subject. They might, with appropriate caveats, and a sensitivity to countervailing arguments, even restate the case for the primacy of politics and strategy, and for the state as the critical unit of analysis. They must reassert the validity of the governing concepts of power, both as a measure of mobilizable resources and of control over outcomes, of force, order, stability, and equilibrium. Afterall, when environmentalists, ecologists, and futurists have had their say, which they certainly must have, when social and economic structures have been examined, when the potato has, for good reason from one vantage point, been afforded greater significance than the Armada and all similar political events, the study of war and its avoidance, of peace and its preservation, must prosper, especially when war as an instrument of policy can threaten the existence of civilized society. It surely follows that the applied aspects of the subject, international history, and for example, its use in the contemporary policy formulation process, is more relevant than ever. The point of departure there is the case study, with its limitations overcome somewhat by techniques of controlled and sustained comparison. Finally, they can, as they refine it, confirm the rigor of a tested and time-honored methodology, as they quarry archives that are multi-cultural, private and public, not confined to those of the state and yet representing the whole bureaucratic structure rather than merely the foreign policy apparatus.[2] Balance will always be a problem for no institution matches the state as a creator and manager of archives.

They must resist, particularly perhaps in the United States, the pressure from a socio-intellectual environment that breeds distaste for, or an idle, conspiratorial fascination with, the study of elites and the exercise of power. In fact, they must confirm the necessity of explaining elite behaviour, the sources of elite power, the way elites come into being, adapt, develop structures of interests, beliefs, values, and doctrines, institutionalize ideologies, fashion operating procedures, develop lifestyles and cultures, sustain themselves as they pursue goals and needs, and are disbanded, co-opted, or brought down. International historians must do so while exploring that subject well beyond both the frontiers of a single state, to see cosmopolitan groups, and the boundaries of pathological behaviour. Internets of collaborating elites function at home and abroad, and have their foreign counterparts; how else, for example, is the North American political economy managed?

Second, from that foundation, from that flow of consciousness and reassertion, historians of the international system can establish the broader substance, the anatomy of the subject, identify its parameters, set its reasonable boundaries, and mark it as a legitimate, coherent, and comprehensive field of inquiry. They can establish an expanded but manageable research agenda and ways to implement it, while avoiding constraints on the heroic. The research agenda must address problems at various levels of analysis; the task of implementation is one of skills and methodologies, of analytical sophistication, of standards. Both endeavours will help consolidate and expand on the considerable achievements of the last fifteen years on both sides of the Atlantic, and require an exploration of the points of intersection with other areas of historical research and with the behavioural sciences that have had such a marked influence on the development of international relations theory in the last twenty years.

The levels of analysis approach, the routine of social science, has much to commend it. If historians continue to view the international system as an intellectual construct, as an abstraction, as 'a metaphysical entity' rather than 'a series of interacting outcomes not readily deducible from a summing up of individual policies,'[3] or as a mere context or environment in which governments operate relatively freely, the preference of a high percentage of the classical literature on the origins of the First and Second World Wars concerned with the responsibility issue, so much of the explanatory value will be missed. The system as a system, with its rules, transactions, structures, repercussions, linkages, influence on the state behaviour, and sub-systems, maintaining itself and changing, must be addressed, without accepting Paul Schroeder's view that, 'It is less important to know why statesmen took certain actions than to know what reactions and results those actions produced in the international arena, and why under the prevailing system they led to these results and not others, and how these actions affected the system itself.'[4]

Furthermore, a systems approach will stimulate, even necessitate, not only analysis of the political-strategic system and the dusting off of the best of geopolities, but also of the economic, socio-cultural, ideological, and technological systems, and bring together, for example, the study of the management of resources and the exercise of power. To date, scholars of the Annales have enjoyed open season, while the functioning of the international economy, the reciprocal impact of societies and cultures, of ideas and values, remain essentially outside the purview, let alone the research, of so many international historians. Too few of them have explored the role of non-state actors, of transnational and transgovernmental as opposed to international transactions and relations, and even of international organizations and regimes. Therefore, questions of status, of the management of dependent relationships and of complex interdependence, of hegemonies, of the relative influence of the small and weak, and the impotence of the large and powerful, go relatively unexplored. Comparative analysis, regional histories, work over longer periods of time, across cultures, beyond national and narrow topical boundaries, and somewhat free from the tyranny of crises do not flourish as they should.

The state, as analytically the second level, is best seen as that area between the government and its decision processes and the boundaries of society where the public, influential groups, individuals, and the media function, defining the nature of the state and embodying domestic policies. From these one extracts the domestic sources of and constraints on foreign and defence policies, themes that have rarely been exploited fully. Yet viewing policy as an expression of social structure, political texture, and economic factors opens up many avenues. The impact of economic, social, political, cultural, ethnic, and racial factors, and the influence of the electorate, party political and legislative processes, and rhetoric, the press, lobbies, pressure groups, corporatists, and publicists, business, trade unions, and missionaries merit, and have occasionally received, due attention. Indeed, where would that sickly child, Cold War historiography be, without the economic foundations and dynamics of American imperial policy? Conversely, foreign policy behaviour may be viewed as a mechanism to reconcile diverse interests and values within a polity, to justify the extraction and reallocation of resources from and to various segments of society, in effect as a contributor to political consensus and social order. In these ways one captures some of the important manifestations of what is described as linkage politics;[5] that is the reciprocal interplay between domestic and external policy needs, goals, and behaviour. That behaviour can be war, diplomacy, or quasi-war and diplomacy called covert operations and 'intelligence', as governments conduct relations with other governments, with oppositions to governments, with colonies of their own nationals living abroad, and with non-state actors.

The third level of analysis is that of decision making within the structure of government. The anatomy and essence of decision, in both crisis and routine situations, set preferably in the context of behaviour that constitutes broad strategy and policy, the determinants of decision, and the decision-making process is in fact at the core of so much recent historical scholarship. It views decisions as outputs of a bureaucracy's standard operational procedures, or of bargaining processes among bureaucrats in the nation's foreign affairs agencies, and of executive choice. These procedures and processes underpin cabinet level decision-making, where domestic political considerations play an understandably significant role. Such historical analysis is a logical extension of more traditional diplomatic history. Foreign policy is viewed less, therefore, as an event which results from the attributes of the nation state or from reactions to the behaviour of other nation states. Bureaucratic and cabinet politics have blossomed more fully than any other area of enquiry, primarily as a result of the opening of the Western and Asian archives; what is seen as a welcome and necessary multi-archival approach has flourished.

The individual, as an individual, as role-player, and as group member constitutes the fourth level of analysis. The research agenda here should include the reconstruction of the official mind, as a whole rather than as a disaggregated unit, with a structured view of domestic society and the international system, the capturing of purpose, intent and motive, the reconstruction of images, beliefs, and ideologies, and the analysis of information processing. It demands the exploration of the relationship between beliefs and behaviour, between thought and action, of the intensity with which beliefs are held, and the distinction between central and peripheral beliefs. Foreign policy is seen, from this perspective, as a choice of goal-oriented behaviour, made by individuals and small groups in analytically particularly relevant circumstances. Opportunities exist at this level to explore psycho-politics and to rediscover that biography has, despite its detractors, analytical as well as descriptive properties.

The promising points of interaction between international history and other areas of historical research on the one hand, and those areas of the behavioural sciences relevant to empirical research and the development of international relations theory on the other, are obvious and need not be catalogued. However, it is worth stating that for those who care to master the language, who are numerate as well as literate, who can consume the research findings, and who are willing to clamber over disciplinary walls that are less forbidding than is often assumed, the social sciences offer possibilities, conceptually and theoretically, at every level of analysis. Systems and region theory, the behaviour of the state and non-state actors, linkage and bureaucratic politics, decision-making theory, and cognitive politics lie in varying states of maturity and disarray, ready to be exploited in a selective and discriminating fashion. In their turn, international relations theorists, having surfed on the third and fourth waves of analysis, are probably more ready than ever, and particularly the empirically minded, to extract from historical research.[6] They are more conscious of the distorting affects of some of their work, and yet rightly insist that historians must be, in turn, more structured and systematic in their thinking, and more explicit in their causal reasoning. This demand is reasonable and justified, even though historical research is rare if ever a quest for theory and prediction.

The advances made by historians in the analysis of the determinants of decision, of bureaucratic and cabinet politics, reflect more than the impact of the opening of archives. A sensitive and discriminating use of analytical perspectives from the social sciences has enabled certain historians to document the significance of organizational processes, administrative procedures, bureaucratic infighting and bargaining, and of calculated and random pressures from within and outside the formal structure of government. They have begun to demonstrate the limitations of models of unidirectional behaviour in search of clearly defined, understood and agreed upon national interests and goals, while for the most part still seeing statesmen conceptually as rational processors of information and decision-makers. They base such analysis on public and private archival sources, on the records of oral and written debate, supplemented by published primary evidence. They assume that the weight and authority of such sources both governed rational decision-making at the time, and gives authority to their own reconstructions. The web of elaborate footnotes provides authenticity. In that sense, historical analysis is driven more by data than by problem, by what the archives are expected to disgorge, and pays particular attention to the logic and coherence of argument in both bureaucracy and cabinet. It constitutes both a defensible and creative form of analysis, despite its limitations. In addition, other historians, drawing on both institutional and organizational history, and political sociology, have very effectively put foreign ministries and diplomatic corps under careful and productive scrutiny. The results of this work is depicted in Model I.

Yet, consciously or not, historians have begun to question some of the assumptions of classical rationalism. The purposeful and calculated acts of unified governments, the enjoyment of full and clear information, the presence of unambiguous values or acts of systematic value trade-off, the logical ranking of alternatives and priorities, choice based methodically on calculations of high utility and low risk, and assumptions of rising learning curves no longer exclude other possible explanations. In assessing the impact of a decision and its implementation on further decisions historians have begun to probe those forms of logic related to rationalization. Was an unwise and disfunctional decision inevitable because of compelling circumstances which, afterall, left no choice; did hindsight somehow demonstrate that an unsound decision was in fact a wise one? Or, after taking a decision that, for example, made war more probable, perhaps reflecting bureaucratic pressure or domestic political forces, did the outcome become so painful that evidence must be distorted to justify the decision and the resulting tragedy,

Model I

Problem → Analysis and information processing by Bureaucratic (Diplomatic, Military, Financial, Economic, etc.) figures → Constraints on latitude → Political Elite decision-making e.g., in Cabinet → Implementation of decision → Evaluation of decision and its implementation

Analysis and information processing by Bureaucratic (Diplomatic, Military, Financial, Economic, etc.) figures
- the problem's history and current status
- development of options, alternatives and choices
- evaluation of risks, costs and benefits, and utility
- evaluation of environment
- relating of means to ends
- evaluation of consequences
- set in terms of broad national interests and goals

Constraints on latitude
- bureaucratic politics, organizational processes, and institutional factors
- role factors

Political Elite decision-making e.g., in Cabinet
- weigh evidence and information in all their aspects from bureaucracy
- cut through detail and expertise
- weigh new evidence
- repeat some of analysis, e.g., set in terms of broad interests and goals—e.g., check consequences of alternative actions
- insert domestic political calculations
- insert own intellectual contribution, perspective, and experience

Implementation of decision
i.e. foreign policy behaviour

Evaluation of decision and its implementation
- good or bad impact
- effective or not; short and long term
- how have antagonist and other actors responded
- provide any needed rationalization, e.g., had no choice especially if outcome was bad
- cumulative impact on next decision

or to enable the leader to argue that his actions would, in the end, produce the desired results?

What social scientists would regard as analytical, systematic study of the individual, independent from bureaucratic structures, still languishes, despite the quasi-biographers, the unrelenting fascination among historians with political, diplomatic, bureaucratic, and military personalities, and the analytical weight given them.[7] This situation continues in spite of the contributions by social scientists, and in the presence of a consensus on the existence of significant relationships between the world of ideas and beliefs and the realm of behaviour. In explanation, one should point out that a majority of international relations theorists isolate the individual in order to neglect him. They question both the relevance and indiscriminate use of psychological and related models, and argue emphatically that systems, structures, organizations, and institutions, overpower or severely constrain the individual. At best the policy-maker is a role-player, with sharply circumscribed impact, and is insufficiently important to warrant the expenditure of scarce resources. Analysis of the individual offers little that is replicable and of predictive or prescriptive value, and, in any case, presents formidable data and methological problems. Only a distinct minority argue to the contrary; the micro for them is the larger picture, which they seek to paint with the aid of cognitive social psychology. Their concern is with information-processing and decision-making as weighty, indeed necessary, variables in explaining foreign policy behaviour. The weight increases in special, nonroutine situations where other than standard operating procedures are required, in crises, in the presence of stress which impairs the ability to perform complex cognitive tasks, in circumstances where leaders experience little restraint from the domestic sphere or the bureaucracy, when long-term planning is at issue, and where leaders can shed routine and indulge in creative unorthodoxy. The relevance to Lloyd George's conduct as prime minister is obvious. Both sides of the debate genuflect, of course, to the need to explore the dynamic, interactive relationship between man and his environment, between the individual and the other levels of analysis.

Yet James Joll, in 1968, was unequivocal. 'But, in any case, it is only by studying the minds of men that we shall understand the causes of anything.'[8] Struck by the disparity between the importance of the decision to go to war and the moral and intellectual ordinariness of those who decided Europe's fate in 1914, Joll wrote of unanticipated outcomes of decisions made in crises that were not fully understood. In such circumstances, leaders 'fall back on their own instinctive reactions, traditions and modes of behaviour. Each of them has certain beliefs, rules or objectives which are taken for granted.' Documentary evidence, he pointed out, cannot capture what, 'goes without saying' and rarely illuminates mood, tone, inflection, and motive. And yet, if we are to understand motive, intent, and meaning, if we are to judge the policies that the documents represent, we must capture the individual, for as decision-makers in crisis fall back on 'unspoken assumptions', 'their intentions can often only be judged in the light of what we can discover about those assumptions'. Thus Joll sought to explain both the 'general ideas in the air', variously expressed as the climate of ideas and opinion, the spirit of the age, the moral and intellectual climate and the general ideological background, the mentality, the Weltanshauung, and its sources, of political elites, and the links between those phenomena which help explain behaviour. Those links, he concluded, were to be found in the minds of elites, and thus he argued that, '... it is on one's reconstruction of what was in their minds that our judgement of their actions must be based.' Joll's language lacked precision but he set out clearly a possible relationship between a climate of ideas, the mentality of a specific elite, and its behaviour in a crisis. He demonstrated the essentially and perhaps unavoidably conservative or reactive nature of such behaviour as he pointed to the existence of belief systems, of governing yet 'unspoken assumptions'. The document he examined was the September 1914 statement of war aims, not one extracted from the July crisis.

Not surprisingly perhaps, Joll, when speculating on how to capture the climate of opinion and the mentality of leaders, and to reconstruct the individual mind in terms of its unspoken assumptions, found little sustenance in the behavioural sciences. Their theories were in his view too general, their evidence too fragmented and their hypotheses either too tentative or quite obvious. While the social sciences might suggest novel explanations and indicate fresh analytical approaches, 'They cannot... provide the precise answers to the historians' questions; they cannot offer precise links between the general and the particular and thus cannot help explain a specific event or act of behaviour.' Joll found certain promising leads, however, in other areas of historical inquiry, for example, in social history and through it clues even in educational sociology and social psychology. Edward Grey's fundamental attitudes stemmed from his boyhood days at Winchester.

> It is to his education and the education of the class to which he belonged that we must look for the key to much of Grey's later political behaviour; and this suggests that we should in general pay more attention to the links between educational systems and foreign policy, between the values and beliefs inculcated at school and the presuppositions on which politicians act later in life.

To tackle the problem of recreating the climate of opinion in which leaders operated, the images and ideas, the philosophies of life and history, to understand the pervasive presence of fatalism, religious pessimism, and determinism, or optimism and enthusiasm, to capture the sense of destiny or relief born of release from tension and anxiety, and to understand feelings of personal and national fulfillment and even joy that accompanied mobilization and the prospect of war in 1914, Joll pointed to the connection between the history of ideas and the history of international politics. After a diversion into the possible links between the art of a society and its political attitudes, between symbols and assumptions, Joll came to the following propositions, which controlled for the passage of time. 'If we want to understand the presuppositions of the men of 1914, to reconstruct, so to speak, their ideological furniture, it is to the ideas of a generation earlier as filtered through vulgarizers and popularizers that we must look.' In that way, Joll suggests, we will see how ideas survive and change, and have their impact; how, for example, Darwinism, the work of T. H. Huxley and F. Nietzsche, the ideology of imperialism, themes on the role of the state, the nature of conflict, the impact of nationalism, and the necessity for war, and the actual decisions in 1914 are connected. Similarly, and in the presence of a 'reversal of all values', one can relate the ideas, beliefs, and actions of dissenters and revolutionaries. Thus one captures the spirit of the age and is not astonished by resulting behaviour. In conclusion, Joll called for forms of historical enquiry that were discriminatingly eclectic in origins and unifying in execution, goals that were clearly more easily stated than achieved. He omitted any reference to psycho-history, but unwittingly perhaps, suggested that those who seek to understand the relationship between beliefs and behaviour may find richer results from studying those who dissent rather than those who govern. The former operate, perhaps, with fewer constraints, whether or not they resort to terrorism.

Joll's call for eclectic analysis has not been adequately addressed. Few match his grasp of the relationship between intellectual, political and international history. Fritz Fischer's work dissolved into the responsibility for war issue; Paul Kennedy's thoroughly admirable if not entirely successful attempt at another form of integrationist writing stands virtually alone.[9] Joll's scepticism about the transportable value of the social sciences seems to be shared, in comfort, by many. A few historians have indulged in illuminating public debate with international relations theorists.[10] Those who have used bureaucratic politics models and decision-making theories, have demonstrated, at the very least, that Joll's scepticism was challengeable. However, it is time to go further and necessary to dilate historical research to include other approaches and lenses, if only because social scientists are meeting historians on their own archival grounds, as the 30 year rule exposes the Cold War. Those of us concerned with the conduct of foreign and defence policies, the traditional concerns, by, for example, Lloyd George and his coterie, should explore the literature on cognitive politics and its debt to cognitive social psychology.[11]

This is an area of enquiry of relatively recent vintage, dominated by North American scholars. Its lineage goes back to the 1950's and even earlier, to the work of Harold Lasswell, Nathan Leites, Kenneth Boulding, Herbert Kelman, Dean Pruitt, Harold and Margaret Sprout, and others. The generic questions of why individuals in office think and behave in the way they do, and how free they are to behave in preferred ways, have produced ten research problems.

First, are the process of choice for goal-oriented individuals in office and the art of information processing, which constitute the essence of decision-making, indispensable factors in understanding state behaviour? For those who answer in the affirmative the second question is what is the significance of the distinction between an individual's psychological composition and his operational environment, between perception of reality and reality, between the world the individual believes exists and the world in which his decisions will have to be carried out; and do differing perceptions of the environment result significantly in differing decisions? Third, what is the relationship between beliefs, images and perceptions, and behaviour in the form both of decision-making and the implementation of decisions; do decisions, for example, stem in casual fashion from belief systems, or are beliefs constructed to explain decisions already made and to justify behaviour already indulged in, or is the relationship always reciprocal? Fourth, what constitutes subjective rationality and differentiates it from irrationality? Fifth, what are the constraints on rationality and therefore on rational choice theory? These problems force consideration of the analytical significance of logical assertion and phenomenological reasoning. Sixth, what factors constrain latitude of choice, as a set of limitations possibly quite distinct from those that constrain rationality? These factors can be domestic in that they are bureaucratic and political, or they can be international in terms of circumstances existing and behaviour being practised abroad. Constraints on latitude may be beneficial or detrimental; constraints on rationality are always to be deplored. An individual's sense of these limits both in decision-making and in the implementation of decisions compliments the issue of whether an individual is relatively passive and acquiesces in constraints, or welcomes them, or seeks to secure freedom from them. All historians recognize that Lloyd George's answer to the constraints imposed on him was to create his own independent but official bureaucracy. Seventh, assuming that the anatomy and dynamics of decision-making can be understood and the constraints articulated, can an optimal decision be reached and be judged to have been reached, in retrospect? What constitutes a high quality decision, what limits optimality, what causes leaders not to choose the best means to secure desired ends, and what stimulates risk-taking and error, both motivated and unmotivated? Eighth, what is the relationship between motive, and intent and purpose, and how can individual motives, that are personal or situational, be reconstructed and related to beliefs? Ninth, how analytically can and should one use character and personality variables, that complex of attitudes, temperament, and dispositions that relate to role and possibly clash dramatically with it, to the point of making an individual quite unfit for the office held? The tension can occur because of the malfit or, as in the case of Richard Nixon, because office permits maturing to take place and allows the individual's character full play. In both cases, little adaptation occurs, despite the view that the realities of office have their inevitable, significant and usually modifying impact. Caution is necessary but surely it is reasonable to argue that anyone other than Henry Kissinger as Steven Walker demonstrated,[12] or Lloyd George, in the roles they occupied, may not, in some circumstances, have behaved in the same way. Tenth, what are the critical relationships between individual cognitive processes and the cognitive dynamics of a small decision-making group where individuals of necessity function? 'Group think' is an inelegant phrase but a decidedly valuable concept. An individual may dominate a small group, be a synthesizer, or be submerged in the group as options and choices are evaluated. The more choices faced by decision-makers the more complex is the problem of value and interest trade off, and the more indispensable a Lloyd George or a Kissinger may become. The problems of stress-related and anxiety-laden behaviour penetrate these questions, stimulating ranges of conduct from the coolly analytical to the irresponsibly subjective, but no more than does the impact of the cumulative historical experience of individuals, groups, and organizations.

Cognitive variables are analytical constructs; they are *ex post facto* judgements about what an individual, group, or nation believed, developed images of, perceived or misperceived at a point in time or period of history. Misperceptions, for example, are judgements of perceptions, of perceptions judged to be faulty by certain tests and standards. Vocabulary is important because beliefs, images, and perceptions, and even ideologies, while rarely used interchangeably, are seen as parts of a cognitive structure without a clear hierarchy. Images are particular kinds of beliefs, beliefs contribute to perceptions, and perceptions result when information, beliefs, and images are brought together in the individual's mind to preface decision. Yet other factors intrude to help formulate an individual's psychological environment, apart from personality factors. Moreover, that beliefs, images, and perceptions can be held simultaneously by individuals, groups, and the informed public presents problems of their inter-relationship and consistency, and of their relative weights in terms of influence on a decision.

Beliefs and belief systems, and their significance, are central in the literature. Yet relatively simple questions can still be asked about them. What categories of phenomena are important beliefs held? At what levels of generality or specificity are these beliefs? And, what is the relationship of those levels of belief to each other? Lloyd George, for example, may have held beliefs about the nature of politics and the international system, about imperialism and communism, concerning individual state behaviour, authoritarian and democratic statesmen and their craft, and on specific but persistent dyadic relationships or policy questions. What exactly constitutes a belief system; how rich, complex, structured, and sophisticated do beliefs have to be to become a system, and how deeply, completely and consistently held? How are belief systems created, developed, maintained, and even undermined? How can a historian confidently reconstruct them; what evidence can be used and how? How do they function, and what and how much do they explain as individuals in small groups search for decisions and make choices?

A belief system is a way to attempt to structure reality, to bring order to the complex, to organize the external world, and to code and understand information from it. Because of the coherence it brings, an individual can describe and give meaning to the past and the present, sense what will be, and decide what ought to be. Given that decision-making is a necessary act of simplification and ultimately of conformity, which links available choice to possible outcomes, a belief system gives the individual bases for consistency where uncertainty reigns and a measure of order where complexity seeks to dominate. This search for consistency can be, up to a certain point, beneficial.

Individuals develop images which are related to but distinct from beliefs and help determine behaviour.[13] Images are best understood as those intellectual simplifications about self, others, and other's images of self. They conform, it is hoped, to one's own view of reality and contribute to reciprocal understanding. They are formulated in the years of political maturity and, possibly, of office, when high levels of information are available and the need for simplifying constructs is urgent. Images are concrete and specific but can be about and be held by individuals, groups and nations. Indeed images of national character and culture, stereotypes and caricatures for the most part, appear frequently in both the archival evidence and the literature. For example, Lloyd George developed images of his and Britain's role in the war and the postwar period, of enemy and alliance nations and statesmen, of Greece and Venizelos, of France and Clemenceau, and of Russia and Lenin, of influential groups in, for example, the United States and Germany, of the seemingly inevitable hawks and doves who comprised all administrations, of Jews, generals in politics, officials as a breed, and bankers. Enemies grew in malevolence with the telling, England's course was true and moral, a common purpose worthy of broad political support, and allies took on British virtues; backsliding friends revealed evil propensities, and wavering enemies deserved the benefit of each doubt. Above all, Lloyd George believed that his behaviour served national values, interests, and goals. Clearly, images are significant analytically both because leaders, groups, and nations hold them, and because, in many instances, they have a capacity to triumph over the evidence. Lloyd George knew that his enemies at home and abroad regarded him as thoroughly unreliable and untrustworthy; in moments of exasperation he could be tempted to let their images and prophesies be fulfilled.

The role of belief systems and images in choice and decision requires consideration of how leaders process information. Pertinent information received by decision-makers invariably contains, simultaneously, data that is factual but may be excessive or impoverished, and interpretive in that it is ambiguous and dissonant. It has quality and form, degrees of comprehensiveness, and both diagnostic and prescriptive value in that it is also advice and evaluation. It is affected by its source and perceptions of that source; the absence of formal diplomatic representation and channels can be critical, and marks the difference between 1919 and 1945 as the West grappled with Communist Russia. It is sought out, generated, and received from routine and unorthodox channels, and then dealt with selectively, discarded, or given a degree of credibility, verified, analysed, and then stored and retrieved. At some point information is given the status of evidence. All this must be related to bureaucratic structure and decision process, but not mechanically, and over certain issues the Lloyd George administration severely tests credible rules of information processing.

Tracing information-processing brings one to the phenomena of perception and misperception and the ways decision-makers perceive, diagnose, and evaluate their environment and its immediate issues.[14] Perceptions rest on established beliefs and images, and are affected by them. They are dynamic rather than static, fashioned in each circumstance and situation and in the face of every fresh problem, and may thus be transitory. However, they may persist, take on cumulative properties, and have a distinct permanence. Perceptions are developed as decision-makers respond to information about and form judgements of the attributes, motives, intentions, and goals of adversary or ally; perceptions follow from the testing of behaviour, and are what leaders come to believe. How an adversary or ally reacted to a particular proposal or event, and whether that response was reasonable and justifiable or plainly mischievous, is important as leaders decide whether an actor is hostile or not, is seeking real or symbolic, current or future gain, or is attempting to recover from past losses and rectify unacceptable situations.

Misperceptions may occur, persist, and deepen when psycho-logic replaces formal logic. Decision-makers who seek to structure reality so as excessively to achieve consistency, who reach for premature cognitive settlement and then indulge in rationalization, or avoid stress brought on by fear, guilt, or uncertainty in the face of disconcerting developments, and resulting from confronting complex or conflicting values and interests may misperceive. They may behave in a consistent but irrational manner. However, the same outcome may result from flawed intelligence and its analysis, from insensitivity to and miscalculation of events and behaviour, from excessive optimism and undue pessimism, from the pressures and checks from the domestic political arena, from the inflexibility brought about by rhetoric and posturing, and from the constraints on latitude imposed by the bureaucracy as its various parts pursue their goals, or from the freedom permitted by its subservience. Lloyd George, for example, observing threats to the peace settlement, his government, and his career, risked war against Turkey in the fall of 1922 even though such a decision conflicted with his preference to avoid war. He was not able, in office, either to reflect on the problem or to use it as a guide and justification in future crises, but, even as he was ousted, he exaggerated the chance of success, minimized the risks and costs, and berated his detractors. In that way, Lloyd George achieved a degree of psychological comfort in a situation where domestic conditions had not pushed him toward war in any unequivocal way, but the bureaucracy had been less of a constraint than is sometimes supposed.

Misperceptions then are important and dangerous; to overestimate the unrepentant hostility or to underestimate the resolve of one's opponents, to indulge unwisely in threat or concession, to risk or refuse to contemplate war may produce faulty choice, even when goals are clear and interests are obvious. In some ways, the single most dangerous misperception in a crisis is to assume that one has no alternatives left, but that one's opponent has several alternatives and that, therefore, he must make the fatal choice between, for example, peace and war. Thus leaders convince themselves that they are at the mercy of the fateful choice of their opponent, and that history will surely condemn those who force war on the system. They themselves are blameless for they have merely reacted in the face of provocative and even aggressive behaviour.

Few social scientists have attempted to isolate and explore fully the historian in the decision-maker though many recognise that what decision-makers have learned, interpreted, and misinterpreted from and about history is a significant part of his consciousness. Clearly, a sense and reading of history, shallow or sophisticated, and the perspectives it gives affects the construction of beliefs, images, and perceptions. Information is processed in history's context which is also the principal source of analogical and comparative reasoning. A relationship exists presumably between history as a scholarly discipline and the current history of the press, and between personal awareness and actual experience, but with what likely impacts? Does mastery of history promote diagnosis but hinder prescription as in the case of Lord Curzon? He could tell Lloyd George solemnly and authoritatively, and enjoyed the exercise, what had happened in the past, and yet could rarely offer clear cut policy choices. Curzon's grasp of history bred elaborate memoranda and ponderous speeches not decisive advice. Because of this he was suspect, in terms of his loyalty, and value and perspicacity.

Beliefs, perceptions, and images have a relationship to ideologies. An ideology is composed of those principles and values that are coherent and comprehensive, and are expressed in the form of a declaration or manifesto in order to provide a basis for political action to impose or maintain an order of things. An ideology is tested, resilient and autonomous, and integrates views relative to domestic society and the international system. Indeed, a mature ideology, a grand design, cannot stop at a domestic or cultural boundary. In its operational form it becomes doctrine, a combination of beliefs, values, behaviour, and rhetoric. Woodrow Wilson, by this test, was an ideologue; Lloyd George was not.

Social scientists have constructed three types of individual belief systems. They are, in descending order of generality, Operational Codes, comprehensive beliefs about one antagonist or ally and its ideology, and Cognitive Maps about a specific set of policy problems. The operational code of an individual leader, for example, Kissinger's, John Foster Dulles's, or Ramsay MacDonald's, is constructed in order to identify and organize the most politically relevant views and attitudes, and to conceptualize them so that they become a set of general beliefs about the nature of political life and how to operate in the political environment.[15] The code is assumed to be in existence before office is reached, and is thus free of role, but is not necessarily unique in every aspect. It should be constructed, but has not been to date, from an analysis of primary published and unpublished documentary sources, the records of the written and spoken word, either by qualitative or quantitative content analysis. Only then can the possible tension between private and public behaviour, and between the speech and the letter or diary, be evaluated in terms of validity. An operational code is developed by seeking answers to the following questions, which are seen as either philosophical in that they constitute a diagnostic and prescriptive rationale for behaviour, or instrumental in that they determine patterns of conduct:

The Philosophical

1. What is the 'essential' nature of political life? Is the political universe essentially one of harmony or conflict? What is the fundamental character of one's political opponents?

2. What are the prospects for the eventual realization of one's fundamental political values and aspirations? Can one be optimistic or must one be pessimistic on this score, and in what respects the one and/or the other?

3. Is the political future predictable? In what sense and to what extent?

4. How much 'control' or 'mastery' can one have over historical development? What is one's role in 'moving' and 'shaping' history in the desired direction?

5. What is the role of 'chance' in human affairs and in historical development?

The Instrumental

1. What is the best approach for selecting goals or objectives for political action?
2. How are the goals of action pursued most effectively?
3. How are the risks of political action calculated, controlled, and accepted?
4. What is the best 'timing' of action to advance one's interests?
5. What is the utility and role of different means for advancing one's interests?

When the code is in place the question becomes one of imaginative rather than mechanical application to decisions and their implementation. If information received in the decision-making process rarely changes a belief system then the operational code acts as an assimilator, as a filter or lens for processing and interpreting information. The belief system remains static, rigid and changes only dramatically, and functions primarily as a critical, intervening constant which helps reduce ambiguity and inconsistency, and, therefore, tension. Throughout caution and caveat should rule, in terms of the code as a concept, its internal logic and the relationship of the two sets of questions to each other, the means of its construction, and its use in explaining decisions and implementation. It may indicate tendencies and predispositions better than it predicts decisions.

Few social scientists dismiss the proposition that beliefs may be constructed after decisions have been made and implemented, but most explore the significance of the relationship in Model II.

In the critical 'space' between information and beliefs, the decision-maker may seek to produce harmony between beliefs and information. Beliefs will play a role in the establishment of perceptions, and in that critical 'space' between perception and decision leaders will attempt to reconcile values and interests, or choose between them. At these points the psychological factors constraining rationality operate. In addition, bureaucratic and domestic political considerations constrain latitude. There risks are evaluated, costs weighed, priorities determined and then choices made, hopefully in the solemnity of a cabinet room, but possibly at Lloyd George's

Model II

Domestic Political Influences

Bureaucratic Influences

→ Problem → Information → Operational → Perceptions and → Decision- → Implementation → Consequences and
　　　　　　and Advice　　Codes　　　　Misperceptions　　Making　　　　　　　　　　　　Evaluation of them

- its essence
- its context
- its significance

Information and Advice:
- on background and perspective
- on current status
- estimates/ evaluations
- policy options and recommendations
- i.e. from bureaucracy

Operational Codes / Images

Decision-Making:
- on policy options

Implementation:
or failure to implement fully or in part

breakfast table. Subsequently, and crucially, the policy-maker deals with the actual consequences of success or failure, and does so cumulatively the longer he is in office. Rhetoric explains and justifies publicly; bureaucracies become wedded to or repelled by specific courses of action and policies. In these ways the weight of recent experience takes its toll or edifies. Clearly, the historian seeking to cope with these processes must, rather than seek new evidence, view the central, primary evidence in a different light and from a different perspective.

Historians may not find the operational code particularly operational in terms of explaining specific behaviour. A second type of belief system, more specific, more functionally dyadic may well prove more attractive. Deborah Larson analyzed from archival sources the flow of information to four United States decision-makers on the post-war problems of managing relations with the Soviet Union.[16] These policy-makers processed and interpreted this unified body of information, to which all four had the same access but did so differently. The initial critical 'space' was that between the information and their pre-existing, well-established, and central beliefs, where information processing took place and where the influences were reciprocal. Their beliefs concerned the sources, methods, aims, and legitimacy of Soviet policy, its stability or inconsistency, the degree, speed, and direction of change, and the relationship between the current ideology of Communism, Soviet domestic politics, and foreign policy. These beliefs dealt with the Soviet elite, their values, interests, and intentions, their malevolence or trustworthiness, the predictability of response and behaviour, their view of the United States, the gaps between their oratory and behaviour, their methods of calculating risk and costs, their sense of vulnerability, whether they were dominated by hawks, doves, or waverers, how they responded to different kinds of treatment, how malleable they were, and what would deter them from irresponsible and pre-emptive behaviour, and war. From that basis beliefs were developed about the litmus tests of friendship, of the available options to deal with the Soviet Union, and the requirements imposed by the international system. As information and beliefs interacted on each other the latter were altered sufficiently to produce belief system change. Then, in the 'space' between the reconstituted central beliefs and the decisions made on how to manage relations with the Soviet Union, the problem-solving rational processes, the constraints on rationality, and the constraints on latitude were operative, as in the analysis of an Operational Code. In this case, however, the intellect of the decision-makers had full play, and was not discounted excessively to make room for psychological explanations. Post-decision processes and feedback followed logically, rhetoric provided legitimacy, bureaucracy institutionalized the policy, and doctrine was enunciated as the Cold War deepened.

Dr. Larson thereby challenges the assumption that belief systems are rigid and unyielding to a new information and to the realities of their operational environment. She does so in part by neglecting the broader categories of belief in the Operational Code. She also questions the assumption that decision-makers search primarily for consistency, in order to preserve beliefs and relieve psychological stress. She elevates the role of information processing and the decision-maker's flexibility as he seeks to solve the problems associated with the Soviet Union. The decision-maker is made more ingenious but only to become captive, for he is not ultimately freed from constraints on either rationality or latitude. However, the model is amended in Model III as Dr. Larson dispenses with perceptions as a discrete category, and uses image in order to construct her level of belief system.

This mode of analysis has much to offer that is attractive and promising for historians who will test its cognitive social psychological dimensions. It can only be attempted sensibly from primary historical source, and is obviously transportable, for example, to Lloyd George and the post-war problem of Bolshevik policy. It offers explanation which is multifaceted and integrated, rather than reductionist, and involves factors from the international system and the domestic arena, while weighing the significance of the bureaucracy and the individual. To answer Joll's criticism, it demonstrates that social science can offer the degree of specificity required by the historian and does so, in this case, by meeting the historian on his own archival ground. This study provides a plausible explanation of the relationship between beliefs and pragmatism, demonstrating the vulnerability of beliefs while showing that so much is interactive and contingent as individuals react to new realities and formulate judgements rather than merely behave according to old attitudes. Information processing and beliefs take on a reciprocal relationship to each other, information impacting on beliefs, and beliefs mediat-

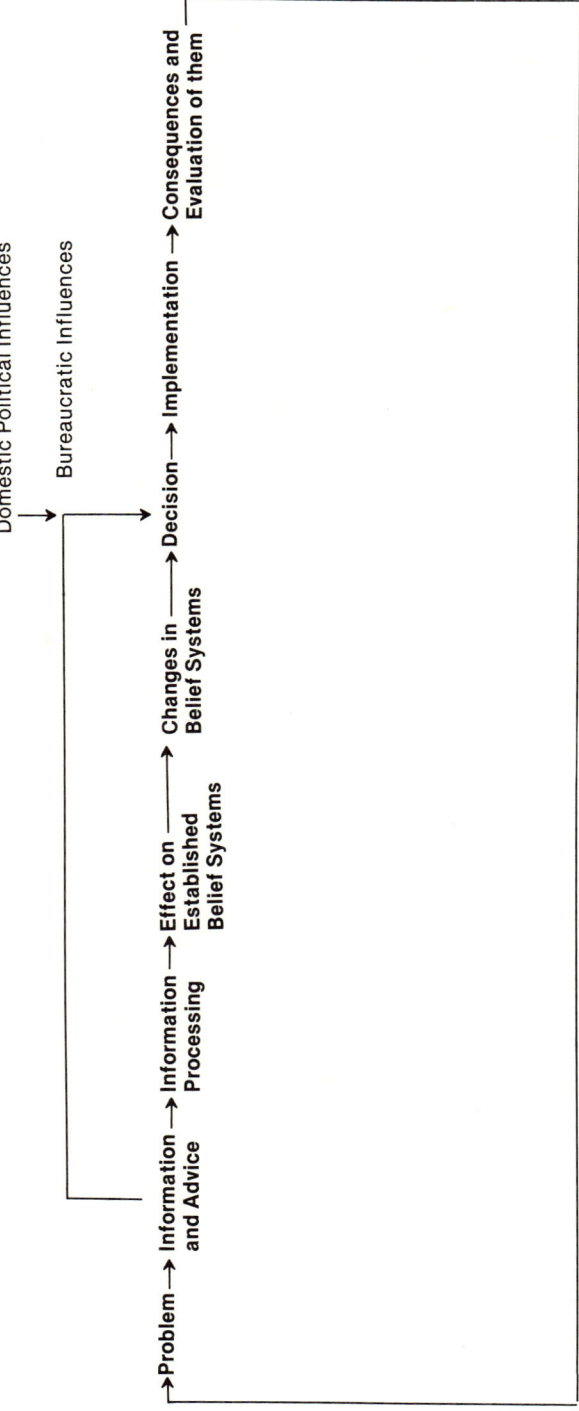

ing and influencing during information processing. Additional problems about belief systems are raised. Is it significant, analytically, to distinguish between central and peripheral beliefs particularly when tracing change in belief systems? How do individual belief systems impact on each other within a small group, and what is the impact of a new member or of wastage? How, when, and to what extent do belief systems change? Are there watersheds and turning points, real drama and bold conversion accompanied by new levels of conviction, or gradual, piecemeal change of beliefs, a process marked by indecision?

Cognitive maps, operating at the highest level of specificity, seek to explain the relationship between belief systems, alternatives and possible consequences, choice and decision on a concrete, limited policy question.[17] Robert Axelrod, in his *Structure of Decision*, assumes, erroneously, that the inter-departmental Eastern Committee of 1918 was a decision-making body, but offers a plausible analysis of its debates, and one which historians may find insightful. Many may struggle with the methodology, some will see the venture as primitive conceptually, others may not recognize their decision-makers wrapped as they are in scientific language, and more than a few may well regard the exercise as wearisome and even unnecessary, particularly if they care little about prediction.

Axelrod is sensitive to the problems of deriving cognitive maps from historical evidence, of constructing beliefs from oral assertions, and the possible loss of nuance. He is cautious about his findings, and reasonably modest about the contribution. He reaffirms the significance of choice, of 'the effects of policy alternatives on valued goals', and of the need for individuals 'to simplify their images of the complexities of their environment in order to cope with it'. He and his collaborators construct mathematical models or representations in graph form, that are paths or cycles, of individual belief systems with respect to a specific policy question, derived from the oral assertions that exist in the historical documentary evidence. These cognitive maps are formulated to capture the causal aspects of those beliefs, the structure of policy-makers' causal assertions, in order to explain decision. The cognitive map has two components; concepts seen as variables and called points, and the causal links which connect and express the relationship between them, showing how one concept affects another. The concepts are seen as cause or effect variables and express policy components and utilities in terms of interests. The links demonstrate their impact on each other in either a positive (+), reinforcing way, or a negative (−), inhibiting way.

For example, the statement, from the minutes of the Eastern Committee, that 'the amount of security in Persia augments the ability of the Persian government to maintain order', contains a policy and cause variable (the amount of security), a utility and effect variable (the ability of the Persian government to maintain order) and a link of positive value (augment), giving a positive causal relationship. The statement 'the ability of the British to put pressure on the Persian government inhibits the removal of the better local governors in Persia' demonstrates a negative causal relationship between the two concept variables. These relationships are demonstrated in the following way:

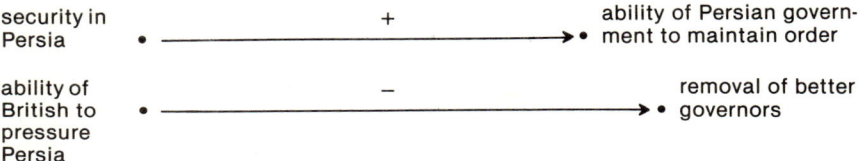

When beliefs are inter-related and effect variables become cause variables a path from, for example, the 'policy of withdrawal', via the amount of 'security in Persia', to the 'ability of the Persian government to maintain order' is constructed.

policy of   −   security in Persia   +   ability of Persian
withdrawal •ーーーーーー→• ーーーーーー→• government to preserve order

Additional complexity produce the following paths:

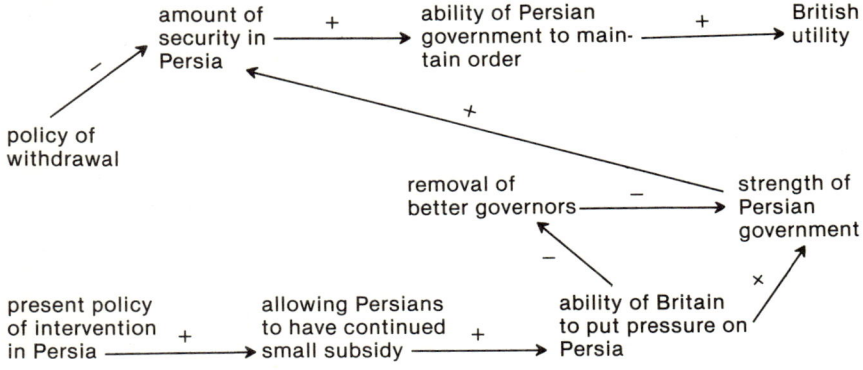

The sum total constitutes the cognitive map, the whole set of interrelated beliefs, of 'portrayed assertions', which represent a flow of thought and analysis as an individual develops a policy posture, holds to or reverses it, and ultimately decides. The degree of stability of the map and the extent of the consistency between it and the decisions made indicates the predictive value of the model. Inconsistency, resulting perhaps from domestic political considerations, may cause individuals either to restate their beliefs or change their behaviour in order to achieve conformity.

The model is a rational one in the sense that 'if it accurately captures a person's beliefs, [however complex], that person should make decisions that correspond to those generated by the model'. Axelrod concludes that '... individuals do express choices... that are consistent with the functioning of the cognitive maps corresponding to their assertions about their beliefs'.[18] Thus beliefs via choice predict behaviour through the process captured by the cognitive map, and not surprisingly, given the narrow policy issue being analysed. He insists, however, that such behaviour does not represent unconstrained rationality for constraints on rationality are found in the limitations in the structure of beliefs, in the representations of the operational, policy environment, in the necessary simplifications asserted by the decision-maker. Distortions result, some intricacy is lost, some complexity is understated, internally as it were, not operationally, as decision-makers function with normal cognitive limitations. Subsequently they may rationalize as well as simplify. Yet, in the critical 'space' between asserted beliefs and choice, consistency ruled. 'For example, Marling's cognitive map is completely consistent with his stated preference for continuing the present policy of "dragging along" and his disapproval of the policies of complete British withdrawal or conciliating the Persians.'[19] Axelrod thus elevates the intellectual, logical qualities, even the 'honesty', of the debate within the Eastern Committee. Many historians will not be surprised.

Most analysts of belief systems readily acknowledge the importance of, but leave relatively unexplored, the area between decision and implementation. Yet they virtually assume, without explanation, that slippage frequently occurs. In other words, even when beliefs lead to decisions, rational and complete acts of implementation often do not follow those decisions. This phenomenon becomes part of the evaluation of the consequences and efficacy of policy, of the judgement of behaviour of others, of cumulative feed-back and impact, of justification and rationalization for domestic and international consumption, of the development of doctrine and rhetoric that binds, and bureaucratic behaviour that influences further decisions and behaviour. It can also lead to brooding, blood-letting, and scapegoating. Attempting to explain the failure of implementation is beyond the scope of this paper, but the significant factors will almost certainly include those that constrain rationality and latitude, both domestic and international, and the question of process, involving, for example, the nature and significance of the issue, its past history, the source of the decision, the form of the instructions, and the circumstances of their receipt.

Finally, as a preface to Lloyd George, the relevant strands of social psychological theory must be identified.[20] Attitude change theory posits that opinions and attitude change through the impact of manipulated, persuasive communication which presents fresh information. Cognitive dissonance theory, given the existence of well-established and firm belief systems, argues that the presence of inconsistency and ambiguity of information and values, or of behaviour inconsistent with beliefs, causes stress. This, individuals and groups seek to reduce or eliminate, in a search for consistency, by ignoring, disregarding, or reinterpreting evidence in order to preserve beliefs, or by altering beliefs to match behaviour. This search for cognitive consistency leads to rationalization. Attribution theory seeks to explain how individuals, as problem solvers, grapple with the combination of changing events and constant factors they experience and observe. Personal dispositions and situations, perhaps interacting, are assumed to guide behaviour, and are therefore used to explain it. Individuals and groups tend to assume that situation provokes, controls, and necessitates their own conduct; personality characteristics, deep designs, and calculating motive govern the behaviour of their opponents, be they individuals, governments, or states. After attributing behaviour in that way, one generalizes about and predicts future behaviour. Self-perception theory suggests that behaviour actually represents what individuals really believe, and stimulates the development of those beliefs by providing evidence of their existence. Beliefs become, in fact, summaries of what persons have already done. Concrete developments thus change beliefs as individuals react to reality. Finally, schema theory suggests how individuals use experience and information to create categories and mental constructs, which influence judgement. Schema are created and stored in memory, and are activated to provide illustrative fits for current situations and actions; they are categories that help one simplify and recognize. Episodic, historical scripts, for example, of Munich and the behaviour associated with it, metaphors, and personnae, which are stereotypes and fixed caricatures of individuals are schema. The link with analogical reasoning and the abuse of history are obvious.

From December 1916 to October 1922 Lloyd George was the decisive figure in British and European politics. His attributes, his character, and personality-rooted needs, the sum preparatory total of his political and social experience, and his ideas and beliefs, have been analysed as 'the education of statesmen'. Attributes are given, achieved, and ascribed. Class, family, religion, culture, socio-economic roots, intellect, dispositions, instincts, health, and temperament form the well-springs. Upbringing, education, political socialization, and participation develop skills, preferences, and style, and the reverses thereof. The relevant essence of the man is his sense of vocation, proportion, paradox, priorities, history, ambition, and destiny; his ability to cope with stress and with impossible burdens, and to adapt, learn, and grow; his interpersonal, tactical, administrative, communications, and leadership abilities; his presence, confidence, and perceptiveness; his principled idealism, philosophy, imagination, vision, and pragmatism; his judgement and courage; his constancy and contradictions; his work-habits, curiosity, perserverence, powers of analysis, synthesis, and contingency-thinking; his nerve, combativeness, compassion, and magnaminity. His ability to persuade and inspire trust as well as confidence helped determined what attributes others ascribed to him; his demonstrable need to satisfy self-esteem, personal desires, impulses and compulsions affected his conduct and judgements of it. He became as controversial as Joseph Chamberlain and Winston Churchill; distrust of him was fashionable. Lloyd George was a well-versed politician and an experienced and creative minister, holding cabinet rank from 1908. He was as prepared, eager, and fitted as any colleague to become prime minister in December 1916. The layers of his personality were set-down; a composition of ideas and beliefs was in place but remained vulnerable, and likely to evolve, expand, and contract.

Development of his operational code can help confirm the content and hierarchical structure of his politically relevant belief system, and test its stability. A grasp of his images and second order of beliefs, of his perceptual skills, and his ability as a processor of information can help guide one through his performance in cabinet and conference debate, and as a decision-maker. Lloyd George, the evaluator and rationalizer, in the face of the implementation and the consequences of policy decision, turned with little respite to the next phase of the problem, or a new issue. As the record unfolds one sees the critical relevance of small group structures, their composition and processes of decision-making, and the attendant problems relating to their efficiency, effectiveness, and cohesion. In Lloyd George's informal and formal groups, and because of the relationship they bore to each other, were options tested sufficiently, was information and advice fully available, were debates comprehensive and cumulative, and were risks and costs adequately weighted? Did the bureaucracy constrain as it should or gear advice to the beliefs it knew Lloyd George held; did the official bureaucracy compete effectively with the improvised? Lloyd George established a coterie of advisors and informants, but which ideas and beliefs were central, cohesive, and structured as opposed to being peripheral, and which helped guide action? Did excessive conformity and cohesion develop; did Lloyd George dominate too easily, or erratically and insufficiently, or act as an effective and creative catalyst? Were solutions reached to serve conformity's needs or was vision maintained? In those circumstances of uncertainty and ambiguity, did Lloyd George's governments rush to decision and yet convince themselves that they had met the needs of the nation, party, and bureaucracy, while furthering their personal, political lives?

In the face of these analytical challenges cognitive dissonance theory, attribution theory and schema theory are valuable aids, particularly the latter two. Yet there is no easy solution, no simple alternative to tried and tested historical analysis. Decision-makers are not abstractions or objects of experimental research. Kissinger's behaviour, for example, may be bewildering but, in time, historical analysis will do much to explain it. Lloyd George had motive and purpose, intellect and vigor, a grasp of issues; a creative pragmatist, he behaved in substantially rational ways and demonstrated logical qualities of argument. Yet undeniably, constraints on his rationality, and latitude, were present, and not all his conclusions followed from their premises. Yet, on balance, Lloyd George emerges more as a serious problem solver, a gifted processor of information, than a leader bound by rigid images, and acting from alarmingly false perceptions as he presided over the conduct of British foreign and defence policy in war and peace.

NOTES

1. Michael Kammen, ed., *The Past Before Us* (Cornell University Press, 1980); and Responses Symposium, *Diplomatic History*, 4(Fall 1981): 353-382.
2. W. N. Medlicott pointed the way over twenty-five years ago in his 'The Scope and Study of International History,' *International Affairs*, XXXI, 4(October 1955): 422. Unfortunately oral history projects languish, short of interest, and funds.
3. Charles S. Maier, 'Marking Time: The Historiography of International Relations,' in Kammen, *The Past Before Us*, p. 386. A distinction should always be drawn between the system as identified in systems analysis, and the environment in which, for example, decisions are made and executed.
4. Ibid.
5. Michael G. Fry and Arthur N. Gilbert, 'A Historian and Linkage Politics: Arno Mayer,' *International Studies Quarterly*, XXVI, 3(September 1982): 425-444.
6. H. Starr, 'The Quantitative International Relations Scholar as Surfer: Riding the "Fourth Wave,"' in *Journal of Conflict Resolution*, XVIII, No. 2 (June 1974); Charles McClelland, 'On the Fourth Wave: Past and Future in the Study of International Systems,' in J. N. Rosenau, V. Davis & M. A. East, *The Analysis of International Politics*, pp. 15-40.
7. Maurice Cowling, despairing of the biographical approach, pursues the thought-worlds, temperament, use of rhetoric and relationships between 'situational necessity' and political intentions, and between oratory and reality in ways that are not unrelated to this essay. (M. Cowling, *The Impact of Labor 1920-1924* (Cambridge University Press, 1971), and *The Impact of Hitler 1933-1940* (Cambridge University Press, 1975). See also Michael Bentley, *The Liberal Mind, 1914-1929* (Cambridge University Press, 1977).
8. James Joll, *1914 The Unspoken Assumptions* (London, 1968), p. 24. All quotations in this review of Joll's argument are from this pamphlet.
9. Paul Kennedy, *The Rise of Anglo-German Antagonism, 1860-1914* (London, 1980).
10. See the debate between Paul Schroeder and Richard Rosecrance et al., *The Journal of Conflict Resolution*, XXXI, 1(March 1977): 3-74.
11. I disagree here with Maier's view. (Maier, 'Marking Time', p. 360-361.)
12. Stephen Walker, 'The Interface Between Beliefs and Behaviour: Henry Kissinger's Operation Code and the Vietnam War,' *Journal of Conflict Resolution*, XXI, 1(March 1977): 129-168.
13. O. R. Holsti, 'The Belief System and National Images: A Case Study,' *Journal*

of *Conflict Resolution,* VI(September 1962): 244–252; K. J. Holsti, 'National Role Conceptions in the Study of Foreign Policy,' *International Studies Quarterly,* XIV(September 1970): 233–309; and R. Mandel, *Perception, Decision Making and Conflict,* (University Press of America, 1979).
14. Robert Jervis, *Perception and Misperception in International Politics* (Princeton University Press, 1976); I. L. Janis, *Victims of Groupthink: A Psychological Study of Foreign Policy Decisions and Fiascoes* (Boston, 1972); R. N. Lebow, *Between War and Peace. The Nature of International Crises* (Johns Hopkins University Press, 1981), chapters 5 and 6; and Janice G. Stein and R. Tanter, *Rational Decision Making* (Ohio State University Press, 1980), pp. 3–87. Janice Stein's work is extremely valuable and takes the reader well beyond the scope of this paper.
15. Alexander L. George, 'The Operational Code: A Neglected Approach to the Study of Political Leaders and Decision-Making,' *International Studies Quarterly,* XIII(June 1969): 190–223; his 'The Role of Cognitive Beliefs in the Legitimation of Long Range Foreign Policy: the case of F. D. Roosevelt's plan for post-war cooperation with the Soviet Union' (unpublished paper 1977), and his *Presidential Decision-Making in Foreign Policy: The Effective Use of Information and Advice,* (Westview Press, 1980); O. R. Holsti, 'The Operational Code Approach to the Study of Political Leaders: John Foster Dulles' Philosophical and Instrumental Beliefs,' *Canadian Journal of Political Science,* III, 1(March 1970): 124–157; D. Kavanagh, 'The Operational Code of Ramsay MacDonald' (unpublished paper 1971); and Walker 'The Interface Between Beliefs and Behavior,' and his 'The Motivational Foundations of Political Belief Systems: An Analysis of the Operational Code Construct' (unpublished paper, 1980). The problems of constructing an operational code from primary evidence that is partial, possibly unrealiable and insufficient, are little different from those normally confronting historians.
16. Deborah Larson, 'Belief and Inference: The Origins of American Cold War Policies' (unpublished paper, 1982). Dr. Larson did not establish a sequence of information processing, using marginal comments and other documentations. One cannot, therefore, trace reciprocal influences between the four decision-makers, i.e., Averell Harriman, Harry Truman, James Byrnes and Dean Acheson.
17. R. Axelrod, ed., *Structure of Decision: The Cognitive Maps of Political Elites,* (Princeton University Press, 1976).
18. Axelrod, *Structure of Decision,* p. 56.
19. Ibid., p. 90.
20. This brief survey follows that of Dr. Larson in her paper cited here.